CLEAR VISION

CLEAR VISION

THE STORY OF

CLEAR CHANNEL COMMUNICATIONS

BY

REED BUNZEL

BRIGHT SKY PRESS
ALBANY, TEXAS

Bright Sky Press, Box 416
Albany, Texas 76430

10 9 8 7 6 5 4 3 2 1

Library of Congress Cataloging-in-Publication Data

Bunzel, Reed.
Clear Vision : the story of Clear Channel Communications / by Reed Bunzel.
p. cm.

ISBN 978-1-931721-98-1 (jacketed hardcover : alk. paper)
1. Clear Channel (Firm) — History.
2. Radio broadcasting—United States—History. I. Title.

HE8698.B86 2007
384.54065'73—dc22

2006101943

Cover design by DJ Stout and Julie Savasky,
Pentagram Design, Austin, Texas
Book Design by Julie Savasky

THIS ONE IS FOR DIANA AND JENNY,
WITH MUCH LOVE AND APPRECIATION.

TABLE OF CONTENTS

9   INTRODUCTION

17   CHAPTER ONE
        CLEAR CHANNEL: IN THE BEGINNING

41   CHAPTER TWO
        IN THE PUBLIC EYE: CLEAR CHANNEL FROM 1984–1996

59   CHAPTER THREE
        OPENING THE FLOODGATES

93   CHAPTER FOUR
        POST CONSOLIDATION: THE MORNING AFTER

107   CHAPTER FIVE
        IT'S NOT ALL ABOUT RADIO

129   CHAPTER SIX
        BEWARE THE EVIL EMPIRE

141   CHAPTER SEVEN
        THE INCIDENT IN MINOT

153   CHAPTER EIGHT
        A MATTER OF INDECENCY

187 CHAPTER NINE
     THE DAY THE MUSIC DIED (. . . OR NOT)

205 CHAPTER TEN
     INSIDE THE BELTWAY: WASHINGTON AND POLITICS

221 CHAPTER ELEVEN
     THE STORM OF THE CENTURY

235 CHAPTER TWELVE
     SERVICE TO THE COMMUNITY

249 CHAPTER THIRTEEN
     ALL IN THE FAMILY

269 CHAPTER FOURTEEN
     FORGING A NEW INDUSTRY LEADERSHIP

283 CHAPTER FIFTEEN
     BACK TO THE FUTURE

297 CHAPTER SIXTEEN
     A CLEAR AND CLOSELY HELD VISION

301 SEGUE

305 ACKNOWLEDGMENTS

INTRODUCTION

WITHOUT QUESTION, CLEAR CHANNEL COMMUNICATIONS TODAY STANDS as the world's largest "out-of-home" media company, with a portfolio of 1,005 U.S. radio stations and close to 900,000 outdoor advertising displays throughout the world. No business (or industry) stands still, of course, and as the orbit of the traditional, analog media world crosses that of new, digital media, the company is poised to alter significantly the communications universe. By merging innovative digital technologies with tried-and-true broadcasting practices and a solid business plan, Clear Channel stands to be a leading player on a number of media platforms for years to come.

Before we look into the future, however, it is worth reflecting on the recent past, because the entire communications industry has — like Clear Channel — transformed itself relatively overnight. Consider all that has unfolded in a relatively short time:

It was just about a century ago that the introduction of electricity and telephones into homes and offices across the country provided light, warmth, and the ability to communicate with friends and family who lived miles away — or right around the corner. In the early 1920s, the radio medium began to invite newscasters, actors, and musical artists into living rooms that previously had served as places for quiet reflection in front of the fireplace. Over the ensuing years the programming that emanated from these receivers — and later from the dashboards of automobiles — improved and expanded to satisfy a newfound thirst for all things entertainment. Long before "must-see TV," "appointment television," and personal video recorders, families gathered each week at precisely the same time to hear their beloved radio programs. It was in this environment that Orson Welles' famed "War Of The Worlds" broadcast sent a nation into panic. Radio was the "master communicator."

Then, as the mid-point of the century approached, the introduction of television provided a seismic shift in the world of electronic media, as much of the comedy, drama, sports, news, and musical programming that once had been the exclusive province of radio made a mad rush to the tiny screen. This mass emigration forced radio broadcasters to reassess the significance of their craft, and those enterprising men and women who believed in the inherent value of an audio medium stuck it out, trusting that television would not displace radio simply because the ear is more demanding than the eye.

As we now know, radio was not dislocated from its position of prominence, and it has co-existed alongside television for more than 50 years. During this half-decade of co-habitation the media landscape has changed markedly — first with the introduction of cable, in-dash 8-track and cassette players, the Sony Walkman and Discman and, more recently, satellite radio and TV services, iPods, cell phones, and the Internet. In an environment in which constant innovation plus corporate dexterity equals time-to-market, established members of the "old guard" often are perceived as too slow and too arrogant to compete in this new world order. The lack of speed and enthusiasm with which the recording industry greeted the new digital distribution systems of the late-1990s — and the volume of litigation it employed in an attempt to outwit and outlast them — is a glaring example of the corporate propensity for trying to keep the status quo as much as possible.

Today, with all these new technologies mingling with traditional delivery systems, the media playing field has become increasingly crowded, and as younger generations of consumers gravitate toward those things with which they can identify the most, many companies — and some entire industries — are being pressured to change the way they do business.

This rapid technological evolution in part was fueled — some might say exacerbated — in February 1996 when President Bill Clinton signed the Telecommunications Act into law, opening the floodgates on media consolidation. Prior to deregulation, U.S. radio companies were restricted to owning only several dozen stations, a limitation that ostensibly provided for greater competition, market diversity, music selection, and personal choice. In fact, in the years just prior to the passage of the Telecom Act (as it came to be known), 60 percent of the commercial radio stations in the U.S. were losing money and threatening to go dark. But when the ownership restrictions were eased and companies were permitted to own up to six, seven, even eight stations in a single market, growth-minded broadcasters immediately recognized the fiscal opportunities that existed, while others were presented with the prospect of cashing out and leaving the game for good. Within days of its passage, the Telecom Act unleashed a giant radio land grab almost unparalleled in the annals of business, with broadcasting companies trading stations as if they were mutual funds, buying and selling "assets" and amassing "operating clusters" in a way that only the sudden release of 80 years of restrictive regulatory pressures could produce.

The result was a veritable feeding frenzy that was viewed by listeners and media watchers alike with varying degrees of shock, apprehension, and awe. Pundits, critics, commentators, and (later) bloggers all drew attention to the vast changes that were underway, and in a world where change is great until it happens to you, the companies that were responsible for these tectonic shifts came under close and often-venomous inspection. Because the news media by their very nature tend to accentuate those events that test the *status quo,* radio consolidation quickly came to be viewed as a black cloud hovering over the U.S. broadcasting landscape.

Consequently, the topic quickly became an equal-opportunity mud-fest, with praise and condemnation being flung far and wide, and launched from almost all quarters. Depending on one's point of view (and labor, political, regulatory, or financial agenda) the radio industry within a few years was accused of becoming bland, as critics claimed that the lack of format rivalry between stations served to cool the "programming wars" that often defined the competitive climate within a market and often led to more than one station targeting the same audience with the same format. Men and women who had spent their entire careers in radio suddenly found themselves standing in the unemployment line, faced with the prospect of trying to find a job in a contracting marketplace — or, even worse, having to move into another industry entirely. By contrast, it also was said that the radio business finally achieved a critical mass that allowed operators to provide services that cash-strapped broadcasters previously could only dream of. And since owners of multiple stations in a single market had no intention of competing with themselves, a much broader range of music formats was becoming available in a single market. Stations could avail themselves of medium- and large-market talent whose skills far exceeded those available in small markets, and significant cost-efficiencies could be achieved by the elimination of redundant facilities and the related personnel.

Monumental change by its very nature inspires intense scrutiny, which often incites critical debate — and that debate typically demands a "straw man" onto which proponents of the "way things always have been done" can vent their frustration and dissatisfaction. Rapid-fire media consolidation that resulted from changes in broadcast ownership rules was a text-book case of this scenario, and San Antonio-based Clear Channel Communications quickly emerged as the primary target within the radio industry.

If an end-game is judged by the person (or company) that amasses the most toys (or stations), Clear Channel without a doubt emerged as the victor. By mid-2000, just four and a half years after the Telecom Act was signed into law, the company found itself operating well over 1,200 radio stations throughout the U.S., not to mention dozens of television stations and hundreds of thousands of outdoor advertising displays. And, while Clear Channel's portfolio of radio properties represented just over 10 percent of the commercial radio stations in the U.S., that volume was enough to mess with the sensibilities of many of the medium's purists and its harshest critics.

A groundswell of indignation, resentment, and anger quickly served to cast the company as the poster child for all that was wrong with media consolidation. A growing number of newspapers, magazines, and countless websites and personal web logs (also known as "blogs") continuously pointed to this multi-billion-dollar corporation as the "evil empire" and "big bully" that had consumed the radio industry virtually overnight. To this end, myriad individuals with political or social agendas scrambled to point out Clear Channel's excesses and errors wherever they could find (or manufacture) them. As a result, such disparate locales as Minot, North Dakota, and Columbia, South Carolina, were thrust into the national debate, as were such contrasting personalities as Howard Stern, The Dixie Chicks, Bubba The Love Sponge, and Glenn Beck. Any complaint — whether valid or manufactured — of indecency, minimized news coverage, political conspiracy, unemployment, or other commission of alleged sin was held up as yet another contemptible example of a wicked corporate megalith run amok. Within a constricted mindset where big business equals bad business, and in which the airwaves were claimed to belong to "the people," Clear Channel was cast as the baddest of them all.

Readers who have picked up this book with the anticipation that it will either confirm or deny one or another of these viral "truths" are bound to come away unfulfilled. Certainly, the rumors and innuendoes that continue to swirl about the company are explored at great depth, and this book is very much focused on the incidents and events that have sparked such extraordinary persistence. And it looks at the warts, the mistakes, and the miscalculations that were made by a corporation that, in just 20 years, grew its annual revenue from $26 million to $6.6 billion.

Perhaps even more important, though, this book is about separating fact from fiction, and identifying where there is a profound difference between the two.

The story begins with two businessmen who in 1972 turned a defaulted loan into a company that currently enjoys a market cap of over $17 billion and employs over 40,000 men and women. In that regard, this book is about the people who have been painted — sometimes tarnished — with such broad brush strokes that they have become vilified in the process. It's a story about individuals who recognized their opportunities, assessed their risks, took their chances, and eventually transformed a single blemished lemon into a tankerful of lemonade. It is a story about people possessed of a strong sense of personal integrity, fiscal responsibility, corporate leadership, and family pride.

That side of the Clear Channel story begins with Lowry Mays and Red McCombs, both of whom — through considerable dedication and hard work — became two of the wealthiest men in the Lone Star State. But measuring either of them strictly by his financial means would be a mistake. Despite their business acumen, they remain very much possessed of the drive and determination that first "brought them to the dance." Lowry Mays is a Texan with a towering presence and gravelly Texas drawl that can cause all conversation to stop as soon as he enters a room. A brilliant businessman, he's also a strong leader, a patient listener, a creative visionary, and very much the guiding force of the company. Above all, however, he's proud of his family — his wife Peggy, his sons and daughters, and their 16 grandchildren. People who have worked closely with him for years are awestruck — and maybe a little bit intimidated — by the tall shadow that he casts. When you shake hands and sit down with him in his office you can't help but agree, for you know that you are speaking with a man who has never been afraid to take an idea and turn it into something real and genuine. More than anyone, he is the man behind Clear Channel, and as you spend time with him you quickly get the sense that the "Darth Vader" accusations are completely misdirected, nothing more than the tired judgments of people whose purpose in life is to bring others down to their own level.

Then there's Red McCombs: not entirely the polar opposite of Lowry Mays, but distinctly different enough to be painted with a brush all his own. The son of West Texas sharecroppers, Red was fascinated by all things business almost from the time he could walk. Educated in a one-room schoolhouse, this future billionaire attended college on a football scholarship, eventually gravitating away from a career in law and into the used car business. Well on his way to riches by the time he was 25, McCombs has always been his own boss, keeping his fingers in as many lucrative pies as he could find. The embodiment of the American entrepreneur, McCombs is open and direct, candid and gracious and, when he speaks, his mellifluous baritone voice resonates with an understandable pride and honesty. A true salesman at heart, within moments of meeting him you know why he was such a success on the showroom floor — you simply want to do business with this man, hoping that just a touch of his success will rub off on you by osmosis.

Inside Clear Channel's executive suite it's very much a generational thing, and occupying the two offices next door to Lowry Mays are sons Mark and Randall. Mark, Clear Channel's CEO, probably is the more affable and personable of the two. When you meet him you are instantly at ease. He's very much the family man who usually arrives at the office at sunrise just so he can go home at a reasonable hour to spend quality time with his wife and six children. Mark today runs Clear Channel's daily operations. While he's genuinely warm and easy-going, he's totally focused on business and the cash flow of the company, and within the executive offices it's been said that it's best never to quote a number to him because he will never forget it. Above all, in an industry that's not known for effecting change, Mark is not afraid of taking risks in order to lead his company — and the radio business — into a future whose waters have yet to be charted.

Younger brother Randall is the finance guy, and serves the company as its president and chief financial officer. As much as Mark will never forget a number, Randall will remember them all — and in a company with a market cap of approximately $16 billion, that's a lot of numbers. In this role he is decidedly more reserved than his brother, but within that reserve there's a relaxed camaraderie waiting to get out. Well-spoken and precise in selecting his words, Randall is possessed of a brilliant business sense, and he has an encyclopedic brain that keeps track of virtually all aspects of the company's finances. He also has an innate ability to dissect a problem, working through the various layers of the situation with the skill of a neurosurgeon.

Occupying the office next to Randall is, perhaps, the most influential person working in the radio business today. In a sense a "made man" within the Clear Channel family, John Hogan is a career radio station manager whose star clearly rose during the early days of consolidation. Tapped to take over the company's Radio division in late 2002, Hogan's job has been far from painless. The lingering effects of an economic recession and the emergence of new technologies have served to keep industry advertising revenues and stock prices virtually inert, and competitive forces have led many to believe that the entire radio industry must make a giant paradigm shift in order to survive, much less thrive. In a business where few individuals are inclined to take that first step toward change, John Hogan has led the charge without hesitation, despite a fair amount of industry-wide skepticism and doubt. Soft-spoken but confident and driven, Hogan exhibits no trepidation in his role as the agent of forced evolution and, as his efforts have begun to show positive results, he has emerged as a respected leader within the radio industry.

In the end, a company is nothing more than its people, and this book essentially is the story of the men and women who have made Clear Channel what it is today. Not just the five individuals mentioned above, but the dozens and hundreds and thousands who are part of a company that, through its radio stations alone reaches over 110 million people each week. Certainly, neither the company nor the people who work for it are perfect, and this is a story about those imperfections, as well. In other words, "the good, the bad, and the ugly." To that end, the following chapters rely heavily on the personal experiences of a number of individuals, told through their eyes and, wherever possible, using their own words.

But — as you will learn in the coming chapters — it's a story that almost never happened....

CHAPTER ONE

CLEAR CHANNEL: IN THE BEGINNING

IT ALL STARTS WITH TEXAS.

If you haven't lived it, you've probably encountered it in the movies, maybe in *The Last Picture Show* or *Giant* or *Tender Mercies.* Or perhaps you've driven through it on I-10, that 879-mile-long ribbon of asphalt that cuts through such lonely West Texas outposts as Ft. Stockton, Ozona, and Sonora or, coming from the east, passes through Beaumont, Houston, and San Antonio. However you may have experienced it, you know it by the land: rain-carved arroyos, wind-borne sage bowling across the vast prairie, oil rigs nodding toward the earth in a steady, constant rhythm. A scorching summer sun bakes the earth during the day, while clear black skies at night create a dazzling display of stars that stretch across the horizon. Detour off the Interstate and you find small towns with dusty main streets and storefronts offering everything from cowboy boots to fishing rods to all things barbecue, and the ever-present Dairy Queen. Pickup trucks and eighteen-wheelers downshift in the distance, Class A football is played under the lights on warm Friday evenings, and church choirs sing the music of the gospel on Sunday mornings.

Of course, to paint the Lone Star State with such broad, earthen strokes would be to diminish the significance and scope of its commercial vitality in the twenty-first century. With an economy that grew out of oil and ranching and banking, Texas has established itself as a business leader on the world stage. Two of the last three U.S. presidents call Texas home, as do 102 of the companies on *Fortune's* list of the 500 largest American companies. The glass and steel high-rises in Houston and Dallas serve as testimony to the state's permanent place in the burgeoning global economy, and whether they produce energy, laptop computers, bank statements, or airline tickets, these companies are guided by men and women who have an innate sense of Texas pride. One of these companies is Clear Channel Communications, a true Lone Star corporation founded by two native Texans who, as skilled entrepreneurs often do, were presented with a once-in-a-lifetime opportunity and ran with it.

In a greater sense, Clear Channel's story dates back to the 1920s, when radio was still in its infancy and the U.S. was a country re-emerging from the devastation of the first World War. These years — portrayed in popular culture as the "roaring twenties" — often are characterized by images of "flappers," Fords that could be had in any color as long as they were black, silent movies on silver screens, and an overwhelming exuberance that all was right with the world — or at least it would be soon. And as the "roaring twenties" truly began to roar, the state of Texas — like much of the rest of the United States — entered into a decade-long period of economic expansion. At the start of the twentieth century the Lone Star agricultural industry had been focused primarily on cotton, but as the war drew to an end a substantial lumber industry had begun to take form in the piney woods of East Texas. At the same time, the development of a public irrigation system in the Rio Grande Valley fueled a profitable and rapidly expanding economy based on truck farms and citrus groves, which today still yield a bumper crop of the state's trademark Ruby Red grapefruit. More than anything, however, the end of the war and the availability of newly discovered oil fueled America's newfound fascination with the automobile and created a strong nationwide thirst for "Texas tea." Wildcatters were sinking holes throughout much of the state, and tales of gushers spewing forth from the high plains and sweeping prairies created a population boom unlike any the state had ever seen. In fact, in the decade that ended in 1929, more than one million people had moved to Texas, representing more than a 25 percent gain in the state's population.

Of course, much of the state's financial growth came to a screeching halt on October 29, 1929, when a paper-fueled stock market plunged nearly

40 points — the equivalent of a 1,150-point drop today. By the following summer the market had lost nearly 90 percent of its value, and many companies and top corporate executives had been wiped out. A lingering demand for cotton, oil, and beef kept the Texas economy bumping along for another year and a half, and many of the state's newspapers reported during this uncomfortable period that the state's increased construction, oil production, and livestock sales were stabilizing, if not actually growing. In Washington, President Herbert Hoover tried with great political aplomb to explain that the crash was a paper loss, bound to impact only the greedy financiers on Wall Street and whose effects would not extend to the common American family. But this optimism rang false to the hundreds of thousands of workers whose fortunes already had hit the skids, and a deep economic and psychological depression soon gripped the country. Devastating infestations of crop-loving insects and an unrelenting multi-year drought only compounded the suffering and despair as the good times of the twenties quickly slipped into a decade-long period of hunger and desolation. While some men and women were fortunate enough to remain gainfully employed during these hard times, many others were faced with the prospect of relocating wherever the all-elusive dollar might take them. Sometimes they would load up the family truck like the Joads in John Steinbeck's *Grapes of Wrath* and head west to California, while others pulled up their roots and fled the farm to the big city, where more often than not they would fall into the anonymity of soup lines, street corners, and tenements.

It was against this depressed landscape that in 1931 a young salesman named Lester Mays married a young Texas woman named Virginia Lowry. Given the dire economic conditions, Mr. Mays was fortunate enough to be earning a modest living as a sales representative for Kansas City-based Sheffield Steel, an upstart company that had carved out a niche business by buying scrap iron, much of which came from discarded railroad rails, and melting it down for use in the production of a variety of industrial products. Later, during World War II, the plant produced heavy-duty bolts that were used to manufacture Jeeps, as well as an alloy that was used in armor-piercing bullets and explosive shells. Despite the difficult economic times that persisted through most of the thirties, the steel business remained a constant, and Lester Mays did well enough as an account manager to begin a family. In 1933 the young couple welcomed a daughter, whom they named JoAnn, and two years later — on July 24, 1935 — young Lester Lowry Mays came into the world.

More than seventy years later L. Lowry Mays does remember moving to Dallas at age five when his father was promoted to general manager of the company's southwest region. "My dad was an outstanding salesman," he says. "He grew up on the sales side of the steel business, which was why he was made manager of the company. He worked in downtown Dallas in one of those tall buildings, and I used to go to the office with him every Saturday morning. I'd play at the Dallas Athletic Club while he worked, which is probably the reason I've always worked on Saturday mornings."

Those early years are somewhat a blur today, more than six decades later, but Lowry says he fondly remembers family excursions to the Gulf Coast or the mountains — memories made much more vivid over the years because his father recorded them on movie film. "We would go on trips together, either down to Galveston to the beach or out to New Mexico," he says. "One of my mother's brothers had a place in the mountains, and my father always took these movies of those vacations. I still have those movie pictures of myself when I was two feet tall, running around, and pictures of him, too. Without those movies I wouldn't have the clear memories of him that I do."

Good thing, too, because those home movies came to an abrupt stop in 1947 when Lowry's mother received word that her husband had been killed in an automobile accident. "It was very hard on all of us, but it was particularly hard on her," Lowry recalls. "Fortunately, my father's extended family lived in and around the Dallas area. They were all born on a farm in Frisco, which is about 30 miles north of the city. My dad was one of twelve children, and they all grew up on that farm, raising cotton and anything else that would grow." Lowry's father — as well as his aunts and uncles — all attended a tiny one-room school about two miles from the farm, and as they were growing up they lived very much like the Waltons on television, pitching in and working on that farm to benefit the entire family. When Lester Mays was killed, one of his brothers — Avery Mays — stepped in and became somewhat of a surrogate father to Lowry, who to this day remembers him with great affection. "Avery kind of mentored me through the years," he says. "Because of him I didn't have as much of a vacancy in my life when my father was killed as I would have had if he had not been there — along with all my other aunts and uncles."

Without the family's chief bread-winner coming home from work every night, money grew pretty tight very quickly. As tragic as her husband's death had been, Virginia Mays knew without question that she had to continue putting food on the table, so she found employment in the real estate business and did a brisk business selling houses in and around Dallas — including new post-war homes that were being built by one of her late husband's brothers. "My mother had quite an active real estate business," Lowry recalls. "She was able to provide the wherewithal to raise us in the best school district in Dallas, and she did a wonderful job at that." Hard work and the value of a dollar were emphasized throughout his childhood, and Lowry says that as far back as he can remember he always worked on the family farm in Frisco during the summer, picking cotton and doing whatever odd jobs needed to be done. Later, when he was attending high school, he worked at the local market, stocking shelves and bagging groceries. "A strong work ethic was one of the family values that was instilled in both my sister and me at a very early age, and during the summer I always found a job," he says.

When it came time for Lowry to head off to college he elected to attend Texas A&M University, which offered a degree program that focused on the oil business. "In those days it was not very expensive to go to a state school, and my mother was able to help both my sister and me," he remembers. "Still, during the summers that I was in college, I worked in the oil fields as a roughneck to help defray expenses. I mostly was employed in southern Louisiana and, depending on where I was working, I'd rent a room in the closest town and go out to the rig every day with the rest of the crew. I worked all shifts — morning, day, and night — usually on the drill floor with the lead tongs, breaking the pipe down when we were coming in and out of the hole. Those guys who grew up in the oil business in the '50s were tough cookies, and south Louisiana was no exception. It was a rough lifestyle, but the pay was very good and it was exciting. I felt like I was really accomplishing something, and I was helping to pay my expenses in college. It wasn't easy, but I was 18 years old so I didn't know any better."

It was that experience in the oil fields that led Lowry to earn his bachelor's degree in petroleum engineering at Texas A&M. "I always believed I would end up in the oil business," he says. "In fact, I did start out in the oil business as a reservoir engineer." That aspect of his career was interrupted, however, when the U.S. Air Force came calling, part of an ROTC commitment he had made while in college. "A select group of us in school were in a pre-flight program, and we had learned how to fly fixed-wing single engine airplanes at an airfield near the university," he says. "In my senior year I got my private pilot's license, and from there I thought I would go on to flight school." Just before graduating, however, the Air Force brass changed the rules, now requiring pilots to remain in the service for five years rather than the three years that previously had been required.

"For a kid who was barely 22, five years was a lifetime," Lowry says. "I didn't really want to be in the Air Force for five years. My commitment was always three, so I decided to bypass flight school and instead go directly into the Air Force and fulfill my commitment in a non-flying status." To complete his service obligation Lowry was sent to Brooks Air Force base in San Antonio where, as a second lieutenant, he initially served as the base petroleum officer, responsible for storing all the fuel for the aircraft and making sure that all the planes' tanks were filled. The Air Force had bigger plans for young Lowry Mays, however, and in an exchange program arranged with the Nationalist Chinese government on the island of Taiwan, he was assigned to take charge of the construction of a new oil pipeline that was being built from the northern to the southern end of the island. In 1949 Chiang Kai-shek had moved the government of the Republic of China to the island formerly known as Formosa, and had declared that Taipei was the new provisional capital of the country. The Chinese leader expressed his desire to return to the mainland within a few years, but the leaders of the Communist Chinese regime made it clear that they had other ideas. As it became more and more evident that "free China" would remain on Taiwan for some time to come, the U.S. government agreed to help the Nationalist Chinese build an oil supply line that would connect the ports at either end of the island.

"At age 22 I had 10,000 people working for me," Lowry Mays remembers. "They dug that pipeline by hand, and I lived in a jeep for a year and a half, just going up and down that line. It ran from Chi Lung, which is the port on the north end of the island, all the way down to Kao-hsiung. The air bases were located along that main north-south route, so we built the pipeline right down the main highway from the top of the island to the bottom. That way you could bring a tanker full of jet fuel into either port and pump it north or south to supply the air bases."

But let's back up a moment: One warm afternoon shortly before being sent overseas to Taipei, Lowry and another second lieutenant stationed at Brooks Air Force Base went out on a pre-arranged double blind date. Lowry recalls that the girl he had been paired up with was sweet and pleasant, but it was his friend's date who really caught his eye. "I had a brand new ski boat and my own date didn't know how to water ski," he says. "However, my friend's date did — and I drifted over to her pretty quickly. Her name was Peggy, and we started dating. Within about 20 or 30 miles of San Antonio there are two or three lakes where we'd go out to launch my boat and go water skiing." Weekend dates evolved into a full-fledged romance and words of marriage were whispered back and forth, but then Lowry's pipeline number came up and he summarily was shipped off across the Pacific. Love would have to wait.

"Peggy did not go to Taipei with me at that time, because she was scheduled to be the queen of Fiesta here in San Antonio and had a bunch of social engagements," Lowry remembers. "But the following summer I came back from Taiwan so we could get married, and then she moved with me back to Taipei. We had our honeymoon in San Francisco and Tokyo on the way back to Taiwan."

During that final stretch in Taipei, the newlyweds began working on a family and, shortly after returning stateside to San Antonio, Kathryn Mays was born. With a baby daughter at home and an honorable discharge in his pocket, Lowry understood that it was time to decide which direction his career would take. "When I got out of the Air Force I knew I wanted to go back to school and get an advanced degree," he says. "I was either going to get a master's degree in petroleum engineering, or I would go to law school or business school. Fortunately, while I was stationed in San Antonio before I was sent to Taiwan, I had taken law courses at St. Mary's University and business courses at Trinity University, just to see how I would like them." In one of those decisions that ultimately affects not just one's own destiny but the futures of many others, Lowry determined that business school would give him a broader diversification of his skills, something he thought would be "more rounding and beneficial."

To pursue this career track, the family headed north to Boston, where Lowry had been accepted to attend Harvard Business School. While the young family enjoyed the city's cosmopolitan feel and academic climate, the idea always had been that they would return to San Antonio when his education was finished, and by the time Lowry earned his MBA and the Mays family came back home to Texas a second daughter, Linda, returned with them. The following year baby Mark arrived, and quickly on his heels came Randall, the youngest of the brood. "When we moved back here to San Antonio we settled in easily," Lowry says. "I went into the investment banking business with a local firm that at the time was called Russ &

Company, and I was with that firm until 1970, when I left to form my own boutique investment banking firm."

During the 1960s and early '70s the city of San Antonio was viewed by many people outside south central Texas as little more than just another dusty cow town — and home of the Alamo. Hardly recognized as a center of financial enterprise, it was well off Wall Street's radar screen. In truth, the city's economy largely was based on a hefty military presence, supporting — and supported by — five Air Force bases and Fort Sam Houston, the massive army outpost that had been the base of Black Jack Sherman during the Mexican American War. "San Antonio's economy today is much more based on the hospitality and tourist industries," Lowry says. "One of the big Air Force bases has been closed and the rest of the city has continued to grow in different directions. The military remains an important part of San Antonio, but the tourist industry is tremendous and vibrant. And while we have a few major companies like AT&T, Clear Channel, and Valero headquartered here, the city is not known for its Fortune 500 firms."

By 1970 Lowry Mays was operating his own financial banking firm in downtown San Antonio, and one of the individuals he had come to know through both financial and social interests was a local businessman named Red McCombs, who was growing a chain of automobile franchises and investing in a number of other entrepreneurial opportunities. Eight years older than Lowry, McCombs was born in the West Texas town of Spur, a community of 1,300 located amidst the dust and scrub and dry washes on State Highway 70, sixty miles east of Lubbock in Dickens County. Young Billy Joe — tagged at an early age with the nickname "Red" because of his bright orange hair — was the oldest of four children born to Willie and Gladys McCombs, two young Texans who both had grown up the children of sharecroppers. Despite the hard luck and tough times of the thirties, Willie McCombs rode out the Great Depression working as an auto mechanic at the local Ford dealership, always managing to provide for his family as well as the itinerant farm workers who routinely came through Spur on their way west.

"I've always felt as if I'm one of the luckiest men alive," Red McCombs says today, some 79 years later, sitting behind his desk on the top floor of the office building from which he runs his vast array of commercial enterprises. "First, I was born in America and second, I was born in Texas. If I hadn't been born in Texas I would have run away from home and come to Texas. But on top of all that, I was born to loving and caring parents."

McCombs says he also was born with an almost innate entrepreneurial spirit and a strong desire to make a buck. "Before I ever knew what the word 'entrepreneur' was — certainly before I could spell it — I was fascinated with how business worked," he observes. "I was fascinated with our little town because it was obvious that four or five businessmen made all the decisions. As a result, I wanted to know how the bank worked and how the drugstore worked. As a kid I was never content with having one kind of odd job; I was always trying to do something else. And ever since then I've always been involved in more than one business activity."

McCombs remained in Spur though the eleventh grade, at which point the family moved to Corpus Christi. Red finished his senior year of high school on the Texas Gulf Coast, earning a scholarship to play football at Southwestern University in Georgetown, Texas, just north of Austin, and later transferred to the business school at the University of Texas. "I did my time in college, but the fact is, I never graduated," he says, noting the irony that the U.T. business school today is named after him. "While I was at business school there, I had served 16 months in the service right at the end of World War II," he explains. "Veterans were able to go to law school if they had completed three years of college." McCombs took advantage of the offer and enrolled in law school but, after completing his second year of classes, realized that the life of a lawyer was far from what he had in mind. "I loved going to law school, but once I really found out what lawyers did all day, I knew it would be too confining for me," he says. "I realized I really didn't want to do that as a job."

Instead, McCombs gravitated toward the automobile business and was offered a job selling new Fords in Corpus Christi. It was not by accident that the burgeoning Gulf Coast city also was the home of a young woman named Charline Hamblin, who had hit Red's radar screen several years earlier when he had arrived from Spur during high school. "It was a nice little business town, Charline was nearby, and I was very happy to start my career there," he explains. In short order Red married the love of his life, opened his own insurance company, became involved in building post-war housing, and eventually persuaded a local bank to loan him enough money to build his own used-car dealership. "You have to remember what that period was like," he says, a glint of nostalgia in his eye. "The U.S. economy was great just about everywhere, there was a pent-up demand for consumer products, and just about everyone had good credit. It was a very good time for business."

It was also during this period that McCombs got his first taste of owning a sports franchise, a minor league baseball team known as the Corpus Christi Clippers. "It was a Class B league team that had gone into bankruptcy," he recalls. "I owned that team for four years, taking it out of bankruptcy to positive cash flow in my first year of ownership. I made $50,000 the first year, and the second year I made $100,000 — and that was very serious money back then. Then the next year it was a bit tougher, and the following year I lost money. The problem was, by the mid-'50s people had discovered Jackie Gleason and *I Love Lucy,* and almost overnight it became a different world."

The McCombs family remained in Corpus Christi for eight years after they were married, but in 1958 an entrepreneurial opportunity took the couple northwest to San Antonio. "The only man I'd ever worked for selling cars had purchased his own Ford dealership in San Antonio," he explains. "Unfortunately, he had run into some very tough financial times, and he invited me to come up and help him out. I told him I would stay just two or three weeks until he was able to work through his difficulties, but while I was there I fell in love with the place. My two used-car lots in Corpus Christi were doing well, but as I began to help him work out of his problem I became fascinated with the franchise business. Within one week I began a complete turnaround, and within one month I'd put the business back to where we needed to be from a sales perspective. At that point I was getting kind of full of myself, being able to turn the business around like that, and by the second month I realized that I'd probably play this hand out." Three or four months later McCombs agreed to go into partnership with his former employer, and ultimately was able to buy him out and hang the McCombs nameplate above the dealership door.

IN A STATE WHOSE HORIZONS ARE SO BROAD AND VAST THAT THEY CAN accommodate virtually every visible star in the night sky, it seems almost inevitable that the confluence of those stars eventually would cause Lowry Mays and Red McCombs to find a way to do business together — and eventually they did.

"Red was — and still is — your typical wheeler-dealer type of businessman," Lowry remembers with a fond grin. "I was becoming active in the San Antonio business community, trying to do business with all the movers and shakers in town, and Red was one of the biggest of those movers and shakers. I met him through my banker, who was my next-door neighbor, and we got to know each other and did some business together. What struck me about him at the time was that he was a real deal junkie." "I met Lowry after he'd been here in town a few years," McCombs recalls. "He's eight years younger than I am, and we had met on a social level. At that time he was still in his primary business as an investment banker and I was into all my various ventures. I don't remember exactly where or how we were introduced, but we developed a very strong personal relationship and did some real estate and oil deals together — and we became very close friends. We both liked doing deals."

One of the deals that McCombs had tried to pull off was the purchase in 1970 of WOAI-AM, a 50,000 watt clear channel radio station with a signal that could be heard throughout much of the southwest. Technically speaking, a clear channel station is defined as an AM facility operating at a specific frequency that could not be shared with any other facility in the U.S., meaning that no other station licensed by the Federal Communications Commission was permitted to broadcast at that bandwidth. The WOAI deal never came to fruition, but McCombs still suspected that the radio industry held some intrinsic value, particularly since he saw how radio advertising successfully drew customers to his car dealerships throughout the San Antonio metro area.

Two years later opportunity knocked on Lowry Mays' office door. A local acquaintance and business colleague named Tom Moran presented Mays with an opportunity to go in with him on the purchase of KEEZ-FM, a "financially challenged" San Antonio FM station with 13 employees and virtually no cash flow. "Tom said he knew about this great radio station and invited me to buy it with him," Mays recalls. "The price was $125,000, which at the time was a lot of money. I told him I didn't know anything about the radio business, but he was somewhat persistent. Now, in the same building where my office was located there was a bank, and while I told him that I wouldn't buy the station with him, I did suggest that if he went down four floors to the bank and got a 90-day note, I'd co-sign it. Tom assured me that 90 days would give him more than enough time to raise the earnest money he needed, so we did the deal."

Of course, events didn't quite work out exactly as planned, and 90 days later the bank notified Mays that Moran had not been able to secure the cash he needed to fund the acquisition. With no other recourse, Mays made good as co-signatory of the note and, as *Forbes* magazine would describe it 20 years later, became the "accidental broadcaster."

It should be noted that in the early 1970s, creative programming on radio's FM band was a complete oxymoron. For all intents and purposes FM was a non-entity. Developed by Edwin Armstrong in 1934, "Frequency Modulation" produced a significantly higher-quality broadcast signal (with much less static) than AM's "Amplitude Modulation." Despite the positive results of numerous field tests and listener research, a confluence of events delayed the deployment of FM radio for decades. Many broadcasters for years had viewed FM as a direct competitive threat to AM radio, and at least one corporate executive was suspected of stalling Armstrong's FCC application to procure an experimental FM license. It wasn't until the 1960s that the Federal Communications Commission seriously began approving construction permits for FM radio stations, and by 1972 several thousand were on the air. Still, because very few radio receivers were equipped to pick up an FM signal, most of the programming that was being broadcast by these small facilities fell on deaf ears. FM radios most often were installed in such places as elevators and doctors' offices, and typically played what was known as "Beautiful Music."

It was against this backdrop that Mays found himself, literally by default, the owner of a struggling FM station with no idea what to do with it — or on whom to pawn it off. When Tom Moran first had come to him with the idea of buying it together the station was running an Easy Listening format, but by the time Lowry took possession of the license the format had switched to Rock. "While I knew something about the radio business, at the time it was not an industry I had ever been exposed to, from either a work or investment standpoint," he says. "Essentially, I had to learn it from scratch." Not sure quite where to turn, Lowry remembered the volume of advertising his friend Red McCombs was buying in order to sell his automobiles, and he decided it was time to pay his old friend a call.

"Lowry came to me and said, 'You like radio; why don't you buy this FM station?'" McCombs recalls. "'It's only $125,000.'" And I told him I didn't have any interest in it, but I said that if he would commit to me that he would really get serious and try to buy WOAI, we could own the station together. I didn't think we could make any money from the FM, but I suspected that if we someday could get WOAI, maybe we could make a few bucks."

Lowry was not particularly interested in becoming a broadcaster himself, but McCombs assured him that he personally had sufficient knowledge of the radio industry to make it work — a claim that Lowry says turned out to be a bit of a stretch. "I asked Red if he knew anything about the business, and he said, 'Sure,'" Mays recalls. "But the truth of the matter was, he knew less about it than I did. As an auto dealer here in San Antonio he had bought radio advertising, and he knew it could make money for him. But that was all. Still, he convinced me that it could be a good business, so we got together, discussed the opportunities, and eventually we agreed to buy the station together." Having convinced themselves — and each other — of the potential upside to investing in a business that enjoyed such historically solid cash flow margins as the radio industry, the two businessmen co-signed the bank loan necessary to do the deal.

Thus, in 1972, San Antonio Broadcasting was born.

Lowry says he understood from day one that buying a single FM station easily could be a quick lesson in disaster, since very little radio listening at that time was on the FM band. "Still, I sensed that — because the audio quality of FM was better than AM — there was going to be a big change coming over the next few years," he says. "I also did some research, and believed that there would be a degree of deregulation at some point because of the arbitrary number of radio stations a broadcaster was allowed to own."

In 1972 U.S. broadcasters operated under what then was known as the seven-seven-seven rule, which meant that no company or individual was permitted to own more than seven AM stations, seven FM stations, and seven television stations. The rule further stipulated that in one metropolitan area a single entity could only own one AM, one FM, and one television station. The original AM limits initially were put in place as part of the Communications Act of 1934, which reorganized two previous provisions of law: the Federal Radio Act of 1927, which dealt specifically with the regulation of the burgeoning broadcasting industry, and the Mann-Elkins Act of 1910, which concentrated primarily on reregulating the U.S. telephone industry.

During the 14 years between 1920, when KDKA in Pittsburgh transmitted the Harding-Cox presidential election returns in what is widely regarded as the first commercial radio broadcast, and 1934, when the 73rd Congress replaced the Federal Radio Commission with the Federal Communications Commission, the number of AM radio stations had grown from just a handful of stations to over 1,000. At the same time, several companies, including the Hearst Organization and the Radio Corporation of America (RCA), were thought by many people to be amassing too much control, or "public voice," within their respective communities. Additionally, by the early 1930s there had emerged a debate between commercial and non-commercial broadcasters over spectrum access. The Federal Radio Commission had determined that educational broadcasters constituted a "special interest," which meant — among other things — that they were forced to share frequencies. In 1934 several senators introduced an amendment to the pending Communications Act that essentially would guarantee that 25 percent of all radio licenses would be granted to non-profit organizations, while still allowing them to sell advertising. The amendment died an inglorious death, and the newly created FCC ruled that commercial stations had sufficient time during the broadcast week to air educational and other public information programming — and mandated that they do so. The 1934 Act further granted broadcasters fixed-term, renewable licenses that allowed them to broadcast at a specific frequency, provided they served the "public interest, convenience, and necessity."

Thirty-eight years after passage of the Communications Act of 1934, the number of radio stations in the U.S. had grown at a near-logarithmic pace. By 1939 there were 1,465 AM stations (and no FM stations) on the air; by the end of 1972 that number had almost tripled to 4,354 AMs, although only 2,777 FMs were on the air. Still, the 1934 Act held that in order to ensure that communities maintained a diverse voice of public opinion, radio companies were limited to owning just a handful of stations nationwide. Many of those stations were run by what fondly had come to be known as "mom and pop" operators, some of whom owned a single AM station that more often than not employed just three or four full-time staffers. These individuals often performed a variety of mind-numbing tasks, doing everything from selling advertising to fixing the transmitter to changing the tapes that ran through the reel-to-reel automation machine. Program formats often were determined simply at the whim of the station owner and changed at the discretion of whatever disk jockey was spinning records at the time. Dayparting — the practice of playing one genre of music during one segment of the day, then switching to another format at a later time — was widespread, and listeners often had no idea what kind of music or spoken-word programming they would find on the dial. This meant that audiences (and ratings) tended to shift erratically from one station to another throughout the broadcast day — and week.

Of course, not all radio stations fit this scenario, and it was one of these properties that Lowry Mays and Red McCombs found themselves owning as 1972 came to a close. As a rule, FMs were still considered part of a secondary radio medium that was trying to establish some sort of business model, making up its programming rules as it went along. A few innovative program directors and air personalities had grown tired of mainstream formats like Top 40, which was best characterized by its tight playlists of mainstream pop hits and rapid-fire deejays. These creative programmers began to experiment by playing harder-edge rock music and album cuts, a practice that was frowned on by record labels that were cashing in on the 12-24-year-old consumer's love of the 45-rpm single. But, just as Edwin Armstrong had demonstrated in the 1930s, FM had a signal far superior to the static-filled AM band, and it was much better suited to transmitting high-fidelity, music-oriented programming than its older counterpart. As a result, the Henry Mancini, Mantovani, Ferrante and Teicher, and Perry Como records that were a dentist's office staple were forced to share spectrum space with the likes of Led Zeppelin, The Who, Cream, and the Grateful Dead as younger listeners began tuning in to the great new music that only could be found on this thing called FM.

When San Antonio Broadcasting purchased KEEZ-FM, the station was running a poorly conceived rock format, which the two new owners determined was a big part of its ongoing cash-flow problem. "When Red and I went into partnership he told me he could help me find a manager for the station," Lowry recalls. "There was this local fellow named Doug McCall, who was the general manager of KTSA, the big AM station here in town. I promised Doug that if he came to work for the company and served as general manager of this little FM station we had bought, I would buy more stations; otherwise I couldn't have attracted him to come work for the station. He came to work for us and did a great job, but the station continued to lose money."

STATION IDENTIFICATION

Lowry Mays made good on his promise, and with Red McCombs' blessing he began to shop around for more radio properties. "Red primarily was interested in buying WOAI in San Antonio, but we weren't able to do that — not yet," he says. However, two stations in Tulsa came to my attention through a business associate. They were owned by a company called Tracy-Locke, which was an advertising company — and still is. One of the company's principles was a friend of mine here in San Antonio, and we used to talk a lot about the radio business. One day he told me, 'You know, we own these stations up in Tulsa that you really ought to buy because, as an advertising agency, we shouldn't be in that business.'"

Lowry decided to kick a few tires and traveled north to Tulsa to take a look at the two properties. He and Red almost instantly saw the inherent value in the AM station, but — based largely on their ongoing cash-flow challenges at KEEZ — they had no interest in purchasing the FM. However, the two stations were being sold in tandem, so the broadcasting neophytes agreed to purchase the pair (KBBJ-AM and KMOD-FM) for $750,000. "The FM didn't have any revenue at all, and the AM was losing money," Lowry says. "After we bought them we changed the AM's format to News/Talk, then sold the real estate under the tower for a lot more money than we paid for both radio stations." Despite this bit of creative financing, "we now had three stations that were losing money," he grins.

Because San Antonio Broadcasting's cash flow was a bright red hue, Lowry knew he had to remain with his investment banking firm until necessity dictated otherwise. "I needed that business to pay the bills, because that first radio station was losing so much money," he recalls. "The next stations we bought also lost money. I kept going down to the bank, telling the manager, 'I need to borrow some more money,' and he kept saying, 'I don't think this is a very good business you're in.' But he loaned me the money anyway, and we kept going."

Eventually Lowry elected to close the doors on Mays & Co. and devote his time and energy full-time to the radio business. "He really had become fascinated by the operational side of the radio business, as well as the investment side," Red McCombs remembers. "One day he came to me and said, 'What would you think if I were to get out of the investment banking business and just go into operating stations?' And I remember telling him at the time, 'I would kiss your feet.' He was so good in his investment banking business that I never dreamed he would do that, but when he did do it, it was a huge breakthrough."

It was during this period that the opportunity to purchase WOAI finally materialized, and Lowry and Red jumped at the chance. Not only was the station a "heritage" AM in San Antonio; it was one of just a few "clear channel" stations that the FCC had authorized to broadcast at full strength of 50,000 watts at nighttime. As a result, its signal covered much of the United States, and on a cold winter evening the station's programming could be heard from coast to coast, and well into Canada and Mexico, too. "When WOAI became available I thought it would be a good property to pair up with the FM we already owned," Lowry says. "I also knew exactly what I wanted to do with it as far as the format was concerned. At that time it was the second- or third-ranked rock station in town and it, too, was losing money."

More than a year passed while Lowry and Red tried to put a deal together and close the acquisition, largely because of some oppositional pressure that was applied by a local resident who had considerable influence within the San Antonio community. "There was this fellow named Victor Sota — I never will forget his name — and we met with him once a week for a while," Lowry says. "Eventually those meetings tapered off to once a month, and then I just stopped hearing from him. One day I decided to give him a call to see what was going on, and he said, 'Lowry, I have a new business. I'm selling and installing burglar bars. One day I'm going to be rich like you, so I don't have time to mess with that station stuff anymore.'"

Without further local opposition, Lowry and Red closed on the acquisition and brought in veteran broadcaster John Barger to run the AM-FM combo, part of a handshake agreement that had been part of a plan to merge the station with KRLD-AM in Dallas. That deal never materialized but Barger — who had been managing KRLD and had agreed to come down to San Antonio and turn WOAI around — consented to stay on with the company. Prior to running KRLD for five years, Barger had served as general counsel for Gordon McClendon's radio operations, which at the time was considered one of the most dynamic radio groups in the U.S. McLendon had launched KLIF-AM in Dallas in 1947 and, with the assistance of a young programmer named Todd Storz, virtually wrote the book on Top 40 radio. McLendon also was credited with developing the all-news format, and at one time even experimented with an all-commercial format.

"Lowry interviewed a number of people to manage WOAI, but he never really hired anyone," Barger remembers. "Then he struck a handshake deal with Philip Jonsson who, along with his brother and sister, were the owners of KRLD, which was going to merge with WOAI. However, there was a distinct culture difference between the two parties. Lowry and Red were stand-up Texas guys who shook hands on deals, while Jonsson — whose father was the founder of Texas Instruments — was an MIT honor grad, an engineer and was raised with lawyers around him. There wasn't anything dishonest about anyone or anything that went on in that deal; it just never happened." When the agreement to merge with KRLD fell through, Lowry and Red approached Barger and explained that they still wanted him to remain on board and manage WOAI anyway. "They asked me what it would take to get me to stay, and I said that all I would need was

10 percent of the station's net operating profit," Barger says. "Because the station was losing money every month it was not difficult to reach an agreement. As it turns out, the last month the station had been operated by its previous owner, it lost $50,000. So I told Lowry and Red that I might have to write them a check for $5,000 the following month if I replicated that poor performance."

With his management incentive in place, Barger began the process of converting the station's format from "really bad Top 40 and a mix of agriculture news" to a News/Talk format similar to the one he previously had instituted in Dallas. The format switch was a gradual one, with the introduction of a news block in the morning and, the following week, a similar news block in the afternoon. "During the rest of the day we toned down the Top 40, and still ran some 'ag' news because it was making so much money," he recalls. "It would be another year before we implemented the talk portion of the programming."

One of the first moves Barger made was to hire a former Gordon McLendon disciple named Stan Webb to serve as sales manager at WOAI. At the time, Webb was working in sales at another San Antonio station, but Barger convinced him that if he "crossed the street" to work at Clear Channel he would have greater autonomy and be able to participate in the creation of a "cash cow." "Our sales model was based on us calling directly on clients instead of going to the advertising agency," says Webb. "After a time that particular format tends to attract an older, more upscale audience, including a number of business owners. I figured that out pretty quickly and I started calling on the owners of businesses, because chances were pretty good that he or she was a listener to the station. It was a lot easier to sell a product to someone who already was connected with it. As a result, we quickly began to build a big client base in spite of poor ratings."

"John and Stan did an excellent job for us," Lowry says. "The first month we owned the station it started generating the kind of cash flow we needed to accomplish the expansion we wanted to achieve. Of course, I was already working with the radio company full-time because I had so much money exposed through the funds I had borrowed at the bank." It was during this period that the San Antonio Broadcasting name was changed to Clear Channel in recognition of the fact that the company now owned WOAI. "We were very proud that we owned a 'clear channel' station, so we decided to change our name from San Antonio Broadcasting to Clear Channel," Lowry explains. "While we thought that still might be a limiting name, it certainly wasn't as limiting as San Antonio Broadcasting."

By the mid-'70s the radio business was well into its sixth decade, but Barger says that the industry was overrun with nonprofessionals who really had no idea what they were doing. "The great thing about radio at that time was there were no real business people involved in it," he explains. "It was a collection of egomaniacs, newspaper publishers who couldn't care less, and people with limited education and foresight who liked the comfort of an air-conditioned studio." As a result, he says, any company that had a solid business plan and a team to put it into action could win the marketplace, even if they lacked the financial resources of the competition. "That's how Clear Channel looked at the business," Barger recalls. "Our basic approach was that of zero-based budgeting. I had worked for the U.S. government for about 18 months, making grants on the war on poverty, and one thing I taught the grantees was to act as if they were never going to get any more money, so they had to figure out what they could do without. Also, there was this long-held belief that a news station had to have a wire service, and it had to be Number One in the ratings in order to make money. These were pieces of wisdom that were handed down, and none of it was important."

What *was* important, Barger stresses, was to determine a specific focus for the business and then super-serve the people who were critical to the success of that business plan. "After we bought WOAI Lowry asked me, 'Are you going to make us Number One?'" he recalls. "He and Red both were great cheerleaders, so I said to them, 'Yeah, we're going to be Number One.' And Lowry said, 'Really ? Number One in San Antonio?' And I said, 'Hell, no — we're not going to be Number One in San Antonio. We're going to be Number One in *Alamo Heights*. Because that's where all the money is. That's where the 55-year-old guy with 500 employees — including ad managers and ad agencies — is located. I want to program to him.'" The result: in its second year, WOAI was out-billing every other station in San Antonio by a margin of $1 million.

What about Barger's compensation based on 10 percent of the net operating profit? "By the second year I was making more money as manager of the station in San Antonio than any other broadcast manager in America," he boasts. "Some of the New York stations were making a lot more than we were, but they weren't paying their managers 10 percent of the net. Lowry and Red never approached me to renegotiate my deal, either. They were both honorable guys. They never were concerned about what anybody who worked for them was making. Lowry had been a stock broker and had run a brokerage operation where, for many months, his top salesman made a lot more money than he did. McCombs, being a car guy, was always on the lookout to find the next great salesman, and if that person could sell enough cars, he would keep writing the checks to him. So they didn't really care how much money I was making, because they knew how much they were making."

By 1978 WOAI was turning a tidy profit, but cash flow at the two Tulsa stations was almost nonexistent. To rectify this situation Lowry Mays tapped Stan Webb to move up to Oklahoma and turn the two properties around. "Essentially the AM had a poor signal and was broadcasting a News/Talk format similar to that at WOAI, but it was not doing well and losing a lot of money," Webb says. "The FM station was Album Rock, and it was struggling, as well. What we did have were some really good people, so we refocused the radio station a little bit. I figured the quickest way to ramp up the revenue was to get the FM format going well and simulcast it on the AM. Within a year's time the FM had skyrocketed in ratings and revenue; it had become one of the top-five rated Album Rock stations in the country. KMOD was a fun project; I was able to do a lot of promotions you really can't do in a News/Talk format, which tends to be a little more staid and conservative. The rock format was always based on fun, younger adult listeners."

With the company turning out positive cash flow, Lowry and Red began to look around for other stations to acquire. They didn't have to look very far, as properties in both Port Arthur and El Paso came on the market. They bought the El Paso station — KELP-AM — in 1977, but as attractive as the market initially appeared, the property never generated the level of cash flow that Clear Channel had been anticipating. "We owned the El Paso station about five years, but it never was a very good fit for us," Lowry says. "At the time, it looked like a great market to get into, but it really wasn't. That was the only radio station we sold in the first 30 years of our history."

Port Arthur turned out to be a different story altogether. In January 1978 the company purchased both KPAC-AM and KPAC-FM, whose call letters were switched to KHYS-FM, an early take on the "Kiss" moniker. The following year, in 1979, Clear Channel acquired KPEZ-FM in Austin, bringing the number of company-owned-and-operated stations to eight.

"In those early years we talked about the stations every day," Red says. "We were business partners, but I was never active in the management of any of the properties. I would tell Lowry what I thought he needed to do about programming and business, and I became an expert without knowing anything. I was fascinated by that business — the fact that you had 24 hours of airtime and all you had to do was put on programming that was good enough so people would listen and advertisers would buy commercials. You didn't have any inventory, and you didn't have to worry about manufacturers seeing your product on shelves. It was all on the airwaves. I was very involved in offering advice, but it was not my role to run the business." McCombs insists that, while he was a partner in the company, he did not necessarily consider himself a radio broadcaster. "At that time I was a principal in at least 20 different businesses, and radio was just one of them. The radio business was being run very well by Lowry and John."

Interestingly, while Clear Channel's first acquisition was an FM station that was all but broke, the development of the FM band during the 1970s began to drive more and more cash flow to the bottom line as the decade progressed. "The FM conversion began in 1970 or '71 but, in Texas, FM really came of age in Dallas in 1973," Barger recalls. "When I started at WOAI in 1975, FM had taken over in Dallas, but it would be two more years before that shift occurred in San Antonio because, as they said at the time, there were no FM radios in '57 Chevys." To rectify this problem, Barger teamed up with some after-market audio retailers and provided FM conversions: "We'd give them some free spots so they could sell these converters that came in on 1010 on your AM radio," he says. "I'd run the same routine ten years earlier when I was at a television station in Austin, where we were trying to launch a UHF station against the powerful VHF facility owned by the Lyndon Johnson family."

As Clear Channel began to drive more and more profit to the bottom line, Lowry Mays began to conduct extensive analyses on other markets that the company might want to enter. "We put together a broadsheet that showed us everything we needed to know about a given market," he says. "We looked at revenue per market, revenue per station, revenue per population — all sorts of different statistical data that would identify to us those markets that had more profit potential than others. Of course, none of this was a secret — it was well known that great markets like Atlanta were very high on everyone's list." The downside was that stations in the larger markets generally carried an equally large price tag — usually out of reach for a growing company like Clear Channel. "It took money to get into the larger markets, and that was a resource we didn't have a lot of,"

Lowry says. "We really believed we could have more impact on the medium-sized markets, because we really built our whole company on the concept of directly selling our customers' goods. I always used to say, 'If I can't hear the cash registers ring when I walk through the door, then our business doesn't work.' It's all about being able to meet face-to-face with the customer and hear his cash register ring."

Mark Mays, who was still in junior high school when his father and Red McCombs were assembling the building blocks of the company, remembers radio being his father's passion during those early years. "Dad was always very focused on sales and programming," he says. "He knew about the formatics of News/Talk and how you can be creative with music programming on FM. At the same time he really focused on the business side as well. He was always cognizant of how radio connects with the audience and the advertiser, and he made sure that our listeners were customers of our advertising clients."

"We never had any plan to build this company any larger than we could operate profitably," McCombs says today from behind his massive wood desk, surrounded by historic memorabilia from Texas' colorful past and his own experience as owner of the Minnesota Vikings, the Denver Nuggets, and the San Antonio Spurs. "What we both thought we'd do was get up to the seven-and-seven ownership limits, get some cash flow in them, and then sell them. There was never any plan to make this a big company — not ever. But then other opportunities came along, and Lowry became very active in the industry. He was very good at that. And as those opportunities came to us we began to expand outwards, although we had no idea at the time where this was going to take us."

CHAPTER TWO

IN THE PUBLIC EYE: CLEAR CHANNEL FROM 1984 TO 1996

IN THE CLOSING MONTHS OF 1983 LOWRY MAYS AND RED MCCOMBS increasingly realized that to obtain the sort of funding they needed to make additional acquisitions, they were going to have to look beyond private financial institutions and venture into the public market. "I knew that if we were going to grow this company and consolidate portions of the radio business, we had to have greater access to capital," Lowry says.

Of course, because the radio industry was severely restricted in the number of stations a company could own, very few radio groups had the size or critical mass necessary to make an impression on Wall Street. "Pure play" radio companies could hardly even achieve "micro cap" status, and while several publicly traded media corporations owned and operated radio stations, those radio properties contributed only a minor share of revenue to those companies' bottom lines.

The task that lay ahead for Lowry Mays was three-fold: he had to convince the financial institutions that radio could be a viable player in the public marketplace; he had to demonstrate that the radio industry — which was still tightly bound by constrictive ownership regulations — could deliver the kind of margins that sustain investors' interest; and he had to show that Clear Channel fit both the above scenarios. "The process of going public was one of interviewing several investment houses," he recalls. "I had been in that business and I had been successful in bringing companies public in other industries, so I knew a lot of people in the business." One of Lowry's banking colleagues, John Williams, was the managing director of a regional New York Stock Exchange member called Snyder Burnett & Hickman. "John was a close friend, and I got him interested in doing a public offering," he recalls. "Then we went to a company called Blythe Eastman Dillon & Company in New York, and they agreed to manage the IPO jointly."

1984

In October 1984 Clear Channel went public with an offering of 784,600 shares of common stock issued through an underwriting syndicate headed by Paine Webber Inc. "We sold 25 percent of the company at around $14 a share, which today — because of splits and additional stock offerings — works out to about ten cents," Lowry Mays recalls. "It was hard to let go of that much of the company, but it served the purpose of gaining us access to the capital markets. It wasn't easy. In fact, in the very early days I had to really change the whole investment community's perception of how to value radio stations. I concocted this metric called 'after-tax cash flow per share,' which the analysts grabbed hold of. All it really was, was fully taxed cash flow per share, and it emerged as the standard for the radio industry throughout the 1980s and the '90s."

Initially Clear Channel was traded over the counter but, because of the poor markets in OTC stocks and excessive spreads, several years later the company joined the American Stock Exchange. "They promised they would trade us with a quarter-point spread, so we went with them," Lowry says. "Later, when we qualified for the New York Stock Exchange, we moved over to that."

At roughly the same time the company went public, it also successfully completed the acquisition of Broad Street Communications, which added six stations to Clear Channel's portfolio. These stations included WQUE AM-FM in New Orleans, KTOK-AM and KJYO-FM in Oklahoma City, and WELI-AM in New Haven, Connecticut, which had just celebrated its 50th on-air anniversary.

According to the first Clear Channel annual report issued for 1984, the company's gross revenues increased from $10.3 million in 1983, the last year it was privately held, to $16.756 million. This revenue was derived from a total of 12 stations — six AMs and six FMs — located in six markets, plus the Oklahoma News Network. The original Board of Directors in 1984 included Clear Channel President/CEO Lowry Mays; Clear Channel Senior Vice President and Chief Operating Officer John Barger; Red McCombs, who was identified as a "private investor"; Alan Feld, partner in Akin, Gump, Strauss, Hauer, and Feld; Theodore Strauss, chairman and CEO of First City Bank of Dallas; and John Williams, regional vice president of Thomson McKinnon Securities, Inc. (and the colleague of Lowry Mays who had initiated the public offering).

1985

In 1985 the FCC voted to relax the seven-seven-seven ownership rule to 12-12-12, making it possible for broadcasting companies to own a total of 12 AM, 12 FM, and 12 TV stations. This increase was spearheaded by the National Association of Broadcasters, whose members repeatedly had maintained that a limit of seven stations in any one band was prohibitive in building a company that could deliver the kind of cash flow that was sustainable year in and year out.

"Back when you could own only seven AMs and seven FMs, you didn't have a large revenue-producing business that would generate the interest of investors, private or public," recalls William Stakelin, former NAB board chairman and current CEO of publicly traded Regent Broadcasting. "I remember operating in one small market where we had fourteen separate owners at one time, and that kept the economic base from improving because all these individual companies were competing against each other, either selling commercials cheap or just trying to get enough money to pay the light bill." As more and more broadcasters continued to lose money, it became apparent at the FCC that an increase in ownership limits would be necessary if the industry was going to be self-sustaining.

Certainly, such companies as Clear Channel were driving enough cash flow to the bottom line in order to remain profitable enough to attract investor interest. But the conservative fiscal thinking of Lowry Mays and the Clear Channel board of directors was more of an exception than the rule at that time, and the radio membership of the NAB determined that ownership relief was very much needed. "The NAB played a big role in convincing regulators in Washington that radio was really a very important service to the American public," Stakelin observes. "This was free, over-the-air broadcasting that Americans depend on, and economically it was not proving to be tremendously viable. We had to show that if there were to be some ownership rule changes, it wasn't a matter of the rich getting richer; it was a matter that this service to the consumer could be greatly improved by expanding the limits, because it would solidify the industry financially and people would be able to do more to serve the public."

For the record, Clear Channel's revenues in 1985 increased to $26.278 million, a gain of 56.8 percent over 1984's numbers. While the company made no acquisitions during the calendar year, it did receive a license from the FCC to develop a low power television (LPTV) facility in Bryan/College Station, TX. The 1985 annual report notes that the company also had filed eight additional LPTV applications, and had 17 Multipoint Distribution System licenses pending, as well. Additionally, Clear Channel held a minority interest in the new San Antonio Cellular Telephone Co., which was expected to be operational by the year's end. While the company made no direct radio asset purchases, it did change the call letters of WQUE-AM in New Orleans to WMKJ-AM.

1986

During 1986 Clear Channel's revenues increased 4 percent to $27.420 million. In September the company purchased WHAS-AM and WAMZ-FM in Louisville, KY, for $21 million, an acquisition that effectively increased the number of Clear Channel's radio stations to 14. In the annual report that year Lowry Mays wrote, "The size of the investment and the economic diversification [this purchase] represents makes it an important one for the company. WHAS is our second clear channel frequency and is the number-one-rated station in the market....WAMZ, the number two station in the market, was recognized nationally as the best country music-formatted station in the nation in 1986."

"The Louisville acquisition was very similar to San Antonio from the perspective that it involved two stations that had the same dynamics," notes Mark Mays. "They had a big News/Talk station, and we knew we could be more aggressive in selling it. When we bought the station, it was still being operated with the TV stations and the newspapers in town, and we thought we could be more sales intensive and focused. We didn't change the management; we just brought them out and let them do their own thing. The properties were just very attractive."

In 1986 Clear Channel also was granted a license for the construction and operation of a low power television station in Corpus Christi.

Additionally, the company filed an application with the FCC to move the transmitter site for KHYS-FM in Port Arthur west, to a location that would permit the station to include Houston in its service area. Additionally, the company sold its interest in San Antonio Cellular, largely because the fledgling industry was in the early stages of consolidation, a process that would take considerably more cash flow than the company was willing to commit. "I was one of those people who thought that cellular phones would be a big business at some point in the future, so we had applied for a license," Lowry Mays says today. "There were a few other people who also applied here in San Antonio. When it came time to consolidate the market, we sold our interest to Craig McCaw for $1 million. God knows what that million dollars would be worth today." Note: McCaw was the founder of McCaw Cellular, which today is part of Cingular; he also serves as chairman of Teledesic.

1987

During 1987 Clear Channel saw its revenues increase 36 percent to $37.161 million. As Lowry Mays noted in the annual report, this increase was achieved "in spite of depressed economic conditions in Texas, Oklahoma, and Louisiana, where 65 percent of the company's business is conducted. This accomplishment can be attributed to the ability of the company to increase its marketing position in all the markets we serve."
During the mid- to late-'80s merger activity in the radio industry began to heat up as Wall Street began to discover the attractive cash flow and margins that healthy radio stations could produce. Financial institutions began throwing money at existing and prospective group owners, and a veritable land rush began in earnest. A number of radio companies — most of them no longer in existence — participated in this buying spree, using various forms of creative financing to acquire properties that increased the size of their portfolios, as well as their debt.

Clear Channel shareholders who expected the company to join this free-for-all, however, were going to have to wait, as Lowry Mays anticipated that these acquisitions, many of them highly leveraged, would come crashing back to earth. As son Mark observes today, "We didn't get carried away with it because this company has always been very disciplined. In the late '80s we actually zagged when everyone else was zigging."

Clear Channel did acquire two radio stations early in the year, as the company signed a letter of intent to acquire KTAM-AM and KORA-FM in

Bryan/College Station for $4.2 million. KTAM was a News/Information/Sports station, formatted with some contemporary hit music, while KORA programmed mainstream country music. "These stations will be operated in conjunction with our low power TV station, which was recently put on the air in Bryan/College Station," Lowry Mays noted in the 1986 annual report. This purchase increased to 16 the number of radio stations owned by Clear Channel.

Also in 1987 the company was granted FCC approval to move KHYS-FM Port Arthur to a location that would better serve the Houston market.

1988

In 1988 Clear Channel's revenues increased 8 percent, to $40.130 million. Despite what was turning into a feeding frenzy for the acquisition of radio stations, Lowry Mays and company decided to sit tight, still not wanting to over-leverage the company by paying the high multiples that many broadcasters and institutional lenders were facing. Instead, Clear Channel established a television subsidiary and completed the acquisition of its first television station, WPMI Channel 15 in the Mobile-Pensacola market, for $8.9 million. The acquisition was completed on December 31.

"We believed the Fox Network was going to be an interesting supplier of programming, which meant that the audiences were going to grow on the stations," Mark Mays recalls. "More importantly, we thought we could operate these independent TV facilities more like radio stations. We suspected we could put on compelling programming and operate them in such a way that it was sales-intensive. Sales reps in the TV business back then were a lot like order-takers, waiting for the phone to ring. We looked at it a little differently. We knew that if we instituted a real sales-intensive, locally oriented advertising program that focused on direct accounts such as those we had in radio, we could turn those properties very profitable very quickly."

During the course of the year, the company also successfully moved KHYS-FM from Port Arthur to a new $2.5 million broadcast tower near Houston. In the annual report issued for 1988, Lowry Mays observed, "The Company's radio stations continue to hold strong positions in the markets they serve and rank at or near the top in total audience and revenue share.... Although Clear Channel Communications is primarily a radio broadcasting company, and is expected to remain so, a substantial investment has been committed to television.... To that end, Clear Channel purchased its first television station … [and] on February 1, 1989, the company acquired KDTU-TV Channel 18, another independent, in Tucson, Arizona, for $5.9 million. These two acquisitions should contribute 12–17 percent in revenues and cash flow to the 1989 operating plan." The company subsequently recruited Dan Sullivan to head this new television division.

According to Clear Channel's 1988 annual report, the number of members of the board of directors decreased to five when John Barger left the company. At this point Stan Webb, who had joined the company in 1975, was tapped to oversee the company's San Antonio stations, and in 1995 he was put in charge of all the company's radio stations.

1989

The last year of the '80s proved to be a turning point for Clear Channel, if for no other reason than that Lowry Mays' oldest son Mark joined the company. He had just earned his MBA at Columbia University in New York, and had spent the previous summer working at ABC Radio in the affiliate relations department. "Dad's money guy, his chief finance treasurer, had left the company, and he needed someone to oversee that end of the business," Mark says some 17 years later. "I didn't even make it to my own graduation. Dad was way behind on the finance side, and when I came down to San Antonio I had to get everything up to speed pretty quickly."

In 1989 Clear Channel was hovering very close to the radio ownership limits, and the company had begun expanding into independent television in large part because radio properties were selling at impossibly high cash-flow multiples. "We had bought the Louisville stations in 1984, and we bought Bryan/College Station in '87, but we didn't buy a whole lot in the late '80s," Mark says. "One of the reasons for that was there was so much money chasing deals. The banks would lend you money for just about anything, and a lot of companies were putting together really creative financing, which led to the highly leveraged transaction crisis in 1990. Because of the savings and loan crisis, lenders defined any cash flow loan as an HLT, and therefore they had to have much more capital reserved against it. As a result, HLTs became a big disincentive for the bankers to carry those loans on the balance sheets; they just wanted to close them out and almost put them into default. I remember going to the 1989 NAB Radio Show in New Orleans, where you couldn't get out of the way of all the bankers. A year later, at the same show in Boston, there was not a banker to be found.

There was about one year when the banks really wanted to lend money to radio, and then the flood gates slammed shut."

"For a while in the mid- to late-'80s there was significant liquidity in the market," adds Larry Patrick, president of broadcast brokerage firm Patrick Communications as well as Legend Communications, which owns small market radio stations. "There was a lot of money chasing deals, and a lot of venture people came into the market thinking that radio was wonderful. It was a regulated business with very few new frequencies becoming available and, because in those days you could only own one AM and FM in a market, there were lots of opportunities to buy stations. People were buying and selling, and prices kept going up because Wall Street had not discovered radio yet. It was pretty easy in a major market to have a 40 percent margin, which made radio a pretty attractive business to be in."

"The junk bond market loved the media sector because of its high free cash-flow conversion rates," recalls Drew Marcus, who had initiated coverage of Clear Channel for Deutsche Bank in 1987. "There was a feeling in the mid-'80s that the media sector largely was recession-proof, and it had a lot of leverage. Clear Channel was a company that didn't max out its leverage as some of its peers did, so in the ensuing downturn it was one of the few companies that weathered the storm and stayed public. They used that downturn to start buying independent television stations and they aligned themselves with the upstart Fox Network. At that point they were viewed as very savvy investors, buying these TV properties out of favor, the way they bought radio out of favor in the '70s. Clear Channel truly was one of the most aggressive companies to take advantage of market conditions and the ownership rules as they were expanded."

In 1989, Clear Channel's revenues increased 31 percent to $52.413 million. Still reticent to overpay for radio properties, the company acquired two more television stations — WAWS-TV in Jacksonville, Florida, and KOKI-TV in Tulsa, Oklahoma — and created a sports division, Clear Channel Sports. This entity acquired the radio rights to broadcast the football and basketball games of the University of Oklahoma, Oklahoma State University, Iowa State University, and Texas Tech University. Clear Channel also established an in-house research division to "keep the company in closer touch with its audience and advertising customers in order to react swiftly to changes in the marketplace," according to the annual report. Additionally, the company paid a $3 per-share dividend to shareholders.

"As we entered the '90s we really were a pretty small company and not on a lot of radar screens," says Randall Mays, who at the time was still several years away from joining the company. "But the people who did follow us saw that we had good, consistent top-line revenue growth and controllable expenses, and they knew that we could grow free cash flow at a pretty high rate. Still, we were always very careful in that time frame — as we still are today — to say that someone should never buy our stock for any reason other than that we can organically grow cash flow. We never promised people we would do acquisitions and we never tried to figure in potential acquisitions, because we always felt that would put us in a situation where we would be forced to do deals."

As Lowry Mays noted at the time, "The financial strength of the Company led to the payment in July of a $3-per-share dividend. Although the price of your common stock had increased substantially since the initial public offering, management did not feel it truly reflected the growth in the underlying values of the company over that period of time. For this reason, it was decided to return a portion of the investment to the stockholder."

1990

For 1990, Clear Channel recorded revenues of $69.645 million, a 33 percent increase over the $52.413 reported in 1989. During the year the company acquired its fifth TV station, KSAS Channel 22 in Wichita, Kansas, while KOKI-TV in Tulsa was recognized by the Fox Network for achieving the highest audience gain for the fledgling television company. The annual report for that year notes that the FCC granted a waiver to its "one-to-a-market" or "cross ownership" rules, enabling KOKI-TV to "exchange resources and engage in joint promotions" with Clear Channel's Tulsa radio stations. "This has contributed to KOKI's rapid achievement of its aggressive performance goals," the report concludes. By the end of 1990, Clear Channel's Louisville radio properties accounted for 19 percent of the company's revenues; Tulsa accounted for 14.4 percent; San Antonio, 12.9 percent; Jacksonville, 12 percent; and Oklahoma City, 10.2 percent.

The company remained focused on television during 1990 primarily because of the low prices independent TV stations were attracting, as well as the economic conditions that had begun to hammer the radio industry. The U.S. economy had slipped into a recession in July and would remain in an economic downturn until March 1991.

During this period advertising revenue slumped and many radio broadcasters were unable to make their payroll or their debt payments. The financial institutions that had been throwing money around like confetti suddenly realized that they were not able to take possession of the FCC licenses that so much of their capital was tied to. "That's when the prices of radio stations just came screaming down," Mark Mays recalls. "No one wanted to buy TV, and in the late '80s and early '90s we were able to acquire a bunch of independent TV stations, which gave us a lot of growth opportunities. They really provided us the capital to actually buy a bunch more radio stations, many of which were parts of those struggling companies that had leveraged up. The good news/bad news with leverage is that it works both ways: If you pile on a lot of debt you can grow your company but you have to perform, and you're taking a big risk."

1991

Clear Channel's gross revenues increased 6 percent in 1991, growing to $74.142 million. Part of this increase was due to several significant events that occurred during the year, including the acceptance of a management agreement and a minority interest in KLRT-TV in Little Rock; the successful negotiation of the purchase of KEYN-FM and KQAM-AM in Wichita, giving the company its 17th and 18th radio stations; and the execution of a joint venture agreement with KMSB-TV in Tucson, which was owned by the Providence Journal Company. The station was purchased with the intent to combine it with Clear Channel's KTTU-TV in the same market, with the ultimate goal of making "a much stronger market entity," according to the company's annual report. Also in 1991 Clear Channel issued an additional 1.5 million shares of stock at a price of $14.25 per share.

"Radio was not recognized as an industry until the final parts of deregulation, which occurred in the late '80s and early '90s," Lowry Mays recalls. "It was at that time that we did a big public offering, because the industry was in a very bad crunch. Everybody had gone out and over-leveraged themselves, and the economy was highly leveraged. So we went to the public market again, primarily to build a war chest that would allow us to buy stations from the companies that were going to go broke. It was pretty easy to see that's what was going to happen. The banks were all forcing them out of business, so that was another turning point — going on that road show and convincing institutional buyers that this was a real business and there was going to be further deregulation within the industry."

Lowry says he had been reluctant to take the risks that so many other radio companies had exposed themselves to in the late '80s, a decision that kept Clear Channel financially strong while others began to flatline. "It was apparent that prices were getting too high, especially when the banks were coming to me saying, 'We want to lend you another $50 million.' That indicated to me that all this activity was going to stop. In anticipation of what was coming we did our public offering, and we also paid a big dividend to our shareholders, which was a return of capital because we didn't have anything else to do with the money we were generating. I certainly wasn't going to spend it on escalated prices."

By that point Lowry also knew that deregulatory relief was coming because, as chairman of the NAB board of directors, he had helped draft the language that served as its blueprint. As his son Mark recalls, "Dad was very involved with formulating the regulatory environment that allowed radio to really explode in the '90s. He was always a big believer that less regulation was better, because if he owned radio properties, and anybody was able to buy them, that was going to increase the value of his stations. Radio always was his passion — leading radio and reinventing it, and reinventing it again, in any way that we could. The reason he said he never went bankrupt like a lot of those other radio companies was because he exerted personal caution. Plus, he just knew how leverage worked. He knew how to use it to his advantage whenever he could, but never to the extent that he would put the company at risk. That was his mindset: Don't put the company at risk."

1992

In 1992 Clear Channel celebrated its 20th anniversary with revenues of $94.472 million, a 27 percent increase over the $74.142 million reported in 1991. On January 31, the company completed the acquisition of the Kentucky Network, a news, sports, and information network servicing 78 radio stations throughout the state of Kentucky. It also acquired WPTY-TV in Memphis for $22 million, and announced that the company had been awarded the radio broadcast rights to the New Orleans Saints, with WQUE-AM in New Orleans serving as the flagship station.

After watching radio merger and acquisition activity carefully since the late 1980s, Lowry and Mark Mays finally decided the time was right to begin shopping. As a result, during the course of the year Clear Channel announced the acquisition of WKCI-FM New Haven from Noble

Broadcast Group for $14 million; the company also entered into a sales representation agreement with Noble's KMJQ-FM in Houston, combining marketing activities with Clear Channel-owned KHYS-FM. These sales representation agreements became commonplace in the early 1990s as radio groups, which were prevented from owning more than a total of 24 stations, were allowed by the FCC to enter into joint marketing ventures similar to those that local newspapers formed when circulation woes began to make the co-existence of two major papers in the same market overly competitive. These agreements came to be known as local marketing agreements (LMAs), and in the years leading up to the passage of the Telecom Act, provided a way for broadcasters to effectively generate revenue and cash flow from a station without actually having the benefit (and expense) of owning it. In addition to the Noble deal, Clear Channel also acquired WRVA-AM and WRVQ-FM in Richmond, and WRBQ-AM and WRBQ-FM in Tampa, for a total of $18.5 million. Throw in the completed purchase of KEYN-FM and KQAM-AM in Wichita — which was acquired to pair up with KSAS-TV in that market — and Clear Channel's holdings climbed to 24 radio stations and 7 television stations in 18 markets.

In September 1992 the FCC adopted major changes in its ownership rules that increased the number of stations that broadcasting companies were allowed to own from 24 radio stations (12 AM and 12 FM) to 36 stations (18 AM and 18 FM). More important, companies now were permitted to own two AM and two FM stations in the same market, as long as their combined share of the listening audience was less than 25 percent. This dual market ownership came to be known as duopoly, and it introduced a raft of management challenges that the radio business had never before faced, except for when a combined AM and FM were marketed in tandem.

"Duopoly was like an unplanned experiment," observes Gary Fries, former president of the Radio Advertising Bureau, an organization that focuses on local and national marketing issues. "In the pre-consolidation era the big question was how a sales staff should be run. Some people would pit the two sales staffs against each other, and some people would engage them in combination selling. And that really wasn't resolved until consolidation came along."

In fact, duopoly was widely considered to be a major step to even broader loosening of the FCC's ownership rules, almost a regulatory "trial run" to see how complete deregulation would affect the industry.

1993

In 1993 the company reported a 44 percent revenue increase, with total sales rising to $135.680 million. With ownership limits substantially loosened, Clear Channel began eyeing stations that fit strategically with radio and television properties the company already owned. For instance, Clear Channel completed the acquisition of KQXT-FM in San Antonio from Westinghouse Corp. for $8.2 million in February, then paired it with KZXS, a San Antonio AM station that was purchased from Inner City Broadcasting for $1 million. Clear Channel also entered into a local marketing agreement in San Antonio with Inner City's other San Antonio station, KSJL-FM.

But the company did not stop there, as it signed a letter of intent to acquire KHFI-FM in Austin for $3.5 million, to pair with KPEZ-FM. Clear Channel also bought WRXL-FM and WRVH-AM in Richmond, plus the Virginia News Network, for $9.5 million, and announced the acquisition of KEBC-FM in Oklahoma City for $7.5 million. Further, on December 27 the company announced its intention to purchase WAXY-FM in Miami for $14 million.

During the course of the year, Clear Channel also financed a minority broadcasting enterprise, Snowden Broadcasting, 20 percent of which was owned by Jim Snowden, vice president and general manager of Clear Channel's KHYS-FM in Houston, while the remaining 80 percent was owned by Clear Channel. The two parties entered into an agreement to purchase WYLD-AM and WYLD-FM in New Orleans, where Clear Channel already owned WQUE-FM and WQUE-AM. Clear Channel provided $7.5 million in financing to complete the transaction.

Additionally, Clear Channel announced its intention to merge with Metroplex Communications, which owned radio stations in Tampa, Miami/Ft. Lauderdale, Cleveland, and Buffalo. Because of the FCC's ownership rules, Clear Channel was forced to divest some of its radio investments in order to get the deal approved. It also decided to sell some of its stations in smaller markets, including those in Wichita and Bryan/College Station. Additionally, the company contracted with Snowden Broadcasting to transfer ownership of seven stations it owned in New Haven, Tulsa, and New Orleans. These dispositions effectively made it possible to close the Metroplex deal and maintain flexibility within the FCC's ownership limits, which widely were expected to increase in 1994 to 20 AMs and 20 FMs.

On the television side Clear Channel purchased KITN-TV, the Fox affiliate in Minneapolis, for $35 million, and entered into a time brokerage agreement with WLMT-TV in Memphis, WMTU-TV in Jackson, MS, and KTFO-TV in Tulsa. Big news that year was the announcement that the Fox Network had acquired the rights to broadcast the NFC games of the NFL, with play-by-play coverage to begin in the fall of 1994.

In the 1993 annual report, Lowry Mays observed that, "Clear Channel continues to devote significant attention to long-term planning. We remain committed to decentralized, flexible, entrepreneurial business units that place emphasis on simplifying structures and procedures while maintaining sound centralized financial management. We expect to continue to grow through internal expansion of existing broadcast properties supplemented by strategic acquisitions."

That growth was highlighted in October, when Clear Channel sold an additional 1.725 million shares of common stock, raising approximately $58 million, which was earmarked for making additional station acquisitions.

1994

In 1994 Clear Channel posted record revenues of $200.695 million, a 48 percent increase over the $135.68 million reported in 1993. The company also applied for and obtained the listing of Clear Channel Communications Inc. common stock on the New York Stock Exchange, trading under the symbol CCU. During the year the company also engaged in considerable merger and acquisition activity; for instance, in Houston Clear Channel purchased KBXX-FM for $21 million, then acquired KMJQ-FM and KYOK-AM for $38.5 million and immediately spun off KYOK-AM, as well as KHYS-FM and KALO-AM, in order to comply with the FCC's ever-changing ownership regulations. Following that activity, Clear Channel acquired an 80 percent interest in a partnership that owned and operated KPRC-AM and KSEV-AM, a transaction valued at $26.8 million.

"That Houston deal became the prototypical deal of deregulation," says Randall Mays. "We owned an urban station there that we bought from Cook Inlet, and it was a direct format competitor with a station owned by John Lynch's Noble Broadcasting. We really wanted to acquire the station and we had a good relationship with John, who was experiencing some financial difficulty. The station had $2 million in cash flow, and we paid him $38 million, which at that time was a really huge price for it. But the reason we paid that price was we figured that the station was a direct format competitor with our urban station, and that was hurting both of us because the audience was being diluted equally between them. We knew an audience existed for an urban adult contemporary format in the market, but both of us were minimizing what we could program for the audience. Second, from an advertising perspective, the salespeople were so myopic that one sales force would go in to an advertiser and undercut the other sales force. They weren't selling the benefit of their radio station; they were just selling against each other."

Randall says it was obvious that the ratings and ad rates for both stations were well below what they should have been, and it was apparent inside Clear Channel that, combined, both stations not only could achieve some immediate cost efficiencies, but by programming two distinct formats they also could attract a wider audience and boost ad rates considerably. "Everybody thought we were crazy because we paid this huge multiple," he explains. "But we immediately flipped one of the stations out of the urban format and made it an urban adult contemporary. The two stations had been 10th and 12th in the market, and they quickly became number one and two. That turned out to be the single best acquisition we've ever done, with the possible exception of WHAS and WAMZ in Louisville."

That year Clear Channel also completed its $14 million purchase of WAXY-FM in Miami, which then was flipped to WBGG-FM. In October the company completed its $48 million merger with Metroplex, giving Clear Channel another Miami station, WHYI-FM. In Tampa the Metroplex merger yielded WMTX-AM and FM, which were paired with the company's WRBQ-AM/FM; the deal also allowed Clear Channel to enter the Cleveland market, with the acquisition of WNCX-FM and WERE-AM. The company entered into a joint sales agreement with WENZ-FM, also in Cleveland, which complemented the modern rock format of WNCX-FM.

Additionally, Clear Channel announced it would be acquiring the remaining interest from Snowden Broadcasting of New Orleans LLC, giving the company WYLD-FM as a complement to WQUE-FM and WQUE-AM, which it already owned. The company also expanded its ownership in Oklahoma City with the closing of the $7.5 million acquisition of KEBC-FM. After the successful completion of these transactions, Clear Channel owned a total of 20 FM and 15 AM stations in 12 markets, giving it a duopoly position in each of the radio markets where it was permitted to do so by the FCC.

On the television side, 1994 marked the first year in which Fox affiliates began broadcasting NFL games. Strategic investments included the $25 million acquisition of WXXA-TV in Albany; the company also loaned Clear Channel Television of Little Rock $18.9 million to retire its debt and to acquire the remaining 51 percent of that company for what the annual report describes as a "nominal amount."

In that report, Lowry Mays noted that, "In 1987, 27 percent of the company's total revenue was generated from two radio stations in Louisville. In addition, the company had 15 profit centers. Since that time, the company has strategically diversified into many markets and numerous operating units. In 1994, Clear Channel's largest revenue market was Minneapolis, with 10 percent of total revenue, and the company grew to 59 profit centers.... The exceptional caliber of Clear Channel's 1,700 employees is the most important reason for our success. In our decentralized environment, it is not the people at the corporate headquarters who run our 59 profit centers, but the on-site managers who are charged with increasing the revenue and earnings of the company. They are the backbone and key to our business."

In February 1994 the company's board of directors authorized a five-for-four stock split in the form of a 25 percent dividend distributed on February 22 to shareholders of record on February 15; an additional 6,860,300 shares of stock were issued in connection with this split.

1995

Clear Channel's 1995 revenues were $283 million, an increase of 41 percent over the $200.695 million reported in 1994. Radio transactions were few, with the largest M&A radio activity stemming from the purchase in May of a 21.4 percent interest in Heftel Broadcasting, which at the time was the second-largest Spanish-language radio broadcasting company in the U.S. The only other notable radio transaction activity was the purchase of the Voice of Southwest Agriculture in San Angelo, TX.

Still, in May 1995 Clear Channel made its first foray into international broadcasting through the acquisition of 50 percent of Wesgo Ltd., the second-largest radio broadcaster in Australia. By entering into a partnership with the Australian Radio Network, the two parties created a new venture known as the Australian Radio Network Pty Ltd. As a result, ARN (as it came to be known) owned half of the FM stations in Sydney and Melbourne, as well as stations in Brisbane, Canberra, and Albury/Wodinga.

This transaction was made possible because the Australian government in 1992 relaxed the country's broadcasting laws, allowing for 100 percent foreign ownership of radio properties. The same legislation allowed for duopoly (ownership of two stations of the same service — AM or FM — in the same market) in radio "down under."

On the television side, the company acquired WHP-TV, the CBS affiliate in Harrisburg/Lancaster/Lebanon/York, PA. This market had two CBS affiliates, making it difficult for either station to attract sufficient audience or advertisers to compete effectively. Clear Channel subsequently entered into an LMA with WYLH-TV, which switched to UPN.

On November 30, 1995, the company authorized a two-for-one stock split, issuing 17,290,188 shares of stock to shareholders of record as of November 15.

As 1995 was drawing to a close, Clear Channel had positioned itself to take advantage of what the entire radio business began to realize lay directly ahead of it. With total ownership caps expected to be eliminated and market-by-market limits significantly relaxed, the industry was poised for the sort of consolidation that had not been permitted for the first 75 years of its existence. "The Telecom Act of 1996 was well on its way to being passed," recalls Randall Mays. "Even back in '94 we knew that it was coming, and through '95 we were working pretty aggressively to figure out how we wanted to take advantage of it. Our stock was performing very well, we had very strong access to capital, and multiples were at such a level that owners were very motivated to sell. We had positioned ourselves so that by the time the Telecom Act became law, we had twelve to eighteen months of running room."

CHAPTER THREE

OPENING THE FLOODGATES

THE FIRST QUARTER OF 1996 WAS A WATERSHED PERIOD IN THE HISTORY OF the U.S. radio industry. The Republican-led 104th Congress approved the legislation for the Telecommunications Act of 1996 in January, and Democratic President Bill Clinton signed it into law on February 8 in the Main Reading Room of the Library of Congress.

Much of the Telecom Act concentrated on revamping telephony and cable regulations, with the basic intention of removing barriers that previously had prevented the telecommunication giants from competing head-to-head and, ostensibly, to offer consumers greater choice in selecting local phone service. Still, the legislation served to redraw significantly the ownership lines inside which existing radio and television broadcasters could operate. Many of the original provisions contained in the Communications Act of 1934 had been replaced by increasingly relaxed rules that seemed much more geared for the 1990s than the years of the Great Depression. Television ownership limits were lifted, allowing group owners to own as many stations as they wanted with a maximum U.S. market penetration of no more than 35 percent of the U.S. population. Likewise, radio station ownership limits were lifted almost entirely, effectively allowing broadcasters to own as many stations as they wanted, although the Telecom Act did impose a loose limit on the number of stations a single entity could own within a single market or geographical area.

Of course, without the considerable commitment and hard work on the part of the nation's broadcasters, the Telecom Act might not have passed at all — and most assuredly not in its final form.

"For ten years, all I did was work on deregulation," observes Lowry Mays. "I'd go to the commissioners and point out that back when [William Randolph] Hearst was in the newspaper business and he started buying radio stations, everybody said there needed to be a limit on the number of radio stations you could own so you wouldn't influence public opinion. I'd look at each commissioner and say, 'At this day and time, if I owned one radio station in every market in the United States, do you think I could influence public opinion?' And they inevitably would say, 'Well, of course not.' At which point I would say, 'I rest my case.'"

Former NAB President and CEO Eddie Fritts, now head of The Fritts Group, remembers the zeal with which Lowry Mays approached the deregulation issue. "I was sitting in a board meeting one day several years prior to the passage of the Telecom Act, and Lowry observed that the radio industry should have no rules governing station ownership, either market-by-market rules or national rules," he says. "No one disagreed with him, so that was the philosophy that was adopted by the entire radio board."

While the telecom and cable industries largely were the headliners in the debate leading up to passage of the Telecom Act, both industries realized they needed votes to get the legislation passed. At that point, Fritts says, a number of members of Congress approached the NAB and asked, "What can we work out with the broadcast industry that would bring your support to this legislation?" At that point the radio industry welcomed deregulation, while the television industry was a little less eager, due in part to network growth issues, so the NAB responded, "If you moderate your enthusiasm on the television side and deregulate radio, we're in."

Naturally, some lawmakers on Capitol Hill opposed deregulation of any kind, but by the mid-'90s cable and telephone companies were consolidating rather rapidly, so some members of Congress agreed that radio and television needed some relief in this area, as well.

"Senator Ernest Hollings [D-SC] was opposed to any deregulation, but he'd used up most of his persuasion on the television side," Fritts remembers. "By the time it got to radio deregulation he had spent most of his powder. Now, Hollings was a ranking member of the committee, and however he voted, the rest of the Democrats would vote, by and large."

Ultimately the legislation was passed by Congress and signed by President Clinton, and was hailed as a historic move designed to allow telephone companies into cable and allow the cable companies into telephony. Of course, passage of the Telecom Act swung the floodgates for radio M&A activity wide open, and within the span of a few short years many of the stations and groups that had struggled through the first half of the '90s were swallowed up by those that were less leveraged and better equipped to grow.

For example, Pyramid and Broadcasting Partners were folded into Evergreen, Viacom Radio picked up Sonderling, and Colfax acquired Sundance. Meanwhile, Radio Equity Partners purchased Wilks-Schwartz and NewMarket; Paxson Radio absorbed Guy Gannett and Metroplex; and Jacor picked up Nationwide, Noble, Citicasters, Champlin, Tsunami, and Gannett (not to be confused with the afore-mentioned Guy Gannett). At the same time, Capstar acquired such companies as SFX Broadcasting, Triathlon, Gibbons, Quass, Benchmark, Osborn, Commodore, Patterson, and Community Pacific; eventually Chancellor Media merged Evergreen with Viacom, Shamrock, and a host of other companies — and then, with Capstar, transitioned into AMFM.

What often is lost when focusing on this period of fast-forward consolidation is the fact that, as intended, telephone and cable companies also experienced their share of industry compression. Most notably, Bell Atlantic and NYNEX merged; Southwestern Bell and Pacific Telephone merged to become SBC (which then bought Ameritech); AT&T bought TCI; a larger Bell Atlantic merged with GTE to become Verizon; and MCI Communications merged with WorldCom to become MCI WorldCom.

"The net result of all this in the radio business was an accelerated growth pattern for Clear Channel that was nothing short of breathtaking," recalls Fritts. "None of us imagined that they would expand as quickly or as broadly as they did, or that any one company could borrow as much money as it did in order to buy stations and companies that had already expanded."

Because Clear Channel was the darling of Wall Street, and because Lowry, Mark, and Randall Mays had an acute business sense, they knew the financial markets better than anyone else, says Patrick Communications' Larry Patrick. "More than anybody, Lowry Mays understood what it would take to build his company over the next few years. He knew he needed a tremendous war chest, and he saw that Wall Street was going to be that war chest. Lowry and his sons had a plan to build and operate market clusters across the country, and they proved to be very good at it. They rolled through 200, 500, 800 stations, and in a very short time they created the blueprint for radio consolidation."

"I don't think anybody got the license number of the bus that Lowry Mays was thinking about driving down the road," adds former RAB president Gary Fries. "As consolidation began and kept moving, people started buying companies right and left. It was sort of like the perfect storm, all those forces coming together at exactly the right moment."

1996

At the beginning of 1996 — five weeks before the Telecom Act was to become law — Clear Channel owned, programmed, or sold airtime on 43 radio stations and 16 television stations in 21 U.S. markets. During the year the company began acquiring properties as if the Mays triumvirate was shopping for Kmart "blue light" specials, picking up 35 FM stations and 14 AM stations in 20 markets. By the end of the year, the company reported revenues of $398 million, a 41 percent increase over the $283 million reported in 1995 — and almost 38 times the revenue reported when the company went public in 1984. Some, but not all, of these transactions included:

Acquiring the assets of WOOD-AM/FM and WBCT-FM in Grand Rapids, Michigan, for $42 million; Clear Channel subsequently closed on the acquisition of WCUZ-AM/FM and WAKX-FM (now WVTI-FM), also in Grand Rapids.

Purchasing KOAS-FM and KQLL-AM/FM in Tulsa.

Buying WTVR-AM/FM in Richmond.

Acquiring additional stations in Louisville, including WWKY-AM, WTFX-FM, WHKW-FM, WKJK-AM, and WQMF-FM, increasing the company's ownership position in that market to four FMs and three AMs.

Agreeing to acquire U.S. Radio for $140 million. At the time U.S. Radio owned or operated 19 stations in eight markets, including Milwaukee, Norfolk, Raleigh, Reading, Memphis, Little Rock, Houston, and El Paso.

Entering into an agreement to buy WOKY-AM and WMIL-FM in Milwaukee; WMYK-FM, WDUR-AM, and WZZU-FM in Raleigh; WLAN-AM/FM in Lancaster, PA; and KJMS-FM and KWAM-AM in Memphis.

Completing the acquisition of Radio Equity Partners, which had operations that overlapped with Clear Channel stations in New Orleans, Memphis, Oklahoma City, and Providence. The REP acquisition also contributed radio stations in Springfield, Massachusetts; Winston-Salem-Greensboro, North Carolina; Columbia, South Carolina; and Fort Myers-Naples, Florida.

Making an equity investment of an 80 percent interest in Radio Enterprises Inc., headed by former Capital Cities/ABC executive Jim Arcara and his son David. The company owned or had entered into agreements to purchase WQBK-AM/FM, WQBJ-FM, and WXCR-FM in Albany, where Clear Channel owned the Fox-affiliated WXXA-TV.

Acquiring a temporary controlling interest in Heftel Broadcasting. (Note: in 1997 Clear Channel merged that company with Tichenor Media System, giving Clear Channel 32.3 percent of the combined entity.)

With the large number of radio stations that had started to change hands — not just those that were being acquired by Clear Channel but other growth-minded groups, as well — the U.S. Department of Justice grew increasingly concerned that companies would begin to dominate audience and advertising revenue within a market. Industry forces at both the National Association of Broadcasters and the Radio Advertising Bureau tried to convince Joel Klein, who was the assistant attorney general for antitrust at the Department of Justice, that — since radio receives but a modest slice of overall market ad revenue — the overall share of dollars that a merged company should be allowed to earn in that market should be viewed not within that small slice, but rather compared against all ad dollars in the market. In other words, if a single daily newspaper can generate 40 to 50 percent of all ad dollars in a particular market, a radio group — through the acquisition of stations — should be allowed to compete for as many ad dollars in the market as possible, rather than being viewed separately within the seven-to-eight percent "slice" of total ad dollars that the radio medium typically draws. This was an important distinction, because the Department of Justice was weighing whether radio antitrust considerations should be based on revenue and audience dominance within the overall market, or simply within its own media sector.

"We had several meetings with Joel Klein and other lawyers for the antitrust division," Gary Fries remembers. "Radio was very foreign to them, and they were trying to decide whether radio was an industry unto itself, or part of the overall advertising community. Our position was that radio was part of the overall advertising pie, and we worked on that angle very strongly."

Klein and his team eventually concluded that radio would be considered its own industry, and further decided that any company that amassed stations in such a way that it "controlled" more than 35 percent of radio revenue (as opposed to overall advertising revenue) in a market most likely would come under Justice Department scrutiny.

Speaking before a group of broadcasters in early 1997 in Washington, Klein observed that, "While I'd like to be able to announce a hard-and-fast rule — say, no more than 40 percent in a market — that would be unfair to you and to us. We've already approved mergers resulting in more than 40 percent market share, such as in Cincinnati. And I can imagine a case, depending on format and signal strength, where even less than a 40 percent market share might allow a company to exercise market power unilaterally when demand and supply side factors are fully considered. But I still think it's fair to say that when you're doing a deal that's in the 35-percent-and-above range — or that consolidates a large part of a particular format [even when that involves less than 35 percent of the overall market] — you should bring in antitrust counsel early on, so that you can be fully advised with respect to any problems the deal might encounter and decide whether you want to take on these problems or restructure the deal to avoid them."

While the antitrust issues wouldn't come into play until early 1997, merger and acquisition activity was beginning to mount. "When broadcasters started to see that they could own two stations and then four stations in the lead-up to the Telecom Act, there was a lot of M&A activity," Greater

Media CEO Peter Smyth says. "Revenues were growing at an incredible clip, and the comment that Federal Reserve Chairman Alan Greenspan made about 'irrational exuberance' really began to take hold at that time. Everyone was buying radio stations in anticipation of flipping them and not really with the anticipation of running them. If you bought a property at a cash flow multiple of 14, you'd sell it at 16 in the afternoon. It was like going to an auction."

As the largest consolidator of radio stations, Clear Channel's acquisitions drew considerable Justice Department scrutiny. Because the company was acquiring a lot of stations in a number of markets, many deals pushed it right up against (and sometimes over) that arbitrary 35 percent line. As a result, Clear Channel on more than one occasion was forced to either step back from a deal, or spin off select stations in order to pass muster with the antitrust attorneys.

As Mark Mays recalls, "We won every fair fight we ever had with the Justice Department. Unfortunately, when you're in the middle of an acquisition, you can't afford to have a fair fight. They know that a delay is going to cost you money in these acquisitions, and their philosophy is to delay things as long as possible and force you to the negotiating table to make a deal you don't want to do. For the most part they were successful in doing that."

The television side of the business did not come under such scrutiny, however, and in 1996 Clear Channel purchased WPRI-TV, the CBS affiliate in Providence, Rhode Island, and entered into an LMA with WNAC-TV, the Fox affiliate in that market. The company also launched television news operations in Memphis, Mobile-Pensacola, Jacksonville, and Albany.

Internationally, the country of New Zealand in 1996 privatized Radio New Zealand Commercial, a broadcasting enterprise that was acquired by New Zealand Radio Network, a consortium consisting of three equal partners: Clear Channel, Australian Provincial Newspapers Ltd., and Wilson & Horton, the largest publisher in New Zealand. At the time, NZRN owned 52 radio stations in New Zealand and controlled some 60 percent of the country's radio revenue. Additionally, the Australian Radio Network, of which Clear Channel owned 50 percent (with Australian Provincial Newspapers, Ltd.), purchased four more radio stations: one in Brisbane, one in Western Sydney, and two in Adelaide.

In December the Clear Channel board of directors authorized a two-for-one stock split for shareholders of record on November 13; 38,496,039 shares of the company's stock were issued. The composition of the board itself remained unchanged from 1995.

1997

Clear Channel's revenues in 1997 almost doubled those in 1996, increasing 98 percent to $790 million. The largest of Clear Channel's 1997 radio acquisitions was the $629 million purchase of Paxson Communications' 43 stations, clustered primarily throughout Florida. The company also either announced or closed on a number of what it referred to as "tuck-in" operations that complemented broadcast operations in many of its existing markets. Additionally, the company closed on acquisitions that added several new markets to its radio portfolio, including Allentown, Pennsylvania; Monterey, California; Dayton, Ohio; and Jackson, Mississippi. As announced in the annual report, by the end of the year the company "operated or sold airtime on" 184 stations in 40 domestic markets.

While radio consolidation continued in earnest in 1997, the year was most notable in that it was marked by the establishment of an entirely new Clear Channel division. In February Clear Channel entered into a definitive agreement to acquire the stock of Eller Media Co. for $1.15 billion. Eller Media at the time was the oldest and largest outdoor advertising company in the U.S., controlling some 50,000 advertising display faces. By '97 Eller Media reached 26 major metropolitan markets including Los Angeles, San Diego, San Francisco, Sacramento, Chicago, Milwaukee, Cleveland, Akron/Canton, Dallas, Houston, San Antonio, El Paso, Phoenix, Atlanta, Tampa, and Miami. Clear Channel announced that Eller Media would operate as an autonomous, wholly owned subsidiary of Clear Channel and would be run by then-CEO Karl Eller. (Please see Chapter 5 for more information on Clear Channel's Outdoor division.)

The company also initiated a stock-for-stock merger agreement with Universal Outdoor valued at approximately $1.7 billion. The proposed merger was expected to close in the first half of 1998, at which time Universal shareholders would receive 0.67 shares of Clear Channel stock for each share of Universal stock held. When these two outdoor deals were completed, Clear Channel essentially became the largest outdoor company in the U.S., with a leading presence in 21 of the top 35 U.S. media markets.

In the second half of the year Clear Channel also announced the acquisition of the Union Pacific Railroad Company outdoor advertising display license portfolio, which included approximately 4,000 licenses to operate displays on railroad right-of-ways. Additionally, the company completed numerous separate acquisitions of outdoor advertising displays in 11 markets, including Los Angeles, Dallas, Chicago, Milwaukee, Houston, Atlanta, and San Antonio.

On the international front, Clear Channel entered the European broadcasting market by acquiring a 50 percent interest in Radio Bonton, a radio station serving the Czech Republic. (The owner of the other half of the property was Bonton s.a., a diversified Czech media company.) Clear Channel also drafted preliminary agreements with Radio Shanghai, which operated 13 radio stations and one cable station in the Shanghai, China market. As part of the transaction Clear Channel announced that it would assist in selling airtime on these 14 outlets, which reached some 50 million Chinese.

During the course of the year, Clear Channel also acquired a 30 percent interest in the American Tower Corp., the leading independent domestic owner and operator of wireless communication towers, in a deal valued at $35.5 million. No television acquisitions were completed in 1997, but plans were made for the conversion of eight stations to digital broadcasting.

In 1997 Karl Eller was named to the board of directors, bringing the number of directors to six.

1998

In 1998 Clear Channel reported revenues of $1.52 billion, a 93 percent increase over the $790 million reported in 1997. The company added 38 radio stations during the year, bringing the total number of stations owned to 204.

The biggest news during the year was the announcement in October that the company had agreed to merge with Jacor Communications, which at the time was the nation's second-largest radio company (as measured by number of stations). Under the M&A leadership of radio industry "wunderkind" Randy Michaels and real estate mogul Sam Zell, Jacor had experienced its own rapid-fire growth since the first days of consolidation, operating 230 radio stations in 55 markets, one television station, and the Premiere Radio Networks, syndicator of such personalities as Rush Limbaugh and Dr. Laura Schlessinger.

Jacor actually was founded in 1981, with the purchase of stations in Cincinnati, Toledo and Baltimore. Five years later the company acquired

50,000-watt WLW-AM and WEBN-FM in Cincinnati; by the end of 1986 the company owned 12 stations and the Georgia Radio Network. The company managed to last through the HLT turmoil of the late '80s, although under different management, and in 1993 it purchased WKRC-AM, also in Cincinnati, making it the first radio group to own two stations in that market on the same band. Jacor continued to make select acquisitions through the mid-'90s, and when the Telecom Act became law the company made some bold moves, including the $190 million acquisition of Premiere Radio, and the $152 million purchase of 10 stations from Noble Broadcast Group. The merger with Clear Channel was structured as a tax-free, stock-for-stock transaction.

Also during 1998 Clear Channel completed the acquisition of London-based More Group Plc, which had 90,000 outdoor displays in 22 countries, most of them in Europe. The company also purchased a 40 percent interest in Grupo Acir Communications, a Mexican radio broadcasting company that at the time owned and operated 157 stations. Additionally, the company in April purchased a 50 percent interest in Hainan White Horse Advertising Media Investment Co. Ltd., a Chinese company that operated street furniture displays throughout China.

In July the company authorized a two-for-one stock split, and Mark Mays, Clear Channel president and COO, was added to the board of directors, bringing the total number to seven.

1999

In the last year of the '90s Clear Channel's revenue again almost doubled, growing to $3 billion from $1.52 billion in 1998. The company also started reporting net revenue rather than gross sales; net revenue in 1999 was $2.678 billion, which also was a 98 percent increase over the $1.4 billion reported the previous year.

The year was celebrated by financial analysts when *The Wall Street Journal* ranked Clear Channel's stock as the best performing in the 1990s, based on issues that traded for the entire decade. To put this in perspective, Bloomberg noted that the total return or price appreciation during the period of December 31, 1989, through December 31, 1999, was 14,326.2 percent — or 64.3 percent annually. Thus, a $10,000 investment made on the last day of 1989 would have been worth over *$1.4 million* ten years later.

"As we were acquiring radio properties through the '90s, the first rule was that they had to be very accretive for us," Lowry Mays says. "We would make those investments on top of each other, and our stock just went through the roof. Of all the companies on the New York Stock Exchange we were one of the best performing, and by a significant margin. And that had to do with buying stations at good prices relative to what we had. That was our basic acquisition philosophy."

Clear Channel made numerous acquisitions through 1999, and by the end of the year owned some 870 radio stations throughout the U.S. The company operated stations in all of the top 10 markets, and 47 of the top 50. Additionally, the purchase of Premiere Radio Networks, picked up through the Jacor acquisition, expanded the scope and reach of the company, adding to its line-up such programs as *The Rush Limbaugh Show, The Dr. Laura Program, Jim Rome's Sports Jungle, The Dr. Dean Edell Show,* and *Coast To Coast With Art Bell.*

Arguably, the company's most notable acquisition came late in the year when it signed a definitive agreement to merge with AMFM Inc. in a deal valued at $23.5 billion — including coverage of all outstanding debt. As Steve Hicks, who served as president and CEO of AMFM at the time of the merger, observes, "It definitely was the right thing to do. Aside from our bank debt we took it all in Clear Channel shares, so we obviously were betting on the management skills of the Mays family as well as our firm belief of what a platform of 1,200 stations would mean to the business."

The son of a radio broadcaster who had competed against Clear Channel in several Texas markets in the '70s and '80s, Hicks in 1990 was named president and chief executive officer of Bob Sillerman's SFX Broadcasting, which went public three years later. Hicks left the company in 1996 to form Capstar Broadcasting with funding from Hicks Muse Tate & Furst, which was co-founded by his brother Tom. Capstar initiated a public offering in 1998 and shortly thereafter merged with Chancellor Media, which had evolved out of Evergreen Media and also was funded by Hicks Muse.

While Clear Channel undoubtedly is viewed as the master of consolidation, AMFM by late 1999 actually had "rolled up" more stations than any other company in the business. In the 42 months between the passage of the Telecommunications Act and the announcement that it was merging with Clear Channel, the company had acquired no fewer than three dozen individual radio groups. Through Evergreen it had picked up a number of companies mentioned earlier, including Colfax, American Media, Shamrock, OmniAmerica, Malrite, Broadcasting Partners, Pyramid, Sonderling, and Sundance Broadcasting. The Capstar connection yielded

SFX Broadcasting, Triathlon, Gibbons, Knight Quality Stations, Quass, Benchmark, Osborn, Commodore, Patterson, and Community Pacific, to name just a few.

As Tony Sanders wrote in the December 17, 1999, *Radio Billboard Monitor,* "It took less than a year for five of radio's top-billing groups to merge and emerge as just two separate groups. The recently announced Clear Channel-AMFM merger will reunite radio's former number one (AMFM Inc.) and number 3 (Clear Channel-Jacor) billing groups."

"We were trying to create a national footprint, which really had not been done before," Steve Hicks recalls. "When sweeping deregulation passed in 1996, the initial focus — particularly of the larger groups — was on buying stations in all of the major markets. Our philosophy, however, was to look at markets 100 and smaller, because there was very little merger and acquisition competition outside of Jacor, which was our biggest competitor in the markets we were interested in. We were looking at cash flow and creating clusters of stations in attractive markets across the country."

Hicks insists he would have preferred to keep AMFM as an operating company, but the Hicks Muse partners decided there would be more synergy — and financial upside — in combining the company with Clear Channel. "We had AMFM for such a short time — just a little over a year — that the actual combination of stations never really allowed us to create a combined culture," he recalls.

Still, in the brief period that AMFM led the radio industry, the company developed some operational practices that never had been attempted before — or at least not to the extent that consolidation now allowed. "We came up with ways to share content among the stations that had not been done before, using our local area network [LAN] system to move content between stations," Hicks says. "We wanted to maximize the use of our content over our platform, and we knew that if we had a great morning show in one market, it made sense to use that same talent in other markets, as well."

This practice, which came to be known as voicetracking — and was vilified by the powerful AFTRA union and others as one of the sins of consolidation — led to some genuine seat-of-the-pants innovation. "It was an interesting time because all this new technology was emerging at the same time that there were significant changes in the rules and regulations," Hicks observes. "The ability to put radio programming on a computer and distribute that to a number of stations simply didn't exist just five years before."

Despite the number of stations the company gathered into its portfolio that year, Lowry Mays says that he and his acquisition team definitely passed on some choice properties. "We missed a lot, because in many cases people were willing to pay higher prices than we were," he observes. "Some of those deals we ended up buying the second time around. For instance, Jacor had bought some companies in competition with us, but we ended up with those properties when we bought them. Same thing with the Hicks Muse group. We ended up paying a higher price the second time around, but that's how the market was working at the time."

In 1999 Clear Channel also expanded its international presence in several ways, including the acquisition of outdoor media companies in seven European countries. In Belgium the company successfully merged six companies under one roof; in France it acquired Dauphin, the leading billboard company, which was merged into four previously owned French companies; and in Italy the company purchased a controlling interest in Jolly, the outdoor market leader in northeast Italy. The company also acquired Affitalia, Italy's largest national billboard operator. Additionally, in Norway Clear Channel purchased 50 percent of Radio One's ten radio stations, which served the country's four largest cities; in Switzerland the company acquired Plakanda and OFEX, the number two and number three Swiss outdoor companies; and in the U.K. Clear Channel bought Atlantic Media, Postermobile, and Rock Box to strengthen its number one position in outdoor advertising in that country. The company also entered the British radio market by acquiring a 32 percent equity stake in Jazz FM, and created the U.K.'s only independent radio sales house, Clear Channel Radio Sales. Additionally, the company strengthened its "Adshel" division, the company's global street-furniture brand, which provided "urban solutions to municipalities in return for curbside advertising rights." Founded in the 1960s, Adshel at the end of 1999 operated 150,000 outdoor faces in 28 countries around the world.

In addition to the 870 radio stations the company was set to own following completion of the AMFM deal, Clear Channel owned 19 TV stations and 550,000 outdoor displays. By the end of 1999, radio was still the company's primary source of revenue, accounting for 67 percent of its gross receipts. The U.S. outdoor and the international outdoor markets each contributed 14 percent of Clear Channel's revenue, while television contributed 4 percent and international radio provided the remaining 1 percent.

2000

In 2000 Clear Channel reported net revenues of $5.345 billion, a 100 percent increase over 1999. Much of this tremendous gain came from the veritable explosion of dot-com companies that, swollen with venture capital, burned through billions of dollars in just a few short years. As each of these firms vied for position in the fledgling online space, they invested heavily in advertising — with many of those dollars going to radio because of the medium's efficiency and effectiveness.

During the course of the year the company completed the acquisition of AMFM, and by the end of the year operated 1,140 radio stations in nearly 300 markets, plus New York-based Katz Media Group. Founded in 1888 in New York by Emmanuel Katz as the nation's first media rep, the firm in 2000 provided advertising representation for over 2,000 radio stations, 368 TV stations, and growing interests in cable. The company got its start in the newspaper representation business, and when those newspaper companies began purchasing radio stations in the early- and mid-1900s, and then the radio companies ventured into television, expanding into electronic media seemed a natural extension of the business. Today Katz strictly deals with radio and television, with annual billings in 2006 of approximately $3.2 billion.

In August the company acquired SFX Entertainment for $4.4 billion to add a new component to the mix of marketing solutions available to clients to reach their customers.

SFX was founded by Robert Sillerman, a maverick entrepreneur who had built similarly named SFX Broadcasting into a billion-dollar public radio company before merging it into Capstar, which eventually became part of Clear Channel in the AMFM acquisition. At the time of its merger with Clear Channel the company owned and/or operated 120 live entertainment venues in 31 of the top 50 U.S. markets, including 16 amphitheaters in the top 10 markets. In fact, SFX was billed as a "leading fully-integrated sports marketing and management company, representing more than 650 professional athletes and is the largest producer and promoter of specialized motor sports shows in the U.S."

When Clear Channel announced it was purchasing SFX Entertainment, the company said it provided "integrated promotion, production, venue operation, and event management services for a broad variety of live entertainment events."

Explaining the rationale of the SFX acquisition, Clear Channel noted that the entertainment company "offers artists and entertainers a one-stop resource for touring, production, and promotion, and has developed a unique lifestyle marketing model enabling marketers to engage consumers in order to build their business and their brands," and "provides consumers a high-quality live entertainment experience at every touch point — from purchasing tickets to attending shows and visiting venues."

As Lowry Mays noted at the time of the transaction, "We consider this acquisition and our entry into live entertainment to be a natural extension of our existing radio operations and a critical part of our long-term strategy…. Ultimately this will allow us to leverage our combined marketing and promotional strength to help our customers sell their products and services."

Randall Mays expanded on the SFX acquisition by commenting, "The acquisition of SFX Entertainment allows us to take further advantage of the natural synergy between radio and live music events. We believe the SFX acquisition brings valuable entertainment assets to our company that, when combined with our other media assets, creates a powerful platform of products to help our clients more effectively and efficiently reach their customers."

Including all acquisitions pending at the end of 2000, Clear Channel owned and operated radio stations and/or outdoor advertising properties in virtually every U.S. market where SFX owned and/or operated live entertainment venues. These marketing synergies, Lowry Mays noted, "allow Clear Channel, through SFX, to gain immediate leadership in the highly attractive live entertainment segment, while taking advantage of the natural relationship between radio and live music events. It leverages the marketing and promotional strength of Clear Channel's broadcasting and outdoor advertising platforms and adds a new component to the marketing solutions, which Clear Channel can provide to its customers to help them sell their products. Additionally, it creates an exceptional platform for Clear Channel to pursue initiatives relating to the Internet and music."

When SFX Chairman Robert Sillerman inked the deal with Clear Channel he said, "Having known the Mays family for almost 20 years and having watched the spectacular growth of the company and performance of their stock, it was a surprisingly easy decision to accept their offer. In the ever-expanding world of media and entertainment, the combination of distribution and content is becoming increasingly important. While what we have created as the world's leader in live entertainment and sports marketing is gratifying, there is no question that the combination with Clear Channel will accelerate our growth and further strengthen our already excellent prospects. This is a classic win-win situation for our shareholders and for Clear Channel's shareholders."

Meanwhile, on the outdoor advertising front, the Eller Outdoor division acquired Ackerley Media's Miami and West Palm Beach display properties. The division also invested in Spectacolor, which was focused primarily on New York's Times Square and was responsible for many of the lighted color displays in the area. Additionally, Clear Channel acquired Interstate Outdoor, which added key displays in the Philadelphia and New York markets; purchased Taxi Tops, which owned some 8,400 taxi displays (tops, trunks, and wraps); and acquired Donrey Outdoor, adding ten new markets to the outdoor portfolio. In South America, the Outdoor division also purchased Chile's leading outdoor advertising company, Procom.

Signaling the realities of the expanding media marketplace and the emergence of new technologies, the 2000 annual report included a new section dealing with the booming Internet sector. The Clear Channel Internet Group was formed in the fall of 2000 and was given the responsibility of developing a "seamless, integrated web network across all of the Clear Channel media and entertainment businesses." By the end of the year it covered some 900 individual station websites and handled 450,000 unique visitors per month.

By the end of the year, 45 percent of Clear Channel's net revenue came from radio, a decrease from 67 percent the previous year. Some 28 percent of revenue came from the entertainment division, 22 percent came from outdoor, while television, international, and "other" drove the remaining 5 percent of the company's business.

Five people were added to the board of directors in 2000: Robert Crandall, former chairman of American Airlines; Thomas Hicks, chairman/CEO of Hicks Muse Tate & Furst, Inc.; Vernon Jordan, Jr., senior managing director, Lazard Freres & Co., LLC; Michael Levitt, a partner in Hicks Muse Tate & Furst; and Perry Lewis, founder of Morgan Lewis Githens & Ahn.

2001

In 2001 Clear Channel reported net revenues of $7.97 billion, a 49 percent increase over the $5.345 billion reported in 2000. The company's major acquisition for the year was that of The Ackerley Group, which held a diversified portfolio of outdoor, broadcasting, and interactive media assets. This was a tax-free, stock-for-stock transaction valued at $765.5 million, including $474.9 million plus the assumption of $290.6 million of debt. The deal was expected to close in the first half of 2002.

During the course of the year the company acquired a total of 183 radio stations, 6,900 outdoor display faces, and a variety of music, sports, and racing events through the Entertainment division. Clear Channel also acquired the licenses of two television stations, both of which the company previously had been operating under a local marketing agreement. Additionally, Clear Channel exchanged one license for two TV licenses and $10 million in cash.

Of course, the third quarter of the year was marked by the tragic events of September 11, when 19 Al Qaeda terrorists launched airborne attacks against the World Trade Center in New York and the Pentagon and other potential targets in Washington, DC. In an unprecedented move, Clear Channel within hours had switched all of its music stations to full news coverage of the terrorist situation, and also established the Clear Channel Relief Fund, designed to raise money for immediate and ongoing relief efforts. Monetary donations were collected at most of the company's 1,200 stations and distributed to such organizations as the United Way, the American Red Cross, the Salvation Army, and other funds set up to directly help the families of those killed in the attacks. Noting the tragic events of that day, Lowry, Mark, and Randall Mays expressed their pride and gratitude for how the "Clear Channel family rallied together to support those in need and each other. The overwhelming success of this fund shows the commitment our employees, consumers, and our customers have to doing good work for our communities. We are all so very grateful to those who made it possible."

During 2001 the radio division reorganized its management structure and hired approximately 600 new sales people. Also that year two individuals — Karl Eller and Michael Levitt — left the board of directors, reducing the number of members to 11.

2002

Clear Channel's revenue in 2002 was $8.421 billion, a 6 percent increase over 2001. This slowdown was primarily due to the economic stagnation resulting from the events of 9/11, the dot-com bust that dried up advertising dollars, and an overall recession. During the year Clear Channel's acquisition activity decreased considerably, with the company purchasing just 27 radio stations and 9,275 outdoor display faces for approximately $241.2 million. By the end of 2002 the company owned 372 AM and 812 FM stations; the Outdoor division owned or operated 716,039 displays; the Entertainment division promoted or produced over 29,000 events, and owned or operated 76 domestic venues and 26 international venues; and the Television division owned, programmed, or sold airtime for 34 TV stations.

The year also was marked by consistent and strengthening criticism of how consolidation and, specifically, Clear Channel was having a negative impact on the entire radio industry. A number of websites promoting this viewpoint appeared quickly and they — along with a few more established online watchdogs — latched on to unsubstantiated rumors that seemed to expand and exaggerate with each repetition. Most notable of these was Salon.com, which gained considerable traction with a series of Clear Channel critiques that cited a substantial number of unnamed sources in an attempt to paint a dark picture of the company that most people now recognized as the largest radio operator in the U.S. and, most likely, the world. While some errors most certainly were made in the years following deregulation, the toxicity of the widespread denigration of Clear Channel was nothing less than remarkable. The majority of the allegations leveled by Salon.com against Clear Channel later would be proven incorrect, but at the time they were carried forward by the media almost without question.

Responding to this new criticism, Lowry, Mark, and Randall together noted, "Much has been written about the size and scope of Clear Channel. Our goal has never been to be big for the sake of being big, but rather to leverage our size to deliver better services to our customers and communities and, in turn, greater value to our shareholders. We recognize, however, that there are some people who need to be convinced of the societal benefit of our business model. Accordingly, during 2002 we intensified our efforts to better educate legislators, regulators, and the public about the benefits of our business strategy and the enormous contributions Clear Channel makes to each and every community we serve." At the same time the company opened an office in Washington, DC and created a senior vice president of corporate communications position — both of them corporate firsts. (Clear Channel's publicity issues will be discussed in greater depth in subsequent chapters.)

In 2002 Robert Crandall left the board of directors, while Phyllis Riggins, managing director of Bluffview Capital, and J.C. Watts, chairman of the J.C. Watts Companies and a former Congressman from Oklahoma joined the board.

2003

In 2003 Clear Channel's revenues were $8.93 billion, a 6 percent increase over the $8.421 billion reported in 2002. During the year, acquisition activity continued to slow, with the company picking up just 16 radio stations in 10 markets for $45.9 million. The Outdoor division acquired 727 outdoor display faces in eight domestic markets and 1,906 display faces in four international markets, for a total of $28.3 million; it also made investments in "non-consolidated affiliates" for $10.7 million, and purchased an additional 10 percent interest in a subsidiary for $5.1 million.

At the end of the year, Clear Channel owned 366 AM and 816 FM radio stations throughout the U.S. The Outdoor division owned or operated 787,575 display faces in over 40 domestic markets and 63 foreign countries, while the Entertainment division promoted or produced over 32,000 events, and owned or operated 74 domestic venues and 29 international venues. Meanwhile, the Television division owned, programmed, or sold air time for 39 TV stations.

2004

In 2004 Clear Channel reported that its annual revenues were $9.419 billion, a 5 percent increase over the $8.931 billion reported in 2003. Acquisition activity for the year remained somewhat muted: The Outdoor division closed a $33.6 million merger with Medallion Taxi Media, whose operations included advertising displays placed on the tops of taxi cabs. The company also exchanged outdoor advertising assets valued at $23.7 million for other outdoor advertising assets valued at $32.3 million. Meanwhile, the Radio division acquired radio stations for $59.4 million in cash and $38.9 million in restricted cash. Additionally, Clear Channel launched four new Spanish-language stations and created the "Hurban" and "La Preciosa" formats. The company also became the nation's largest broadcaster of Progressive Talk programming, launching the format on 22 stations; it also launched Online Music & Radio, hiring away the head of AOL Music and building what would become one of the most popular online music and radio networks.

Then there was Janet Jackson's "impromptu" wardrobe malfunction at the 2004 Super Bowl. For all of 9/15 of a second, a worldwide halftime television audience was exposed to the singer's bare breast. FCC Chairman Michael Powell, who said he was watching the game at home with his young children, was shocked at the display, which was part of an MTV-produced half-time show. What followed was nothing short of a legislative and regulatory election-year spectacle.

Although MTV is a cable network owned by Viacom, the "powers that be" inside the Beltway focused their attention on all things indecent, particularly such increasingly shocking radio jocks as Opie & Anthony, Bubba the Love Sponge, and the "king of all media," Howard Stern. Some members of Congress and the FCC seized on the indecency issue and wielded it as an election-year wedge, putting broadcasters between a rock and a hard place. The commission's rules about indecent programming have always been considered by radio and television programmers as less than specific, and now a lot of contemporary programming — especially that targeting the lucrative young (and mostly male) audience — was being portrayed by politicians and activists as wandering closer and closer to the edge of what could be considered "community standards."

So, during the spring of 2004 — with the presidential election just a half-year off — the indecency issue ignited in the halls of Congress and the FCC. A number of watchdog groups — the Parents Television Council and Focus on the Family among them — maintained a constant vigil over what was being broadcast on the nation's airwaves. While the full implication of this subject is covered at greater length in Chapter 8, it must be noted that several sizeable fines were handed down and the threat of considerably larger fines and possible license forfeitures loomed over both the radio and the television industries.

Until this point, Clear Channel had aired Howard Stern's morning show on six of its stations, but following a substantial assessment (a.k.a fine), the company yanked him from the air in what was one of the only programming decisions ever to be issued as a corporate edict at the company. Lawsuits were hurled back and forth (both of them eventually being dropped), and Stern eventually announced that he would leave terrestrial radio for good, jumping to a satellite radio company in early 2006.

Responding to this new reality, many radio companies quickly developed guidelines to help their on-air personalities understand where and how the new indecency lines were being drawn. While some clearly were not happy with the new restrictions, all understood that they needed to comply, or risk not only their employers' dollars and licenses, but their own jobs, as well.

Clear Channel was one of these companies, and it quickly drafted a "zero tolerance policy" that applied to any programming content on its airwaves.

In the annual report that year, the Mays family commented, "Another example of industry leadership is Clear Channel's recent announcement of a Responsible Broadcasting Initiative in response to the national concern about indecency in programming. Clear Channel has zero tolerance for indecent material on our airwaves and this initiative provides a clear framework for our local managers in regards to indecency. This initiative also calls for the formation of an industry task force to address this important issue. We recognize that with the role of leadership comes increased responsibility. You can be sure that we take our leadership position very seriously and are committed to leading positive change."

Another festering problem in the post-deregulation days of radio was on-air clutter. Many radio companies encouraged their local market managers to squeeze more and more commercials and on-air promotions into an hour, significantly reducing the amount of entertainment or news content while stacking advertisers' messages in "spot clusters" that sometimes ran seven or eight commercials deep. Meanwhile, satellite radio, iPods, and other new media that offered "commercial-free music" were beginning to attract the attention — and dollars — of a younger generation of consumers who were tired of being bombarded by commercial messages.

In a bold and risky move, Clear Channel Radio CEO John Hogan reduced the number of commercial minutes per hour on all the company's stations. Known as "Less Is More," the initiative placed a new and significantly lower ceiling on the amount of commercial minutes that were played per hour across the entire radio group. It also limited the length of commercials in a so-called "spot break," or cluster of commercials, and also limited the overall amount of promotional interruptions.

"Clutter is a major issue in our industry and our decision to limit the amount of commercial time and length of breaks, while reducing promotional interruptions, will benefit listeners, advertisers, and the industry as a whole," Hogan said when the plan was announced. "Despite radio's great underlying listener trends, and the fragmentation in other media, radio is still discounted relative to other media. We're taking this step to close that gap and make radio more competitive, compelling, effective, and valuable. And we actively encourage the rest of the industry to do the same."

"Less Is More" unleashed a virtual firestorm both on Wall Street and on Madison Avenue, and its effects would be far-reaching, both for the company's bottom line and the performance of the radio industry in general. Within a year, the initiative was driving up station ratings as well as the time spent listening by audiences. As a result, advertising prices rose and a new metric, "yield per minute," was introduced to demonstrate the effectiveness of encouraging advertisers to include 30-second commercials within the existing mix of 60-, 15-, and even 10-second ads. But in the beginning, there was widespread resistance to this strategy.

In the 2004 annual report, the company expanded on additional measures it took to ensure the program's success: "We reduced commercial minutes on our radio stations by an average of 19 percent and transitioned to selling more 30-second advertisements instead of the customary 60-second spots. To help speed that transition, we partnered with some of the greatest minds in advertising and marketing today to form a new unit called the Creative Services Group. This group serves as an unprecedented resource for our stations, ad agencies, and advertisers. Its sole purpose is to make commercials more compelling and entertaining. The value for listeners is obvious — more of the programming they love and fewer, better ads. But for advertisers the benefits are equally compelling. Reducing commercial clutter and providing higher quality and more effective commercials increases the effectiveness of radio advertising." (Please see Chapter 14 for more on "Less Is More.")

By the end of 2004 Clear Channel owned 367 AM stations and 822 FM stations throughout the U.S. the Outdoor division owned or operated 151,603 domestic display faces and 671,977 international displays, and the Entertainment division owned or operated 104 live entertainment venues. Radio broadcasting accounted for 40 percent of the company's revenue, while the Entertainment segment accounted for 29 percent of total revenue, and the Outdoor division delivered 26 percent of all dollars. Television, international radio, and "other" entities produced the remaining 5 percent.

Also of note: In 2004 Thomas Hicks left the board of directors.

2005

For 2005, Clear Channel reported company-wide revenues of $6.6 billion, with net earnings of $936 million. Because of the spin-off of the Entertainment division in December 2005, the company's full-year revenues do not include figures for this sector of the business. During the year, the company divested itself of the Entertainment division, increased its regular quarterly dividend by 50 percent and, in a move that would be a forerunner of changes to come, announced it would make 10 percent of its Outdoor division available via an initial public offering.

While acquisition activity was marginal during the year, the company did make strides in solidifying its market position in its radio and outdoor businesses. Specifically, the Radio division intensified its cross-platform distribution of audio entertainment, working with such companies as Apple, Yahoo, Motorola, BMW, and Garmin to distribute programming via the Internet, iPods, cell phones, and in-car mobile navigation devices. The company also held the line on its reduction of the number of commercial minutes and promotional interruptions per hour on all of its radio stations, which led to a measurable increase in ratings at many of them. Time spent listening also improved significantly, although a year-long hiccup in national advertising spending across the radio industry helped to reduce the Radio division's revenues by 6 percent compared with 2004. Still, with an average 19 percent reduction in commercial inventory, and only a 6 percent decline in revenues, the initiative clearly was holding its own.

In August of that year, Hurricane Katrina devastated the city of New Orleans and much of the Gulf Coast, where Clear Channel owned and operated a number of radio stations. Recognizing that millions of local residents were left without electricity, water and, in many cases, habitable homes, the company — in partnership with Entercom Communications and several independent radio broadcasters — quickly formed an ad hoc broadcasting enterprise known as the United Radio Broadcasters of New Orleans (also called URBNO). For several weeks immediately following Katrina's landfall, the URBNO broadcasts provided virtually the only outlet for news and information throughout southern Louisiana, and also served as the primary communications conduit between first responders and government officials — many of whom struggled with how to deal with an emergency of such monumental proportions. For radio listeners around the country who were not directly affected by Katrina but still wanted to help in some way, Clear Channel stations pooled their resources and raised approximately $65 million within 60 days of the hurricane's direct hit. (Please see Chapter 9 for more information on Hurricane Katrina and URBNO.)

On a more technical level, Clear Channel also began its wide-scale rollout of HD digital radio, beginning the conversion of hundreds of stations to broadcast in the new "high definition" technology. The company's goal was to have 90 percent of its facilities in the top 100 U.S. markets broadcasting the improved signal by the end of 2007. In parallel, the

Radio division assembled an army of 200 programmers to create hundreds of new digital audio channels to feed additional digital channels to run alongside the primary HD digital signals. Called "multicasts," the extra signals began broadcasting in January of 2006 and by year's end were available in more than six markets. Clear Channel also spearheaded the formation of the HD Digital Radio Alliance which, in the fourth quarter of the year, united a number of major radio operators in an immediate effort to convince electronics manufacturers to accelerate the rollout of the new technology and retailers to carry the new receivers. The stated mission of the Alliance is to "coordinate the rollout of HD digital radio, including coordinating the formats on new multicast channels known as HD2; work together to secure automotive design wins and lower receiver price points; and jointly market HD digital radio, in partnership with receiver manufacturers and retailers."

"We made strategic, operating, and financial progress in 2005 by investing in our businesses, leading change, and tightening the focus of our company," Mark Mays said when the 2005 numbers were released to investors. "We are pleased with the recent progress in our radio division and have renewed confidence in our long-term growth outlook. Listenership and ratings all continue to trend up, [and] with trends in the outdoor business and our local television stations also positive, we have never been more excited about our future."

2006

For the 2006 calendar year, Clear Channel continued to outperform its peer companies, particularly those in the radio industry. The company reported revenues of $7.07 billion, a 7 percent increase over the $6.6 billion the company earned in the previous year. Income before discontinued operations grew almost 9 percent over 2005 levels, to $688.8 million. The Radio division continued to move the company's content aggressively onto emerging digital platforms including the Internet, mobile phones and even in-car navigation systems, as John Hogan and his team pursued those platforms' tremendous growth opportunities. The company's online platform continued to grow and, as ranked by ComScore/MediaMetrix, the Online Music & Radio Network ranked in the top five of all online music and streaming radio sites on the Internet in the U.S.

Additionally, Clear Channel continued to invest in HD Radio technology, and made significant progress rolling out so-called HD2 digital multicasts in a number of the top 100 radio markets in the U.S. By the end of the year, 360 of the company's radio stations — in 87 markets — broadcast with an HD signal, and the company was projecting that all of its radio operations would have thrown the HD switch by the end of 2008.

On the outdoor front, 2006 turned out to be a year of expansion and acquisition. In May, the Outdoor division purchased Interspace Airport Advertising, an operator of advertising displays in 190 airports worldwide, and also acquired Van Wagner's United Kingdom business. That same month Clear Channel Outdoor brokered a completely new type of relationship with a global consumer brand. Its deal with Coca-Cola was designed, according to the company's annual report, to "create and enhance new and customized outdoor programs for Coke's wide array of brands." The agreement would give Coca-Cola preferred access to prime outdoor properties around the world. It was the first such time a brand had worked directly with an outdoor company.

The Outdoor division's most significant progress, however, came on the digital side of the business. Throughout the year the company rolled out digital outdoor displays in a number of new markets, initiated programs to expand its digital business with 100 new boards in 20 more markets by the end of 2007, and initiated new programs that would culminate in the creation of "SpectacolorHD," which debuted in 2007 with the launch of a high-definition display in New York's Times Square, designed to run multiple advertiser spots in conjunction with streaming news, weather, and live HD broadcasts provided exclusively by CNN.

Still, following a secular decline that began with the dot-com bust in 2000 as well as recessionary pressures following the events of 9/11, 2006 proved to be yet another year of disappointment and frustration for public radio groups and their shareholders. Advertising revenues for the industry finished the year relatively flat to just slightly up, and many public radio companies grappled with numbers that were tinged with red ink. After several years of slipping stock values and Wall Street discontent, it was becoming increasingly evident that the public marketplace was growing impatient with the entire radio sector's earnings performance. While a number of group heads privately were anticipating that investors finally would understand the inherent value in radio's cash-flow margins and reward the sector with a little bit of love, The Street likes tangible evidence of long-term fiscal performance — and in 2006 any such signs were glaringly absent. The hard truth was obvious: public companies were going to have to endure at least another year of stagnant ad revenues and hammered stock prices — or they would have to find an alternative financial market.

Thus, after 22 years in the public eye — and seven years after *The Wall Street Journal* ranked the company's stock as the best performing in the 1990s — Clear Channel's top executives in 2006 elected to entertain offers designed to take the company private. The move effectively would end the constant short-term scrutiny of Wall Street and allow Clear Channel to focus on its core radio and outdoor businesses, as well as provide some breathing room for further investments in creativity and innovation.

A statement released at the time confirmed that the company was "evaluating various strategic alternatives to enhance shareholder value," although it was clear to suggest that "there could be no assurance that this process will result in any specific transaction." Two investment groups interested in taking Clear Channel private quickly emerged: one composed of Providence Equity Partners, Blackstone Group, and Kohlberg Kravis Roberts; the other comprised of Thomas H. Lee Partners and Bain Capital LLC. The latter group eventually won the bidding, promising $18.7 billion — or $37.60 per share — and repayment of $8 billion in debt. The company's 11-member board of directors unanimously approved the merger agreement, although four of those members — Lowry Mays, Mark Mays, Randall Mays, and Red McCombs — recused themselves from the vote.

Reported in tandem with the $26.7 billion leveraged buyout — and potentially more far-reaching for both the radio and television industries — was Clear Channel's announcement that it would be selling 448 of its 1,150 radio properties, plus its entire Television division, which at that time consisted of 42 stations. Collectively, all properties on the auction block contributed less than 10 percent of Clear Channel's annual net revenues, and were not expected to affect significantly the company's overall profitability.

"Our decision to divest these broadcast properties was reached as a result of the ongoing optimization of our diverse portfolio of media assets," commented Clear Channel CEO Mark Mays in a statement announcing the planned sales. "These are profitable and well-managed properties in excellent markets. We believe that the sale of these stations will allow us to position our business to provide even greater value to our listeners and shareholders.

"Now we can really find new and exciting ways to expand and grow both divisions organically," Mark continues. "On the radio side we're obviously focused on lots of new and different revenue streams, like our Clear Channel Online Music and Radio initiatives. For our Outdoor division, this means we'll be making tremendous investments in digital technology and other opportunities that will grow revenues in that business. Clear Channel's growth process always has been very much an evolution, and this is just another step in the process of continuing to evolve the company to prosper in the future."

While the pace at which the LBO was finalized and announced may have taken the communications industry by surprise, the process actually began three years earlier as part of a regular strategic planning session. At that time, Clear Channel's top executives took the temperature of the public marketplace and determined that the equity markets at some point again would recognize the significant profitability of the radio business. In other words, they envisioned a future in which investors once more believed that radio exhibited significant upside as a value play, and stock prices would increase accordingly. Of course, the continued downward trend for virtually the entire sector suggested that this assessment was one whose time had not yet come, and might not for the foreseeable future. By mid-2006 it became clear that the public market was not going to favor radio. "It was our opinion that nothing was in place to break or change that perspective," Mark says. "And that meant we had to look at things a bit differently. As we looked at the current environment we realized that the private equity markets actually did view radio as a good business over the long term, which meant there clearly was an opportunity to go in that direction — and also put some leverage on top of that because the debt markets still like radio, as well."

However, for a company whose stock was in the mid-$50 range a few years earlier — and had topped $90 at the end of the 1990s run-up — a $37.60 exit price did not sit well with some shareholders. At the extreme high end, two Wall Street analysts who covered Clear Channel suggested a $41 per share value for the company.

To those who insisted that Clear Channel should have held out for more cash, Mark Mays is quick to point out that the vast majority of radio company stock prices — Clear Channel's included — had been drifting downward for years, rather than returning to levels of a half-decade ago. "The stock was at $28 in August 2006," he observes. "Sure — everyone would have liked more, me included. But as we went through this process, it became clear this was the most we could get out of the private equity markets. Our choices were to seek an alternative financial market or keep doing what we were doing. If we had remained public in this environment, our stock price would have continued to drift, irrespective of our gains in revenue or how much we outperformed the rest of the companies in our sector."

2007

The planned buyout of the company by two private equity firms had some wrinkles, and it could be said that Clear Channel spent a number of months in the "ironing board room" attempting to smooth out creases in the deal. Originally, the company's shareholders were scheduled to approve (or not) the buyout offer from Thomas H. Lee Partners and Bain Capital LLC in April 2007, but February and March exposed discontent with the terms of the buyout among some of the company's larger institutional investors. Because the company was incorporated in Texas, approval of the deal would require a positive vote from two-thirds of all shareholders. Under Texas law, any shares not voted would be counted as "no" votes.

It became clear in the weeks leading up to the scheduled vote that the buyout at the announced price of $37.60 would not find approval, so Clear Channel's board of directors and the two private equity firms amended the deal to $39.00 per share. That figure represented a premium of approximately 33.3 percent over the average closing share price during the 60-trading-day period that ended October 24, 2006, the day prior to Clear Channel's announcement of the board of directors' decision to "consider strategic alternatives." (It should be noted that Lowry Mays, Mark Mays, Randall Mays, and B.J. McCombs recused themselves from this amendment vote and all subsequent votes that focused on amending the private equity offer.) A vote for shareholders to approve the new offer was set for May 8.

That increase still proved inadequate, and when it again became evident that major institutional holders remained less than elated with even the proposed increase, Clear Channel's board entered into further discussions with the private equity firms. The resulting amendment upped the buyout offer to $39.20 for each share currently held, plus additional "per-share" consideration. In other words, as an alternative to receiving the $39.20 per share cash consideration, Clear Channel's unaffiliated shareholders would be offered the opportunity — on a purely voluntary basis – to exchange some or all of their shares of Clear Channel common stock on a one-for-one basis for shares of Class A common stock in the new corporation formed by the private equity group, plus the additional per-share consideration, if any.

In this amended deal, the total number of Clear Channel shares that would be able to "elect" to receive shares in the new corporation was approximately 30.6 million, with a total value of approximately $1.2 billion (at the $39.20 per share cash consideration).

When this arrangement finally came to a vote on September 25, 2007, the company's shareholders approved it with overwhelming enthusiasm. More that 73 percent of the total shares outstanding and entitled to vote were voted in favor of the transaction, with the final tabulation indicating that an impressive 98 percent of the shares actually voted were cast in favor.

Under the new arrangements, Thomas H. Lee Partners and Bain Capital LLC would each receive four board seats, while Randall Mays and Mark Mays retained their seats; two independent seats would be added. Lowry Mays, who had served as chairman, retained the title of "chairman emeritus."

Almost eclipsed by the ongoing drama of the shareholder vote was the announcement in April 2007 that Clear Channel had entered into a definitive agreement to sell the Television division to Providence Equity Partners for approximately $1.2 billion. Providence Equity Partners had been one of the bidders for the entire company. The sale included 56 television stations, including 18 digital multicast channels, several having robust online operations and located in 24 U.S. markets.

"The stations and management of Clear Channel Television have established an outstanding record of achievement, innovation and community service in broadcasting and web development," Mark Mays observed when the deal was announced. "While we will miss the important role they have played in the Clear Channel family, we are excited that they will be partnered with Providence Equity to continue to pursue growth opportunities in the rapidly changing media environment."

The bottom line is, of course, the bottom line — and from that perspective Mark Mays is optimistic that taking the company into the private sector was the right move at the right time. "Now we might be able to miss this quarter's numbers but create value over the long term," he says. "Wall Street really only cares about the next quarter, but private equity investors are going to be more long-term oriented and less guided by a quarter-to-quarter mindset. They're going to be patient and, as long as we have a good game plan over the next four to five years, they know this is going to be a good deal for them. It's a great deal for our shareholders because they get a good price in today's marketplace, and it's a fabulous deal for our employees because they're going to get a different environment in which to operate. This entire scenario is a win-win-win, and ultimately the company will operate under an entirely different business dynamic. That's just another step in the process of continuing to evolve the company today to prosper in the future."

NEW BEGINNING

Without question, the ten years following the 1996 passage of the Telecommunications Act were tumultuous, unpredictable, and at times capricious. After 75 years of government regulations the industry changed with great zeal. Broadcasters who previously functioned under tight controls and even tighter access to capital suddenly found themselves in the position of writing a new rulebook for not only how to acquire and merge radio stations and groups, but also how to operate the entities they were creating. The mantra at the time was that "one plus one equals three" (sometimes more), and many broadcasters began to see how a consolidated business could result in innovative and creative business practices.

When Randall Mays joined Clear Channel in January 1993 — three years before consolidation's starter pistol was fired — the company ostensibly was divided into two elements: the operations side of the business, which included the vital roles of programming, management, marketing, and engineering — and everything that was non-operationally related. Randall handled everything that dealt with investor relations, accounting, capital structure, capital markets, financing, and acquisitions, while his brother Mark primarily focused on the direct operations of the company.

"Some of the larger transactions were done primarily with stock, which certainly diluted us as owners in the business," Randall says. "But everything we've done was framed by the notion of putting together a collection of assets that would allow us to be in control of our own destiny. There was nobody in this industry who had the ability to do what we did, and none of them had the tenacity to do it."

During the height of consolidation, Clear Channel took great pains to examine specific station clusters, determining how stations fit together within specific markets. "It was no different from what we did with those Urban stations in Houston," Randall says. "Whenever we looked at an acquisition we focused on the cumulative total of what we could do with all of these frequencies. We studied them in terms of attracting an audience with our programming, and we knew that in order to maximize that audience we needed to maximize our format diversity. The more stations we acquired, the more we proliferated formats, because we didn't want to overlap other stations. Of course, there was always a little overlap because we wanted to make sure that we didn't allow someone else to wedge a station in between ours."

Randall scoffs at critics who say that consolidation has served to limit the number of music formats available to listeners; in fact, he says a far greater variety of music is offered on the radio today than in the years before deregulation. "Anybody who has taken an economics class knows that if you owned every station in the market, none of them would play the same format," he explains. "There's absolutely no reason to. If you look at any radio market in 1994 and compare that to today, you can see how formats evolved over the next decade, and you'll see significantly more format diversity than we had before consolidation."

Chief Accounting Officer Herb Hill maintains that Clear Channel maintained a solid entrepreneurial spirit all the way through 2000, when the acquisition period came to a rapid standstill. "Even though the company was growing almost logarithmically, each acquisition and planned expansion still remained an entrepreneurial play," he recalls. "Each station or group that we purchased was viewed as an asset."

As Clear Channel expanded during the peak of consolidation, the company always followed a straightforward accretive formula, Randall says. "Radio stations are tremendous cash-flow entities," he observes. "We knew that if we could acquire them on good financial terms, then we would be able to produce more cash flow, which would allow us to buy more of them. It was that simple. It was never about being big; it was just that we saw these stations as great assets. And in our opinion, the more of them we were able to have, the better."

Looking back, Randall says that there clearly was a point before the AMFM merger that Clear Channel developed a game plan that directed — at least to some extent — how the consolidation game would play out. "It's important to be able to control your own destiny," he observes. "There was no question that if we continued to expand our footprint across the entire country, we'd be able to do things that we couldn't do if we were just another broadcaster in a few individual markets." He concedes that this might not seem like a major revelation today, but maintains that in the coming years, as an explosion of technology continues to shift audiences from one medium to the next, it will be viewed as tremendously profound.

"When people look back at what we've done, it will be obvious how important it was that we built this type of platform," he says. "What's going to set radio broadcasters apart in the future is the same thing that set them apart in the past: the ability to have compelling content that will entertain — and retain — the listener."

Despite all appearances during Clear Channel's late-'90s buying spree, the company was founded not on M&A activity, but on a foundation of broadcast operations. "Internally, we've never thought of ourselves as anything other than an operating company," Randall says. "That's why we've been so successful. We bought stations, we operated them better than the people we bought them from, and that provided us the cash flow that enabled us to buy more stations. It also caused our stock price to increase, which gave us even more access to capital. Those people who say that Clear Channel really is just an acquisition company that met with a slowdown when we had to finally operate all these stations are misguided. We've been an operations company from the beginning, and it was the fact that we were operating so well that enabled us to continue to grow."

Of course, when the stock market plummeted in 2001 and the U.S. hit the recessionary skids, Clear Channel's share price slipped precipitously, as did those of most other companies in the radio sector. "At that point our cash flow also went down and our acquisitions all but stopped," Randall says. "It was very clear that we had to do what we always did best: operate our stations. We've always been an operating company; we just stopped the acquisition side."

CHAPTER FOUR

POST CONSOLIDATION: THE MORNING AFTER

THE ENTIRE STATION ROLL-UP PROCESS TOOK APPROXIMATELY SIX YEARS — from early 1996 to 2002 — a party that followed 75 years of relative calm, and resulted in an industry-wide hangover. While some broadcasters who survived the binge-and-purge period of the late-'80s and early-'90s had anticipated "clustering" several hundred stations, it was almost unbelievable that one company would ever be able to — or even want to — amass 1,200 radio properties the way Clear Channel did when the confetti finally settled to the floor.

"Never in my wildest dreams did I think Clear Channel would get this large," says Lowry Mays. "We built it on a block-by-block process. I remember when I would go down to the Frost Bank here in San Antonio and sign those original notes. In fact, there was a notice in the local paper when we increased our bank line to $1 billion, and Tom Frost, who was the president of the bank, called me and said, 'Did you ever in your wildest dreams think that anyone would lend you a billion dollars?' And I told him, 'No — I had no idea this company would get this big.'"

But it did get big, and it did so at a time when big was not necessarily perceived to be better. During the consolidation growth process, many industry die-hards who had entered the radio business because it was their passion, abruptly found themselves jilted by the business they loved. The much anticipated "cost efficiencies" that were assumed to be a benefit of consolidation often translated to simple job compression that put many people out of work. As a result, a number of career radio professionals woke up from the industry's long night of partying without a place to call home — and instantly resented their sudden displacement. Suddenly looking at radio from the outside in, many of them began vocalizing their displeasure for what had happened. (In fact, it would take several years for most critics to concede that consolidation actually has introduced a number of positive elements to the radio business. More about that later.)

One of the individuals who took much of the heat as the fire of consolidation got hotter was former Jacor Communications head Randy Michaels. Together with real estate tycoon Sam Zell, Michaels built Jacor communications from 18 stations in 1994 to 230 stations when Clear Channel acquired the company in 1999.

Randy Michaels best can be described as a radio industry enigma. Depending on who's talking, some of the words that most often are associated with him are (in no particular order) brash, vibrant, frat boy, radio geek, genius, confrontational, intense, fanatical, impetuous, impatient, challenging, obsessive, and passionate. The mastermind behind Tampa's Power Pig in the 1980s, Michaels arguably was the first broadcaster to take advantage of the 1996 change in ownership rules, snapping up Jacor's first post-deregulation property just days after the Telecom Act was signed into law. Over the next 30 months, driven by the slogan "The Noise You Can't Ignore," the company acquired such companies as Tsunami, Champlin, Gannett, Citicasters, Nationwide, Noble, and Apollo, which had become Regent Communications (not to be confused with the Regent Communications that is publicly traded today).

Despite his larger-than-life image in the radio industry, and the frenetic pace at which Jacor amassed radio stations in the first days after the Telecom Act was passed, Michaels was the antithesis of the corporate wheeler-dealer. "Randy would rather hang around the board op or the engineer than the general manager," says Clear Channel Vice President of Programming Sean Compton, whom Michaels hired fresh out of high school. "He really wanted to touch the people who do the work. Of course, he could be very intimidating to those people who didn't know him very well, because of the way he approached this business."

It was perhaps because of this approach — impatient, impetuous, and possibly a touch reckless — that the Jacor environment took on almost mythic proportions. "Randy's corporate culture was very different from most other companies," Compton recalls. "It was blue jeans every day if you wanted, it was loud, and Randy had a temper."

In the early days of consolidation, some 2,000 radio stations were merged into a handful of hungry companies. Jacor and Clear Channel were two of these entities, and when the two radio groups announced in October 1998 that they were merging, many broadcasters who were acquainted with both Lowry Mays and Randy Michaels started offering an "over-and-under" on how long the "big bang" partnership would last. The prevailing wisdom held that Mays, known for his conservatively fiscal approach to acquisitions and operations, would clash with what was perceived as Michaels' over-the-top, sometimes impetuous business style.

In fact, as the two companies came together in one of the largest mergers ever to occur in the broadcasting business, those who were opposed to consolidation began to search far and wide for evidence that the radio industry was changing forever — and, all too predictably, for the worse. In this process, some critics depicted Michaels as the poster child of everything that ostensibly was wrong with radio. Web postings — most of which, by the sheer nature of the Internet, never can be traced back to their original authors — vilified him as everything from "the antichrist of radio" to "a blight on professionalism" to "representative of the heinous crimes perpetrated by Clear Channel."

Why such venom? Michaels has suggested that this gross negativity largely had to do with an innate fear of change, especially when that change has lasting, personal effects on an individual. Further, Michaels understood that his and Clear Channel's approach toward consolidation profoundly shook a lot of people out of their comfort zones and effectively changed their lives — and their livelihoods — forever. Disparate stations were squeezed together, cultures were forced to blend, people lost their jobs, job responsibilities mounted, and budgets were tightened — all in the name of creating cost efficiencies and generating critical mass. Along the way, some members of the radio community began to lament a loss of innocence — both theirs as well as the industry's — as rapid-fire evolution changed the radio business almost overnight.

Much of that protest came from people who saw their careers change almost overnight. The emotions of radio professionals run deep. Many are self-professed "radio geeks" who, as young adolescents, would sit in front of a record player and pretend to announce songs to an imaginary audience. Still others are those whose love for music and a gift for gab led them to the local radio station, where they worked the boards or "carted" music while waiting for a chance to go in front of a microphone. However they got their start in the business, radio people have always had a passion for what they do.

This, perhaps, is why consolidation in general and Clear Channel in particular initially were so intensely criticized within the radio industry. While some people lost their jobs in the name of cost efficiencies, many were "downsized" because their individual talent level — on-air, sales, or management — was less than the new company expected or required. Still others found themselves unemployed because they reacted to change in a very Darwinian way: they simply could not adapt. As Mark Mays has said more than once at Clear Channel management meetings, "A bend in the road is not the end of the road, unless you fail to make the turn."

"Clearly we let some people go because we didn't need them from a staffing perspective, but more often than not, it was self-selection," says Randall Mays. "Those people just wanted to do business the old way, which is fine — but it was important for them and for us that they go do it the old way somewhere else."

An oil-and-water analogy might be a bit strong, but there was no question that combination of Jacor's Michaels with Clear Channel's Mays triumvirate was much like trying to mix Jose Cuervo with Gentleman Jack. Many industry analysts wondered how long Michaels could continue to run the company's radio operations while ultimately reporting to San Antonio, and the fact that he remained at the helm of the division for almost four years after the two companies merged is reflective of a mutual respect that emerged, despite a clear difference in operational styles. Possibly contributing to Michael's post-merger tenure was the fact that he remained in Jacor's headquarters in Covington, Kentucky (directly across the Ohio River from Cincinnati), a good 1,025 miles from San Antonio.

For reasons that never were publicly explained, in the summer of 2002 Michaels stepped down as CEO of the Radio division, purportedly to oversee development of the company's interactive, wireless broadband, and satellite technologies. "A lot of people have very polarizing opinions of Randy," says Randall Mays. "But you can't take away from him the fact that he knew the radio industry cold, and he had a great vision of how things could work in this business. He really could see beyond the operations of an individual radio station to understand how they could function together in a cluster."

John Hogan, who replaced Michaels as head of Clear Channel Radio in 2002, had worked closely with him as chief operating officer of Jacor prior to the company's acquisition by Clear Channel. "Randy is one of the most unforgettable people I know," he says. "His contributions were absolutely invaluable to us as we grew the company. My style is very different from Randy's and is well suited to what the company needs today, but I have a lot of respect for Randy and what he has done."

Despite disparate leadership styles between Randy Michaels and the Mays family, the overriding goals for both Jacor and Clear Channel were much the same, says Tom Owens, who serves as the company's executive vice president of programming. "Both companies prioritized high-quality service to their respective communities," he explains. "As a result of consolidation, the management of politics and public relations increased as a priority. Due to timing, Clear Channel had to weather many criticisms that Jacor did not. The company also had to make a number of difficult decisions related to content and practices that Jacor never faced."

Among these difficult decisions was the need to combine facilities, staffs, cultures, and operating systems of radio stations that often had been virtual enemies in the marketplace. Prior to consolidation, stations with similar programming and demographic targets often would engage in hand-to-hand combat in order to drive ratings and revenues, sometimes employing on-air and behind-the-scenes tactics that created incredible enmity. All of a sudden stations that previously had been at war with each other had to send up the white flag and make nice, a process that did not sit well among many competitive industry veterans. Even in such "back room" operations as traffic and accounting, systems that had been put in place by one corporation almost overnight were replaced with different processes, creating confusion, frustration, and resentment.

In most situations where stations were combined in a market, Clear Channel placed an emphasis on explaining to employees that it was critical to look at the entire operation, not just specific stations or staffs. Sometimes this strategy worked; sometimes it was less than perfect.

Clear Channel hurtled through consolidation at break-neck speed. While outsiders might have viewed the acquisition process as a game of Monopoly gone wild, Clear Channel had a very distinct — and fiscally prudent — approach to the mergers in which it was engaging. Still, as the company expanded at a faster pace, it couldn't help but suffer from growing pains.

"Our general manager meetings used to be held in a hotel meeting room, and then almost overnight we got to this point where the dinners at those meetings were held in a tent outside the hotel," says Bob Cohen, who currently runs Clear Channel's international Radio division. "Nobody was sure how these mergers were going to work internally; we just had to go with the flow, because we knew there was going to be a lot of change — and we knew that change was going to come very fast. To help handle the sheer size of our radio group, Mark Mays assigned two of our senior general managers to senior vice president roles, splitting the country in half. That worked for a while, but then we got to the next level in size, and Mark quickly realized that we were going to need some more people to do this. The model just kept evolving, like a cell splitting and then splitting again."

Any time two companies engage in a sizeable merger, there will always be collisions of style and culture, and Clear Channel went through an adjustment period during which management and staff had to figure out which culture would prevail with the combination of groups. A quick resolution of the issue was desirable because a lot of political lead started flying through the air in very short order. "One thing we learned was that the quicker you can figure out who does what, and where you can capitalize on people's strengths — and manage those strengths — the better," Cohen observes. "There will always be rough spots, and you just have to sand them down as quickly as you can. There also will be some saboteurs, and you just have to identify those people and get on with it. We were just sorting through the hard details of how to put these groups together, and we all knew that we had to be very creative and resourceful."

One aspect that consolidation brought to the table was the potential for a merged cluster to spread its combined sales staff across the entire market platform. In other words, while account executives prior to consolidation usually had sold the advertising for one station (or possibly two, in the case of an AM/FM combo), market clustering afforded companies the opportunity to offer advertisers sales packages that combined the audiences of several (and sometimes all) of its stations in a market. Additionally, some radio groups would use their weaker stations as packaging tools so they would amass an enormous amount of available inventory, and use it to deliver a larger number of units to an advertiser.

"Again, our approach was to take each of these radio stations and do our best to make it stand on its own two feet," Cohen says. "Each one had its own P&L, budget, revenue requirement, and unique audience, and whether or not it was sold in combination with another station, it was expected to have its own rates, its own spots, and its own marketing approach to customers," he explains.

Of course, the industry also started to attract considerable attention that it never before had received. "We started to get covered by reporters and media outlets that weren't very familiar with the business," Cohen recalls. "We had people writing about radio in the business pages who didn't have a great working knowledge of how this industry worked, and their interpretations and comments were reported in a manner that may have helped some of the myths and urban legends evolve and develop."

As a result, radio played a lot of hurry-up defense in those early years. A lot of individuals and organizations were developing perspectives that were less than informed, and much of the negative media coverage was being fed by agendas of all sorts. "Looking back it would have been better had we been playing a little more offense, explaining the benefits of consolidation a little bit better," Cohen says. "Still, in spite of some of those early perceptions, the radio industry is far better off than it was."

Part of the maturation process during consolidation didn't come from external forces, nor did it come from new technology that began competing with traditional media. The process largely came from within, and a number of people — some of them former broadcasters who got pushed out of station ownership, some of them people who got displaced from their jobs — saw consolidation as a tremendous negative.

"The industry attacked itself, and it took us time to get through that," explains Bill Stakelin, CEO of Regent Communications. "Now that we've seen how consolidation has matured, it's evident that these companies are providing great service and entertainment to their communities. All in all, radio is a lot better off after the growing pains and the transition that con-solidation has brought about."

Station envy also played a huge role in the spread of negative energy and discourse. "As Clear Channel grew, it became a strong competitor of every other radio company in the business," observes former NAB President/CEO Eddie Fritts, who now runs his own lobbying firm in Washington. "Clear Channel literally competes with everybody, so it's likely that they also not only have a lot of competitors, but a lot of people who would like to see them not do well. It's inherent in our business for one to always want to get the upper hand on the competitor."

"In 1996 Clear Channel was a relatively small company, certainly by today's standards," notes Lew Dickey, chairman and chief executive officer of Cumulus Media, which is second only to Clear Channel in the number of stations it owns. "But they grew very quickly through a number of large transactions. I think I can appreciate, more than anyone else, what Clear Channel had to go through to build that company. They bought some large groups that had very disparate cultures, and they had to meld them together and create a business out of it. It's hard for most people to appreciate how difficult it was to integrate 1,200 radio stations into one company, and to build a cohesive functioning business with some basic systems and a sense of purpose and a unified culture. I don't know that anyone else could have done it any better."

While it was focused on building and operating its divisional businesses with an overriding commitment, Clear Channel sometimes displayed an innocence that almost bordered on naiveté. Not only was the company almost oblivious to the mounting criticism that was bombarding it from virtually all directions, but those individuals responsible for its logarithmic growth — Lowry, Mark, and Randall Mays — appeared unconcerned with how consolidation's end game would play out.

"We never really thought about how large this company might become," says Mark Mays. "When we had 12 stations we thought it would be great if we could have 24, and when we got up to around 50 stations I thought we were in high cotton. If you look at the way we grew, we just about doubled the size of our company about every 18 months for awhile. That was a fast-paced moving dynamic, but it was a manageable dynamic. In those days — 1989 to 2000 — we'd always joke at the end of the year, and say, 'Golly, look at everything we accomplished this year.' We reveled in that for about five minutes, and then we'd say, 'Okay, here's what we have to do now.' Everything we did was focused. Dad's focus has always been on a strong work ethic, and then making sure that you have a great capital structure. That's where he was different from a lot of other players, because he always made sure we had that capital structure that enabled us to grow through the ups and downs. As a result, there was never a deal we did that was a 'company bet,' where we could have lost the whole company. We're a public company, so everything was transparent and above board. We were also monetizing it, not only with debt, but with equity along the way. We didn't always do transactions with debt, like a lot of other people did. We did it with both. The secret to our success has been Dad's ability to retain, motivate, and attract really good people. He clearly instilled in Randall and me the idea that you have to surround yourself with the very best individuals, because at the end of the day, all you have is towers and people, and a little piece of paper from the FCC that allows you to broadcast."

Mark also asserts that Clear Channel always has remained an operating company, even during times of intense acquisition. "Because we bought blocks of stations at a time, we usually added management along the way," he says. "The key was making sure that we had the very best people running all of the different stations. We were always evaluating our people, and the cream started rising to the top. It all comes down to what I call the 'operating core' of radio, and letting the local managers make the decisions on how they're programming and selling those stations. As Dad likes to say, "each peanut stand on the prairie thrives on its own merits and its own decisions.""

Indeed, any perception that Clear Channel tried to squeeze out a disproportionate number of its people while operating a lean and mean business ignores the fact that the company today has many more employees than it ever did during the height of consolidation. "We have more people working at Clear Channel Radio today than we had at all the different companies in the late '90s," Mark says. "They're not all the same people and they're doing different things, because the business today requires a different skill set. In the late '90s you didn't have to have an Internet guy, and you didn't really have too many people working in non-traditional revenue. No, we don't always have two receptionists, but we often have an extra sales assistant, because of all the sales people we have. Whenever you have a displacement of people there's going to be controversy, because people hate change. So it's common practice to hate large corporations that are perceived to be the force that generates that change."

Explaining the inevitability of change — and how it affects individuals' lives — is critical when any industry is experiencing a massive transformation like consolidation. As Mark Mays recalls, "In 2000 we said to our people, 'Here's the world we're living in today. Look back at 1995. I can guarantee you that you're going to see as much change in the next five years as you've seen in the last five. We don't know what that change is going to be, but if you're not willing to adapt and you're not going to change — and change quickly — to whatever the environment is going to be, you're doing yourself a big disservice. To paraphrase an old quote, it's not the strongest or the most intelligent species that survives; it's those that are the most adaptable to change. That's true, and it also defines a real facet of human nature. As a result, we really wanted to ensure that our people understood not only that things were going to change, but that they were capable of changing with the times, if they wanted to."

When Clear Channel bought Jacor and then merged with AMFM, three distinct operating cultures suddenly were assembled under one roof that for years had been marked by Clear Channel's climate of fiscal restraint. The company's corporate office knew it was critical to identify the positive aspects of each culture and incorporate them into the overall business structure, while eliminating the negative. "We had all these corporate culture guys telling us that it takes three years to develop a culture," Mark Mays recalls. "And we said, 'That's not true — we don't have three years. We're doing it today.' There was a pervasive mentality that you were either a Jacor guy, you were an AMFM guy, or you were a Clear Channel guy. Everyone in the company had a persona or a stigma, and it took us a lot longer than I thought it would to work through all that."

Mark says that every major company that merged into Clear Channel brought its own distinct cultural brand, and Clear Channel tried to incorporate the best of each. "We used a lot of the sales intensity from AMFM, the programming elements from Jacor, and the sales and capital investment issues from Clear Channel," he says. "We put them all together, and today we've got a pretty good blend of all those different elements."

Still, those operational practices were different, and not always in a pretty way, Mark says. "Those individuals who couldn't come to grips with what we were doing either had to sit in different chairs or exit altogether," he recalls. "The more that happened, the more people became comfortable with a new way of doing business. We didn't try to tell them there was a Clear Channel culture, or a Clear Channel way of thinking. The only thing we insisted on was that we were going to have centralized accounting, because we always want to know where the books are, and what they say. As I always told them, 'we want you guys to play, but we're going to keep score.'"

Good thing, too. "When all that Enron stuff was coming out, everybody in this company was really happy that we had centralized accounting," Mark says. "No one ever had to worry that we were going to wake up one day and find that someone had done something funny in a distant part of our world."

"One of the fundamental challenges was that we had 1,200 radio stations that were acquired from very contrasting backgrounds, systems, expectations, and cultures," says Clear Channel Radio CEO John Hogan. "These people needed to be aggregated into a single company, with a vision, a focus, and a set of expectations. We understood that we had disparate cultures and personalities coming together, some of which were desirable and some that were not. Now, the bedrock of this company has always been performance; our distribution systems, our ratings, and our revenues are all about performance and growth. What we decided to do was to take advantage of the best ideas, the best intellectual resources, and the best experiences that we had acquired."

Part of the task of building a new corporate culture meant eliminating some of the previously existing perceptions and practices and instead developing something that worked across the company and across all platforms. "It was similar to what Mercedes and Chrysler went through when they merged," Hogan explains. "We told our people that we were going to talk about the best way to do things, and we'd probably argue about what those were, but at the end of the day we were going to make a decision and move forward. Those people who could support that decision would remain on the team, and those who had a problem with it would be free to go their separate ways." Resistance to any form of cultural change came in many forms, from the way the company administered health benefits to a difference in traffic systems to the way a salesperson wrote up a client order. "People love change until it happens to them," Hogan observes. "And this was happening to them on a daily basis. Virtually everything was changing in some way, shape, or form — and it continues to change."

Contrary to how some former employees might describe their experiences, Hogan insists that Clear Channel did not institute an "our-way-or-the-highway" scenario. "We didn't tell people to just 'get over it,'" he says. "Instead, we tried to show people why we needed to make some changes in the ways things were being done. While Clear Channel had become the poster child for consolidation, it also had been the poster child for successful acquisition. The fact was, we were far better than any other company out there. The people at this company had a great vision for what they wanted to do, and the company succeeded."

Still, errors were inevitable and Clear Channel, like every other company that was gorging itself on acquisitions, made its share. "We absolutely made mistakes," Hogan admits. "When I was at Jacor, before we were bought by Clear Channel, we made enormous mistakes. We just didn't make them on the same scale and under the same level of scrutiny that

Clear Channel has had to endure. We made operational mistakes, we made social mistakes, and we made systems mistakes — partly because nobody had ever before done what we were trying to do."

Ultimately, consolidation was a learn-as-you-go process, Hogan maintains. "There was no blueprint, there was no path to follow," he says. "Clear Channel has always been about doing better radio: Having a more compelling product, better talent, and better programming is what it takes to win. The key to our culture is that we are radio people. We're broadcasters. We're in it for the long haul, and we have been in it for the long haul since we were founded. That history, that experience, that time in the chair can work against you in a changing environment, and that's what we've had to guard against."

The fact is, consolidation happened as quickly as it did because the industry had endured 80 years of regulation that had prevented it from happening until the Telecom Act was passed. "What might have happened very slowly over a period of time instead occurred very quickly because of artificial constraints that had been in place for so long," Randall Mays says. None of this would have happened as quickly as it did if there hadn't been all the artificial barriers that restricted ownership." He points out that healthy industries tend to have a market leader that enjoys 30-to-40 percent of market share within that industry. On the other hand, at the time radio was deregulated, the industry's market leader had half of one percent of the market. "What helped add so much fuel to the fire is that Clear Channel went from half a percent to twenty percent over a four-year period instead of 80 years," he says. "And if you're an employee who doesn't like change, it's very difficult to be working in an industry that's changing, and for a company that is an agent of that change."

CHAPTER FIVE

IT'S NOT ALL
ABOUT RADIO

WHILE CLEAR CHANNEL UNDERSTANDABLY IS PERCEIVED AS A RADIO BROADCASTING company, half of the company's net revenues are derived from business ventures outside the radio industry. In fact, in 2007, radio drove $3.44 billion in revenue, while outdoor advertising produced $2.67 billion and "other" businesses (primarily media representation and other ventures) earned another $223 million. Put in perspective, radio accounts for approximately 50 percent of the company's annual revenue, while the other divisions produce the other 50 percent.

MOVING INTO TELEVISION

As previously noted in Chapter 2, Clear Channel made its entry into the television business in 1988, when the company purchased WPMI-TV in the Mobile-Pensacola market for $8.9 million. Now, two decades later, the company owns and operates 41 television properties in 25 markets, most of which are small- and medium-community markets ranging from Cincinnati to Fairbanks, Alaska. The division got its start when Lowry Mays, possessed of a contrarian point of view that the television industry could support another prime time network, began picking up inexpensive independent stations and affiliating them with the upstart Fox Network. Mays believed the decades-old business model that had been established by the three alphabet networks (ABC, CBS, and NBC) could be reinvented to support many more viable TV stations that until that point had been relegated to the UHF hinterlands, airing tenth-run movies and game-show reruns. The introduction of such programs as *The Simpsons* and *Married With Children* were critical tools in this transition, as was the push of the cable industry to reach more and more U.S. television households.

"In the late 1980s independent TV was just a sliver of the television business," Lowry Mays recalls. "None of those stations was making any money, because they had to buy almost all of their programming. But I thought if we could purchase some of these independent stations, we could use the programming that this new Fox network was starting to offer. So we started acquiring some really inexpensive independent television properties and affiliating them with Fox. That turned out to be a good source of cash flow for us during the early part of the '90s, and eventually it helped fund some of the radio stations we ended up buying."

"Nobody thought Fox was going to be successful," adds Randall Mays. "At the time, you could buy independent television stations for almost nothing because everybody thought independent TV stations didn't have access to programming. But Dan Sullivan, who was a good television operator, convinced Lowry that we could make a lot of money buying independent TV properties. So we did, and we became the largest Fox Network affiliate, at a time when nobody had ever heard of Homer Simpson." Using the same business model that the company applied to radio in its early years, Clear Channel began to experience tremendous cash-flow gains, which allowed the company to purchase more television stations as well as begin shopping selectively for more radio properties. "Most people don't know that by 1994, 55 percent of the cash flow of our company came out of television," Randall says. "In five years we went from being a pure play radio company to being primarily a television company."

This shift in cash flow illustrates how the company identified dislocations in the marketplace and took advantage of them. "We simply looked for opportunities to buy things that other people didn't necessarily think were in favor," Randall Mays says. "Television involves most of the same skill sets that are involved in radio. It's an advertising-based medium, and we knew from experience that it was all about putting a good product on the air, and then hiring, motivating, and retaining a good sales force. We always knew that there are three legs to the stool in radio: You put a good product on the air, make sure you have a very sales-intensive focus, and have very strong centralized financial controls — all under an umbrella of total autonomy."

Former Television division president/CEO Don Perry, came to the company in 2002, when Clear Channel purchased NBC-affiliated KMOL-TV in San Antonio and switched the call letters to WOAI. "The key for TV stations today is to re-engineer themselves, both literally and figuratively. Literally, in the sense of making sure that you have the human resources and capital expenditures that will allow you to get the most return on investment as opposed to what we've had over the last 50 years. Figuratively, we need to re-engineer the business in terms of our thinking. We need to be able to embrace the future and view the changes that are coming as an opportunity. One of the phrases used internally at Clear Channel is 'there is no such thing as disruptive technologies; there are only opportunistic technologies.'" Perry says that technology is allowing the company to build a variety of businesses on different platforms, including the Internet, distribution to phones, and multicasting through high definition digital channels.

The core business of virtually any local television station is its local news coverage, and with the advances in new technologies, that coverage now can be distributed twenty-four-seven, Perry says. "We really had to figure out how to be platform-agnostic," he explains, noting that the days of broadcasting local newscasts at five, six, and ten o'clock are fading. "In doing news at all hours of the day, we could either push that to the consumer, or they could pull it from us. Clear Channel television stations are going to give them information on a variety of platforms, wherever and however they choose to find it." This doesn't mean that the fundamentals of the television business have changed, Perry insists; in fact, the content and revenue streams are relatively unchanged. "Essentially, Clear Channel provides news programming to its local audiences, and sells access to those audiences. Advertisers are looking to market their goods and services to consumers, and as long as you don't get stuck in the paradigm that says 'we will tell you when to watch the news' and that 'primetime is going to be at a certain time,' you can adapt. If you embrace the idea of digital change, you're going to be just fine. You have to get the mentality out of the current model and think about all the possibilities that exist."

In order to drive ground-up innovation at the local level, Clear Channel instituted a program labeled the "One Percent Solution," which was designed to solve specific challenges facing local television broadcasters. This program invited local broadcasters to identify a forward-thinking idea that would expand a station's best practices beyond the normal business model. Those broadcasters who submitted a winning idea would be guaranteed that one percent of their expenses from the previous year's budget would be set aside and reinvested in the business. Two winners were guaranteed in each of the company's large, medium, and small markets. "We got some tremendous ideas from this program, and the following year it evolved into an innovation contest for the whole company," Perry says. "We got three or four hundred ideas that came in last year, and we put some serious money against it."

The primary impetus behind the program was the understanding that many men and women generate great ideas during the normal course of a work day, but because of normal business pressures those ideas rarely are actualized. "Part of the problem within all of American business is that when it's a publicly held company we have a short-term mentality," Perry says. "There's a constant drumbeat of pressure for what you are doing next quarter. When we came up with this program at Clear Channel we realized it was going to cost us millions of dollars. But we had to look past that and decide to invest in our future." Interestingly, even though only six stations won the contest in their respective markets, every station came up with at least one new idea, and many of those that didn't win still created budgets that allowed them to implement those ideas anyway.

Much of the innovation that resulted from the "One Percent Solution" (and other programs) was driven by the realization that the television audience increasingly is in charge of what it watches when, and for how long. "The consumer now has the ability to access a lot of different platforms," Perry says. "There's a lot more choice involved in how they do that, but research shows that people still want to watch the local news. Now, that doesn't mean they want to watch it specifically at six or ten o'clock. But they do want to know what's going on in their community, so as long as you hold on to the news brand in the local market and can make an emotional connection with the consumer, you can remain relevant."

Perry says that perhaps the biggest internal challenge in shifting from a single platform to one that includes many access points for the consumer is retraining the people who work in the content business. "Reporters have to understand that they're not just working on one or two news packages a day for each newscast," Perry says. "They now have a variety of ways to report the news. We need to teach them how to publish immediately on a webcast, how to do a mobile download, and how to be able to cut an audio report for both radio and TV. They are now content casters rather than TV newscasters."

Simple as this change might appear, putting it into practice was not always easy. As Jack Welsh observed when he was running General Electric, change has no constituency. Nobody embraces change as an automatic human reaction to things; it sometimes has to be forced upon those individuals who often have the best intentions to adapt to their changing environment but have difficulty reinventing their personal identities. "We have to begin with the notion that the customer is not the same person he or she was five or ten years ago," Perry explains. "People don't think of themselves just as a TV watcher, a radio listener, or an Internet user. They think of themselves as all of those things, and they want to have their brand available on all those platforms."

In a world where the living room television set has gone from three basic network affiliates 20 years ago to over 400 cable channels today, plus countless websites on the Internet, maintaining a strong brand helps the viewer cut through the immense clutter. "It's like being pecked to death by ducks," Perry says. "What we did was create and brand our own channels and platforms, rather than having other people do that. We worked to have content on our websites, and to distribute things via our digital signals that will be totally relevant to small portions of our audience."

Reflective of the changes that are coming to television (and, by proxy, radio) is the growing TV audience during the early morning daypart. "Television news is becoming the new radio in the morning," Perry says. "A number of stations are now starting at four or five in the morning and are doing straight news up until the *Today Show* or *Good Morning America*. It's literally increasing the amount of time people are watching TV." Meanwhile, afternoon and evening newscasts are suffering because people are exposed to news from numerous other information sources during the day. "Consumers have many other options through which they can learn what's going on, so we reconstructed some of our newscasts in the afternoon," he explains. "There is an assumption now that the viewer knows the top stories of the day, so we provided a quick review of them and then tried to give a little bit more context." On the other hand, the "late" 10 o'clock newscasts (11 o'clock on the east and west coasts) remain strong audience vehicles, so there's little need to tamper with that content — at least for now.

Still, over-the-air television viewership has been sliced and diced by the explosion of media and programming venues. In the early 1980s cable was still in its infancy and, while most TV broadcasters correctly assessed it as a threat, it was inconceivable that the American consumer would ever stray from the three "alphabet networks" that had provided them with nightly entertainment since the early '50s. But change occurs irrespective of wishes or faith, and as such entities as MTV and HBO drove cable into homes from Maine to Malibu, more and more American families began to sample non-traditional program content. And as they did, the advertising community began to realize — as they had found with radio just a few years earlier — that certain programs attracted certain types of consumers, thus making it possible to target their ad messages to those specific demographics. As a result, primetime network television viewership that in the mid-'80s hovered around 70 percent of the TV audience today has dropped to approximately 45 percent, while cable- and satellite-delivered programming delivers most of the other 55 percent. Considering that the number of viable networks can still be counted on one hand, that 45 percent is impressive. But just as the big three automakers in Detroit have learned, regaining market share is like trying to coax ants back into the anthill.

Most innovative broadcasters refuse to view these numbers as anything but an opportunity, and many have set their sights on the full deployment of High Definition Television as a technology that will give them major traction with the consumer. First demonstrated publicly in the late 1980s, commercial HDTV is designed to provide a high-resolution picture in a 16x9 (widescreen) format with clear, enhanced color. The FCC has set February 2009 — after the next presidential campaign and inauguration — as the point at which all U.S. television stations must fully convert to HDTV. In other words, the analog fuse will be pulled and the digital switch thrown, although many skeptics believe this deadline is far less than firm. The expense for converting TV stations to digital has been extreme, but Perry says that in the long run the money will be well worth it. "Some Clear Channel stations already are broadcasting in digital, and stations are anxious for the date to come, because it means they can literally turn off the transmitter and save a lot of power." Until that February 2009 conversion date — or whenever it comes — broadcasters are transmitting two TV stations for every facility they own, which has led them to incur significant costs.

How the roll-out of HDTV — in 2009 or a later date — affects the overall television industry most likely will have little impact on Clear Channel's revenues or future corporate operations. When it was announced in November 2006 that an investor group was taking the company private, Clear Channel also revealed, in an unrelated move, that it would be selling the entire Television division — along with 448 radio stations. The decision, in part, was prompted by the spin-off in 2005 of the Entertainment division into LiveNation, which yielded significant capital losses and afforded the company the opportunity to sell some assets with great tax efficiency. Company executives took a look at which assets could be sold and which were core to the overall business; they decided that, since the Television division drove less than 5 percent of the company's revenues, Clear Channel could divest those stations without creating a negative impact for any of the company's strategic operations.

THE GREAT OUTDOORS

As an operating and acquisition company, Clear Channel always has looked for ways to diversify its holdings and to use cash flow to invest in new ventures that could provide superior returns. Investing in the television business was one of these ventures, but as the company began to generate revenue in that sector, station prices began to escalate.

"We had a very strong balance sheet and we didn't want to pay any more debt down, so we were pretty active in trying to seek opportunities to reinvest our free cash flow," Randall Mays observes. "In that process, we came across the outdoor industry and spent a lot of time analyzing the business before we ever approached anybody about buying them."

Noting that outdoor advertising had many of the same characteristics as the radio business, Randall says it also had a very fragmented industry structure that lent itself to consolidation.

"Because of the economies of scale, we knew that we could eliminate a lot of overhead," he explains. "Even if we had to pay a big cash-flow multiple, it actually was a pretty small multiple once the company was folded into our operations. We knew that it had great economies of scale and it was a great business."

Almost a full century before Clear Channel had its outdoor epiphany, two enterprising young men named Walter Foster and George Kleiser suspected that outdoor advertising had the potential to deliver solid profit margins. In 1901, less than a decade after the first automobile was introduced to the horse paths of America — and nearly 20 years before the first commercial U.S. radio program was broadcast — the two men joined forces and founded Foster & Kleiser Outdoor Advertising. Their objective was to shift the business away from randomly placed posters and signs that typically were glued to virtually any surface available, moving them to more uniform structures and locations. The development of the automobile helped them build the company, as people were able to venture farther from their homes and places of work. Over time the company prospered and grew beyond its roots in the Pacific Northwest, expanding southward to new plants in San Francisco, Los Angeles, and eventually to the East Coast.

Half a century after it was founded, the company was sold in 1952 to W.R. Grace & Company, retaining the Foster & Kleiser name. This was the same year that a young salesman named Karl Eller joined the firm, where he was responsible for negotiating sign leases for advertising clients. W.R. Grace sold the company to Metropolitan Broadcasting in 1959, and Metromedia, a division of Metropolitan, subsequently sold F&K to Patrick Media, which changed its name to Patrick Media Group in 1986.

Meanwhile, during the 1970s, Karl Eller had begun to build Combined Communications, a diversified media company that had holdings in radio, television, and print. During this process Eller tapped the legal counsel of a young attorney named Paul Meyer, who worked on some of the early acquisitions that eventually were to become part of the growing company. After Eller merged Combined Communications into Gannett, Meyer moved on to pastures that were somewhat greener and, with several other young attorneys, formed his own law firm.

By then Eller had turned his attention to Columbia Pictures, where he assisted the film company with its merger with Coca-Cola. He subsequently became the head of Circle K, which he built into the second largest chain of convenience stores in the U.S. The company was very highly leveraged during a period of rapidly rising interest rates, which caused it to see bankruptcy court protection in 1990 over Eller's objections. (Note: In 1993 international investment firm Investcorp took Circle K out of bankruptcy, and in 2002 ConocoPhillips became the new owner of the company.)

It was during the Circle K bankruptcy proceedings that Eller approached Meyer and asked him to help him work through some financial difficulties that had arisen from his businesses holdings, part of which had failed because of the savings and loan collapse. "We worked Karl through all those issues, and he decided that he wanted to go back to his roots, which was outdoor advertising," Meyer recalls. "So he started to build an outdoor advertising company again, and I represented him on the early acquisitions. In 1995 he and a venture capital firm in San Francisco bought Patrick Media, which at the time was the largest outdoor advertising company in the country. They decided they were going to take the company public, and Karl asked me to leave my law practice and become his general counsel, which I did at the start of '96."

Meyer recalls that later that year, when he and Eller were in the midst of filing with the SEC for the company's IPO, "Clear Channel came along, totally unsolicited, and made an offer to buy the company." That offer was summarily rejected, but Clear Channel came back in January of '97 and made the classic offer that couldn't be refused. In April 1997, Clear Channel acquired Eller Media, retaining the company's name and keeping Karl Eller on board as chief executive officer. Additionally, Meyer was retained as the division's general counsel. He was named President in 1999 with the understanding that he would ultimately lead the division. That transition came to pass in 2002.

"I can't say enough great things about Karl Eller," says Randall Mays. "He was a true visionary for the outdoor industry, and Clear Channel wouldn't be in the outdoor industry if it weren't for him. When Lowry and I first sat down with Karl, he explained why this was a great business, why it was going to grow, and that he was going to take advantage of that growth by taking his company public. He had already hired an investment bank to initiate that process, but we convinced him that because of our access to capital, and because of all of the free cash flow we had, we would be able to better consolidate the industry. Karl always looked at things long-term, so he sold us the company."

Following that purchase, Clear Channel very aggressively began to consolidate the outdoor industry by making a number of acquisitions. "When we started to get into outdoor, people didn't think it was a very good business, partly because it always traded around an eight-times-cash-flow multiple," Randall says. "Tobacco advertising had just been banned from billboards, which meant there was going to be a huge dislocation in revenue streams, and everybody was scared of what was going to happen."

True to expectations, ad revenues did drop when tobacco advertising disappeared, but the Mays family knew that a similar shock wave had been felt by television and radio in the late 1960s, and both media had weathered the moment.

"Ad revenues initially fell about 15 percent, but a year later they were right back, and then they began to grow very rapidly," Randall continues. "Within a very short period the consolidation economics of the outdoor industry dwarfed what we were seeing in radio."

Clear Channel realized significant cost efficiencies almost immediately. This was at the same time that many large bulletins were still painted by hand, and fixed labor costs kept the margins low. However, if two plants could be consolidated, many of those fixed costs could be eliminated, or at least reduced. Incremental margins were able to more than double in some cases, and with a greater inventory of displays, the consolidated company could rotate an advertiser through an entire marketplace, providing greatly enhanced coverage both in geographical coverage and demographic targeting, while offering a more efficient advertising package.

"We knew we could pay healthy multiples to these companies, multiples they knew they could never dream of getting just by operating the business," Randall Mays says. "Those companies were ecstatic, and we were able to consolidate at what we saw as very attractive prices. The only thing that was holding back the industry was the lack of capital needed to fund acquisitions. Investors were petrified of the tobacco ban."

Clear Channel's consolidation of the outdoor business created awareness among investors, which created public markets, which in turn created access to capital.

At the same time, the physical side of the business was changing rapidly, with the introduction of digitally-printed vinyl displays. "That may not sound like a big deal, but it was," Randall explains. "Before digital printing, anyone who visited our Los Angeles plant would have seen huge warehouses of stretched canvases, with artists painting individual signs. If Coca-Cola wanted to do a big billboard display, it was very slow to get to market because we physically had to hand-paint the signs, and every sign was a little bit different."

Coordinating that imaging process for a market the size of L.A. was difficult, but coordinating it for 50 markets across the country was nothing short of a nightmare, Randall recalls. "You simply couldn't do it," he says. "Suddenly, with the advent of digitally-printed vinyl, we could get images that we really couldn't get any other way. We had absolute continuity of image, we had the ability to roll out a campaign very quickly across a market, and we could do it across multiple markets. All of a sudden we started creating a national marketplace."

Over the years, that initial billboard focus expanded dramatically to include other types of advertising that reached people when they were "gone from home." Today, Clear Channel Outdoor has some 50 separate profit centers, including such specialized segments as airport advertising, mall advertising, taxi advertising (taxi tops and in-vehicle video programming), street furniture including bus shelters and other public facilities (an advertising type most popular in Europe and gaining ground in the United States), and spectacular sign advertising, a division that operates under the name Spectacolor and counts crowd-pleasing signs in New York City's Times Square and massive displays within new sports and entertainment complexes such as Westgate City Center in Glendale, Arizona, among its portfolio.

"Our U.S. business has been enormously successful, and one reason for this is that we have a superb management team that's been together for more than five years," Paul Meyer says. "They work together extraordinarily well. We don't have turf issues, we don't have internal politics, and everybody knows their role. At the same time, people pitch in and jump out as needed; it's just a terrific group."

One incontrovertible strength of outdoor advertising is its future widespread and continued exposure to a mass audience. As most other media struggle to maintain audience share, billboards and other forms of outdoor displays will only continue to gain eyeballs as people become increasingly mobile.

"Traditional mass-market media like television and print continue to face huge challenges," Meyer explains. "All these highly competitive media are experiencing audience fragmentation. By contrast, outdoor has an ever-expanding audience. There's no mute button, there's no on/off switch. We're there twenty-four-seven. Every single year people are out of their homes more than the previous year. People are traveling more miles every year, we have more cars every year, and the miles that are traveled are traveled more slowly every year."

While the business model for outdoor advertising is similar to that for radio, outdoor displays are sold to advertisers in a variety of ways. In some cases billboards literally are sold sign by sign, particularly in small communities where outdoor is really more of a directional signage business.

"Historically we've sold what are called 'showings,'" Meyer says. "For instance, a 50 showing theoretically would be a showing that reaches 50 percent of the designated market area (DMA), and this can be done through a variety of ways. It can be done with a poster campaign coupled with a bulletin campaign, and sometimes we sell groups of bulletins strategically located throughout a market in order to provide greater coverage. Sometimes we sell a rotation program, where anywhere from a couple to a half-dozen or more signs are rotated through the market every 30 or 60 days to achieve certain levels of coverage. Increasingly we are able to deliver more targeted, more demographically oriented campaigns."

The technological changes to hit the outdoor advertising world in the last 15 years have been extensive and dramatic, Meyer observes. "Just the change from hand-painting large-format signs to producing vinyl displays with computer-printed copy was remarkable," he says. "We had real issues with consistency and quality, especially because copy on all signs in a single advertising campaign has to be identical. With the advent of digital printing, we became a medium that could post vinyl copy in a couple of days across multiple markets," Meyer says.

Technology advances drove down the cost of a sign, and they also introduced "back office" systems that allow Clear Channel to be much more efficient in executing campaigns.

"Five years ago, if a client called one of our account executives in New York, that account representative would gather all the information about what kind of campaign the client wanted to run," Meyer says. "He or she then would start hitting the phone to see what displays were available in L.A., Chicago, Houston, and other requested markets. Sometimes that process would take days. Today, we maintain a real-time inventory system, accessible on our website to all of our account executives in all of our markets, so that account executives can look at every single market and know exactly what inventory is available, how it is priced, and develop a proposal in an hour."

Clear Channel expanded its use of digital technology significantly in May of 2005, when the company launched a pilot program in Cleveland, Ohio, that replaced seven traditional (14-foot by 48-foot) roadside billboards with digital displays, each containing 449,280 light-emitting diodes (LEDs) that enable the signs to be viewed even in the brightest direct sunlight. The digital billboards would be programmed as a "network," with static images on the boards changing every eight seconds in a continuous loop, giving drivers the opportunity to see a variety of messages on a single sign.

The new technology also gave advertisers the ability to change their ads more frequently than even with digitally-printed vinyl. For example, a fast-food advertiser could display one message during morning drive, another for lunchtime and a third for the commuters' drive home.

"If a retailer wants to do a big holiday weekend sale, he or she can adjust their advertising on the network on a daily — or even more frequent — basis," explains Meyer. "At the end of the first day of the sale they can check their inventory and see what products aren't moving the way they'd like. The next morning they can change the sign, advertising either a new product or showing a lower price for the product that didn't move the day before."

The trial was an enormous success, and the company moved quickly to convert additional billboard networks in other markets. By the end of 2007, the company had 19 digital billboard networks in 16 markets, with some (like Los Angeles and Las Vegas) having more than one network.

"Ultimately, this technology is making outdoor the most flexible of all advertising media," Meyer says. "It is enabling advertisers to deliver their messages by daypart, day of the week, and even time of the month. We are also providing near-instantaneous responses to critical messaging needs like impending major storms, emergency situations, and most recently, Amber and FBI alerts."

Indeed, one of the most significant early uses of Clear Channel's digital billboard networks has been public safety. The approval process for converting traditional billboards to their digital cousins rested with local municipalities and, reminiscent of the success local governments had in specifying that a certain percentage of cable programming be dedicated to community access, Clear Channel Outdoor offered local leaders and community safety groups early on the opportunity to interrupt instantly these networks' continuous advertising loop to post alerts about missing children. Numerous children were identified and returned safely as a result of the digital broadcasts. Within two years, having watched this success, the local Federal Bureau of Investigation office in Philadelphia worked with the Clear Channel Outdoor office there to post similar alerts showing suspects from their Most Wanted list. Again, the digital billboard networks were amazingly effective; in the first 90 days of the program's creation, four fugitives from the FBI's Most Wanted list were apprehended across the United States.

In other novel applications, Clear Channel is using global positioning system (GPS) devices in its taxi top displays in Manhattan and other cities to target advertising to specific demographics. "This technology allows them to change their signage depending upon time of day and where they are," Randall Mays explains. "You have a whole different audience in New York's financial district than if you were in the theater district. If you're on the Upper East Side, it makes a lot of sense to be advertising restaurants in that neighborhood, rather than restaurants on the Upper West Side. The fact is, digital technology radically transforms this business. An advertiser can now have optimal utility across individual dayparts, and clearly advertisers want to reach different demographics at different times in the day."

While conventional vinyl outdoor signs will remain the core of Clear Channel Outdoor's business for many years to come, the march of technology is inevitable. "A large component of our business will remain traditional outdoor," Meyer says. "But the consumer is going to see an increasing number of displays with electronically-generated copy that is crisper and cleaner. Advertisers are going to see more opportunities for consumers to interact directly with Clear Channel displays by downloading information directly to them." Meyer does not see drivers whizzing past signs at 60 miles an hour trying to interact with a billboard at the side of the road, but such venues as street corners, taxis, malls and airports are already hosting an increased amount of interaction between consumers and advertising displays.

And at some point, digital billboards are expected to be standard around the country, providing drivers with messages that target specific areas and dayparts with greater efficiency and immediate public service. "Outdoor advertising right now has an incredible, unique advantage over other media, especially newspapers," Meyer observes. "And the nature of this business is such that technology will always present opportunities for us, unlike any other business that can be rendered virtually obsolete. Technology only enables us to service clients better and provide far more flexibility and responsiveness to our advertising programs."

"Ultimately, the conversion to digital will increase a board's productivity — and its return," sums Randall Mays. "People really are starting to comprehend what this industry can do." Ten years from now, Mays expects outdoor to be the most effective mass medium, and says it very likely will displace television as the most influential global mass medium.

Clear Channel is so optimistic about the future of outdoor advertising, in fact, that in November 2005 the company announced the initial public offering of 35 million shares of common stock of Clear Channel Outdoor Holdings, at a price of $18 per share. When this spin-off was announced, a company statement claimed the IPO would allow a partially-separated Clear Channel Outdoor to "enjoy greater strategic focus and flexibility. Additionally, Clear Channel Outdoor will be able to supplement its attractive organic profile by pursuing selective acquisitions using a currency based on its inherent valuation rather than the blended valuation represented by the company's current common stock. This public currency will also enable Clear Channel Outdoor to better attract, retain, and reward management in alignment with its performance. Moreover, the company believes an IPO will help Clear Channel Communications shareholders more clearly evaluate the inherent value of Clear Channel Outdoor by highlighting its strong leadership position and growth profile."

Clear Channel Communications retained a controlling stake in the Outdoor division.

SIMPLY SPECTACULAR

Within this digital environment, Clear Channel's Spectacolor division is an entirely different animal. Largely pedestrian in habitat, the division thrives in Times Square in a habitat of color video displays that blink, flash, move, and change constantly, entertaining and tantalizing the hundreds of thousands of people who course through the twelve-square-block area every day. "Our world is a different world from the rest of the Outdoor division," says its chief executive officer, Harry Coghlan. "Times Square is an out-of-home advertisers' dream, an anything-goes laboratory for the world's most creative brands."

The Spectacolor division is somewhat limited by its environment in that few areas in the U.S. offer the proximity, the setting, and the atmosphere of Times Square.

So the company has worked with developers to create entirely new concepts in public space. Early and significant success, as one might expect, has been enjoyed in Las Vegas, where the company's projects include a digital "cloud" above four enormous, adjacent displays above the Fashion Show Mall — creating the largest single outdoor display in the world. The installation was immediately recognized as a unique branding medium by major global advertisers, with a major U.S. consumer electronics company being the inaugural advertiser and securing a multi-year exclusive within its product category.

Other projects on a grand scale include a so-called "mixed use" development outside of Phoenix, Arizona, that combines retail, residential, office, sports and entertainment facilities called Westgate City Center. The location played host to the 2008 Super Bowl. Such projects build on the success Clear Channel Outdoor had earlier in the decade with a pier complex built adjacent to the famed Boardwalk in Atlantic City.

Unlike much of the rest of the outdoor advertising world, Spectacolor specializes in long-term iconic displays typically not sold through an agency, but directly to specific corporations. "A CEO doesn't typically sign off on a lot of media buys, but CEOs are making the final decision on all Spectacolor multi-year deals," Coghlan reveals. "That says something about the awareness that our Times Square and other signs create; they've become a statement of the corporation."

ADDRESSING CONTENT

Just as radio from time to time is faced with content issues — many of which involve community standards and concerns about indecency — outdoor advertising also has its challenges with visual imagery. While the FCC maintains regulatory oversight regarding offensive broadcast content, billboards generally are not subject to content regulation. While some advertisers elect to push the edge of controversy with their messages, a few press it so far as to produce severe repercussions from the community.

With over three quarters of a million outdoor faces spread out around the world, this becomes a recurring challenge, and Meyer says that some sort of copy controversy makes its way to the Outdoor division's Phoenix headquarters once every month or two. One example: several years ago the London-based clothing company French Connection U.K. purchased a billboard sporting the corporate acronym FCUK on a sign that towered over I-95 in South Florida, drawing numerous complaints to city officials and Clear Channel Outdoor. French Connection, which has been in existence for a little more than a decade, claims that "any crassness associated with it was simply in the eye of the beholder," but they also concede that the logo may carry "certain connotations."

Meyer's response? "We have taken a fairly aggressive stance on copy," he says. "Some time ago we banned all sexually oriented business ads, such as for gentlemen's clubs. You used to see a lot of those on taxis in New York, but once we consolidated the taxi business in Manhattan, they all came down. That segment of business is extremely attractive financially, because it is one of the best places for strip clubs to advertise — you hit the guys coming out of the airport so the first thing they see is a taxi cab advertising a strip joint — but we don't want to participate in it."

Meyer insists he wasn't making a moral judgment, but rather based his decision on conversations with outdoor buying specialists at several major New York agencies. "They told me that their major advertisers didn't want to be associated with that kind of advertising, so they were reluctant to use taxi tops," he says. "Sure enough, when we took those kinds of ads off, we started getting more quality advertisers."

That said, specific copy decisions, Meyer adds, are made on a market-by-market basis. The copy that is approved for Clear Channel signs in Las Vegas wouldn't necessarily be put up in Des Moines, and copy in New York might not make it in Wichita. "We had enough of these copy controversies that we issued a company-wide policy in which we told our managers to ask themselves a couple of questions when they have a copy issue: First, would they be uncomfortable having their children see it, or having to answer questions that they might ask about it? Second, if it's 'attack copy' that goes after a person or an organization, would they find it personally offensive if it were attacking them or a member of their family? If either question produces a 'yes' answer, they probably shouldn't put it up."

In the summer of 2004, Clear Channel Outdoor faced a very public challenge of its policy. A group calling itself "Project Billboard" contracted to erect a giant spectacular sign on the side of the Marriott Marquis hotel in Times Square. In an event that Meyer describes as a "clear-cut set-up," the company, noting New York post-9/11 sensitivities to depictions of explosives, rejected the ad's imagery: a red, white, and blue bomb. The would-be advertisers, who initially positioned themselves to the media as "housewives" and later admitted they were political activists, complained bitterly to the media that the rejection of the ad imagery was "undeniable proof" that the company favored Republicans, who would be gathering in New York for their national convention later that summer.

"We are totally apolitical," Meyer explains. "I don't care if advertisers are Democrats or Republicans or anti-war or pro-war. As long as the copy meets our standards, we will put it up. The notion that there's a monolithic corporate enterprise that dictates that people adhere to certain political persuasions in making business decisions is totally wrong. I have never, ever, had anybody in San Antonio suggest to me anything about politics in relation to the copy we put up. Never." (For more on the Project Billboard controversy, please see Chapter 10.)

TURNS OUT IT'S EASY BEING GREEN

While many U.S. companies "went green" in the mid-2000s as part of a massive marketing initiative within the top global brands doing business in North America, Clear Channel Outdoor had been quietly transforming its business to consume less energy, increase its ability to recycle vinyl, and minimize waste materials because going green turned out to be good for business.

The initiatives spanned material, electrical, engineering and even posting procedures. For example, Clear Channel worked with their largest printing vendor to develop vinyl materials that are 100 percent recyclable, immediately alleviating landfill burdens; further, the material was 70 percent lighter than traditional vinyl, enabling the company to eliminate the use of the cranes (and small trucks to transport them) needed to hoist heavy vinyl panels up to traditional billboards. In 2006, the company estimated that the elimination of cranes and their transport trucks saved some 30 percent per year on gasoline expenditures.

Separately, the company is nearing the conclusion of a seven-year conversion plan to use light fixtures on billboards that will lower such energy consumption by 50 percent. The fixtures also have less light spillage and a more even distribution of light. The company's conversion is the first step in transitioning to solar-powered energy, which could be fully converted by the end of the decade.

THE GLOBAL MARKETPLACE

As noted in Chapter 3, Clear Channel moved into the international radio marketplace in 1995, when the company and APN News Media of Australia formed a joint venture to launch the Australian Radio Network. Just over a year later, in July of 1996, the two companies again partnered to form the New Zealand Radio Network. Following the Australia and New Zealand acquisitions, Clear Channel set its sights on Europe. Over the next five years the company acquired stakes in Radio Bonton in the Czech Republic (1997); Jazz FM in Manchester, England (1999); the Aller Group in Denmark (Radio 2) and Norway (Radio 1); Q The Beat, an AM station in Amsterdam; and One FM, Lausanne FM, and Media One Contact in Geneva, Switzerland (2000). Additionally, Clear Channel acquired a stake in Grupo Acir in Mexico in March of 1998. "In many countries where per capita advertising was low compared to the U.S., Clear Channel felt there were strong growth opportunities in radio," says Bob Cohen, president of Clear Channel's International Radio division. "In Europe, we saw opportunity in countries where we had a local management infrastructure with our international outdoor businesses, which understood the local culture and the way business was done. Also, in locations where Clear Channel International Outdoor had operations, we were confident that we could achieve some sales, marketing, promotional, and operational synergies."

Naturally, each country the company entered has its own foreign ownership restrictions, and the decision to make acquisitions in these countries largely was based on whether a very real possibility existed that these rules might be eased in the future. "In almost every case — whether Clear Channel, as a foreign company, could own 100 percent of the business or not — the approach was to seek a local joint venture partner that understood the business culture, the societal culture and the political and regulatory environment," Cohen says. "By working well together with a local JV partner and applying best practices while collaborating, innovating, and enhancing our management philosophies about the practical aspects of running a radio business, we sought to unlock value and grow the business."

Despite these unlocked values and synergistic opportunities — some realized and some not — Clear Channel began in 2001 to divest itself of its international radio operations in Europe, and by the end of 2003 the only international radio operations still in the company's portfolio were the properties in Australia, New Zealand, and Mexico. "Our international radio strategy had changed," Cohen says. "And in keeping with this strategy, we elected to exit Europe where our broadcast operations were much smaller, in order to focus on those three countries where our businesses were much larger in scale and upside growth potential." While he insists that financial results increased consistently during the late '90s growth period and "all our experiences have been positive," Cohen maintains that over time the company has learned which situations work best for producing growth and an overall positive cash flow result. "When we have exited businesses it has been for a variety of reasons, but we have been able to take away something positive from every one of these ventures — and continue to do so," he observes.

Despite the company's exit from most of its global radio markets, Cohen maintains that Clear Channel continues to eye strategic acquisitions where favorable market conditions exist. "We hope to grow the division and spend time in pursuit of developing and evaluating those opportunities which fit our strategic goals," he explains. "Needless to say, our experience in international broadcasting over the years has prepared us to do an even better job of deciding where we should be and what structures we should strive for in order to give us the best chance to unlock value and make any acquisition or transaction ultimately successful."

CHAPTER SIX

BEWARE THE EVIL EMPIRE

THE INTERNET IS A WONDERFUL THING. NEVER BEFORE HAS VIRTUALLY EVERYONE (at least those equipped with a computer and an e-mail address) been able to practice First Amendment free speech so easily and so readily, with such a widespread audience. Have something to say? It's easy to dash it off in Outlook Express, hit the send button, and disseminate it to a virtual universe of similarly equipped computer users. Send it to enough friends and colleagues, and your message stands a good chance of circulating the globe at virus-like speed and efficiency. Of course, if you have access to a website or blog, that efficiency and virulence is increased by untold dimensions. Not only is your message permeating the ether of the World Wide Web, but its mere presence on the Internet lends it credibility and standing beyond reason. In other words, in the minds of many people, if it's on the web, it must be true.

Therein lies the challenge, if not the problem. With all its indispensable value and ubiquitous influence, the Internet also over the past few years has become bloated with websites and postings that have made an international sport of impeaching Clear Channel on a wide range of alleged infractions — chief among them, of orchestrating unprecedented consolidation.

But the truth is out there. The simple fact about consolidation is that, based on the Herfindahl-Hirschman Index, the metric often cited by the Department of Justice, the radio business is the *least* consolidated of all media industries. Specifically, the top four music companies account for 85 percent of that industry's market share, while the top eight film companies account for 84 percent of that industry's revenue. Meanwhile, the top cable company accounts for 29 percent of its industry's market share, while the top six advertising agencies account for 65 percent of theirs. Compare that with the top ten radio companies, which account for 43 percent — less than half — of the radio industry's share, and the clear lack of consolidation begins to emerge very quickly.

In 2006, the FCC reported that 13,793 radio stations — the vast majority of them commercially operated — were licensed by the FCC. Despite much rhetoric to the contrary, they were owned by 3,800 individual radio broadcasting companies. Clear Channel clearly was the largest of these groups, owning and operating just under 1,200 stations, while CBS Radio and Entercom were second and third, respectively, according to BIA Financial Networks' annual report that ranks groups by advertising revenue. But even at 1,200, Clear Channel owned — at its height — just 9 percent of the country's radio stations. And on a revenue basis, the company's stations take in 18 percent of the industry's advertising dollars. Neither of those numbers satisfies any legitimate definition of dominance. Nevertheless, a series of articles published in the online journal Salon.com in 2001 seemed to solidify — at least in the minds of the site's avid readers — Clear Channel's image of "The Evil Empire." And, as Jeff Perlstein, executive director of the Media Alliance and co-founder of Indymedia.org, wrote in June of 2003, "Clear Channel is now widely seen as the 'poster child' for what's wrong with our hyper-consolidated media environment and the free-market government policies that are to blame."

In a world where perception often fronts for reality, Clear Channel — rightly or wrongly — found itself stuck in a quagmire of rumor, myth, and innuendo. Because Clear Channel was the big, new kid on the block, everything that was uncomfortable about the "new world order" of the radio industry was laid at the company's San Antonio doorstep.

One of Hogan's immediate responsibilities when he replaced Michaels was to help Clear Channel shed its negative image, or at least draw attention to the fissure between rumor and reality. That task was fraught with challenges, as many radio people continued to find a connection between "big business" and the corporate excesses that had begun to attract scrutiny from the Securities and Exchange Commission and the general media.

Meanwhile, internally, Clear Channel was earning the nickname Cheap Channel. Budgets within the company had always been tight, as the Mays' financial policy followed the strict assumption that any money spent had to be an investment for future dollars earned. The extreme fiscal scrutiny that accompanied the merger process may have exacerbated this philosophy, and many managers found their budgets tightened more than usual.

In fact, Hogan insists that Clear Channel is more than willing to invest any amount of money that will deliver a solid return for the company. "There is a high expectation that our people will operate their stations in the most efficient, most effective way possible," he explains. "Clear Channel is a great American success story, and that's in large part due to smart financial controls and the discipline that goes with that."

Hogan concedes that an unfortunate side effect of consolidation — for Clear Channel and any company in any industry — was the disappearance of many traditional (and often redundant) jobs. "Bringing several stations together under one roof changed the dynamic for station operations," Hogan observes. "We had to let some people go during consolidation, and those people were not happy about that."

Despite widespread mythology that claims the contrary, Clear Channel has always been operated on a decentralized business model that emphasizes local decision making and entrepreneurial thinking. "It is of paramount importance that our local managers run their stations to best serve their communities, listeners and customers. That means that decisions must be made locally," Hogan maintains. "When we first consolidated and brought together various station and company cultures and practices, that may not have been as clear as it is today."

One of the first things Hogan did when he moved to San Antonio was to make it as clear as he could to all senior managers that the task of running the company's 1,200-plus radio stations resided in the individual markets. "In the end, the local manager is responsible for everything that happens at his or her stations. While that is empowering, it also requires accountability. Our decentralized business model works because we have the very best people at the local level, people who have an ultimate understanding of the people they serve, who know what works and what doesn't."

It's because of this decentralization that Clear Channel Radio employs a small corporate staff at its San Antonio headquarters. Not counting human resources, legal, accounting, and other natural support departments, there are just over a dozen employees — including assistants — in the radio executive suite. Hogan says, "We are here to help our managers and to be a resource for them, but it is up to them to make the best decisions for their stations." Local decision making is the foundation of local broadcasting, and that is the way we do business."

If hindsight could be applied retroactively, Hogan says that Clear Channel probably could have worked harder from the beginning to deflect or quell much of the resulting criticism of its size and clout. "Over the past few years, we have worked to communicate the facts about the company and to separate fact from fiction. Could we have done that sooner? Absolutely."

"It's like people talking bad about your children," adds Lowry Mays who, to this day, is stymied by the volume of ill will that his company has drawn. "That was a personal affront to me. Sure, we were big, but the bigger we got in the business, the easier it became to say, 'These guys are just too big — they have too much influence.' But that's just not correct. Anyone who understands the radio business knows that it's a business you can't influence by being big. Still, it was a period that was very hard for me to understand."

Such is the fate of a company that grew so fast and as large as Clear Channel. The largest targets often become the easiest, particularly in an era where communication via e-mail and instant messaging is constant and virtually immediate. Special interest groups of all political stripes have amassed gargantuan databases that within seconds can communicate news of an incident — or even rumor of an incident — to all points of the globe. As a result, this viral process has wrongly tagged Clear Channel as an imperious multi-national company with a strident corporate arrogance — and a politically activist agenda to match.

To wit:

CHICKS AND BALANCES

Late winter in London is cold and damp. More often than not a thick fog folds in around the city, hugging the streets, and sometimes a gentle mist blows in from the banks of the Thames. The evening of March 10, 2003, was one much like this: A light drizzle had fallen on the city earlier in the day, and the streets were still slick with a thick dankness. In Hammersmith and Fulham, a borough of London known for its rugby team, Fulham Palace (the residence of the bishop of London), and the television center of the British Broadcasting Corp. Shepherd's Bush Green, an 8-acre expanse of open grass surrounded by trees and roads, was bustling with activity as concert-goers who had tickets to the Shepherd's Bush Empire Concert Hall lined up to see that night's sell-out performance.

According to *The Guardian,* "The Empire is the best place to see a gig in the capital. It's just about small enough to be intimate but large enough to make a show feel like an occasion." Built in 1903, the theater has been home to thousands of musical performances over the years, and in 1953 it was converted into studios for BBC Television. A full restoration occurred in the 1990s, and since then the London landmark has played host to a virtual Who's Who of contemporary musicians. Artists who have appeared at the Empire over the past decade include Sheryl Crow, Bob Dylan, Black Eyed Peas, Macy Gray, Alanis Morrissette, The Rolling Stones, Tom Petty & the Heartbreakers, Eric Clapton, Paul McCartney, Smashing Pumpkins, Elton John, and Destiny's Child.

On March 10, the theater's marquee announced that American country band The Dixie Chicks would be headlining that evening. As a reviewer for The Guardian explained to the paper's readers, "The Dixie Chicks are the good-time girls the country establishment loves to hate. Too direct, too old-fashioned, too modern — you name it, it's been slung at the Texan trio. The old vanguard liked their women feisty but second-class, preferably wearing cowgirl outfits and a smile. But the Dixie Chicks were renegade ladies of country who sung gleefully about killing abusive spouses and dressed like an older Britney Spears. Add the success they have had selling a progressive bluegrass sound to fans ignorant of banjos and whistles and you have an emasculating threat."

Threat or feistiness, the Dixie Chicks with just a few choice words that evening catapulted themselves into a firestorm that back home in the U.S. polarized red against blue, Republican against Democrat, liberal against conservative. In between songs, the group's lead vocalist, Natalie Maines, told the audience, "Just so you know, we're ashamed the president of the United States is from Texas." Responding to what she saw as a burgeoning anti-American sentiment that was unfolding in Europe, the Lubbock, Texas, native added, in a printed statement, "While we support our troops, there is nothing more frightening than the notion of going to war with Iraq and the prospect of all the innocent lives that will be lost."

Maines' comments coincided with the final lead-up to the U.S. invasion of Iraq. Patriotic sentiment at home, already heightened by the events of 9/11, was strong and building rapidly, and in the southern region of the U.S., where country music is king, such anti-Bush comments were less than welcome.

The backlash against what was perceived as an anti-American comment was quick and fierce. Almost overnight, angry phone calls clogged the lines of dozens of radio stations from coast to coast. Angry country fans were demanding that the Chicks be banned from the airwaves, while others began to organize boycotts of their records. The trio received death threats and were forced to employ security guards to protect their families and their homes.

This mounting uproar finally led the corporate programmer of Atlanta-based Cumulus Media to ban The Dixie Chicks records on its country radio stations for a month. The company also hosted a CD-smashing ceremony outside its Atlanta headquarters, where news cameras captured bulldozers crushing hundreds of the group's records. During tough questioning at a subsequent Senate hearing, Cumulus chairman/CEO Lew Dickey explained that, "This was driven by listeners, and we were responding to their hue and cry. Cumulus has no political agenda."

In an interesting and ironic twist of fate, Clear Channel for months was identified as the perpetrator of Cumulus' reported company-wide ban. (Actually, The Dixie Chicks were only dropped from the Cumulus' country stations; they received prominent "spins" on its Top 40 outlets.) The Internet crackled with outrage and rabid wrath, decrying the obvious corporate censorship and the company's attack on the First Amendment. While some Clear Channel stations did reduce or eliminate Dixie Chicks airplay for a week or two, others actually increased airplay because of a growing anti-war sentiment in certain regions of the country. In fact, according to Mediabase's Airplay Monitor service, Clear Channel Radio played Dixie Chicks records a total of 10,069 times during the two weeks following the March 10 incident, significantly more than any other radio broadcaster. And during a subsequent Senate hearing Simon Renshaw, the Dixie Chicks' manager, verified that Clear Channel did not ban the group's music and had received a "bad rap."

That hearing was held on July 8, 2003, and included four witnesses who offered prepared remarks and answered questions from committee members. Those witnesses were Cumulus CEO Lew Dickey, MediaCom Co-CEO Jon Mandel, First Media Radio CEO Alex Kolobielski, and the Chicks' Renshaw. The primary purposes of the hearing were to determine whether radio was performing better or worse since it was deregulated in 1996, whether the FCC had acted appropriately in replacing an old "signal contour" method of delineating radio markets, and whether Cumulus' —

and other companies' alleged — ban on the Dixie Chicks was an indication that consolidation reflected a "concentration of ownership" problem. Arizona Republican John McCain, North Dakota Democrat Byron Dorgan, and California Democrat Barbara Boxer all excoriated Dickey for his company's corporate mandate to ban the Chicks, with McCain insisting that such a ban could be cause for his committee to reconsider the wisdom of media deregulation.

Looking back, Dickey says that the entire hearing not only was well-orchestrated, but highly politicized, as well. "The entire incident taught me an important lesson about how Washington works," he says. "Don't ever underestimate the length to which politicians will go to create a sound bite for their local news, at whoever's expense. It was a useful lesson in that respect. Senator McCain and his crew were looking for anything but the truth in that hearing, because what I tried to get across — and they just didn't want to hear about it — was that in the very same markets, in the very same buildings, where we weren't playing the Dixie Chicks on our country stations, we were playing Dixie Chicks music on Top 40 radio stations. That concept was completely lost on them." Dickey insists that Cumulus in no way was trying to censure thought or abuse its power, and further maintains that no programmer was forced to ban the Chicks. "There wasn't a single program director who was ordered to take the Dixie Chicks off the air and did so against his or her will," he maintains.

Company-wide ban or not, Clear Channel was assigned the blame, says Tom Owens, who at the time of the incident was Clear Channel senior vice president of programming. "Within Clear Channel we encouraged the country stations to review the considerable music research they were conducting in their local markets and allow it to guide them. Based on that audience feedback some stations diminished airplay, while others increased it. Of course, sagging Sony sales for Dixie Chicks CDs confirmed it to be an issue of merit with many country music consumers. Still, as the biggest radio group in the U.S., Clear Channel became defined by something it didn't actually do."

Despite the commotion about Natalie Maines' anti-Bush statement, the Dixie Chicks' first concert back on American soil following the London performance was a sell-out. At the opening performance of a U.S. tour on May 1, 2003, in Greenville, South Carolina, Maines walked out in front of an audience of 15,000 wearing a T-shirt that read "Dare To Be Free." Not knowing quite what to expect from her fans, she told them, "If you're here to boo, we welcome that. We're going to give you 15 seconds to do that." Instead, the fans cheered. And the following day, Greenville police reported that fewer than ten demonstrators gathered outside the arena.

The fallout from the Dixie Chicks episode is but one example of how a slight misunderstanding can turn into rumor, which evolves into innuendo and eventually results in a form of "urban legend." Just as Jan Harold Brunvand, professor emeritus at University of Utah, first described the spread of such unfounded but popular tales as the poodle in the microwave and the Chihuahua from Tijuana, the rise of the blogosphere, a fascination with sensationalism, and a widespread mistrust of big business served to ascribe many misperceptions to Clear Channel during radio's rapid period of consolidation.

"When you get as big as Clear Channel, you get into the Wal-Mart scenario," says Regent Communications CEO Bill Stakelin. "There are people who think that Wal-Mart is the greatest thing since sliced bread, and there are people who think that Wal-Mart has put thousands of people out of work — and thousands of American businesses out of business. Clear Channel certainly gets the brunt of that type of thinking." Stakelin says that neither Lowry Mays nor his sons have ever shirked their responsibilities as industry leaders, and insists that they work "hard and honestly to try to do things that will benefit the future of the business overall. Like any company, they have done things right and they have done things wrong, but they undoubtedly are the leaders in the industry. They have set the tone, they have set the pace, and because of the honesty and dedication of the Mays family, which is the way they live their lives and the way they conduct their businesses, they have had a positive influence on all of us."

By 2004, however, Clear Channel was starting to fight back. Unhappy with an October 2004 *Forbes* cover story for which he and other Clear Channel corporate staff had agreed to be interviewed, Mark Mays was dismayed not only by the cover headline that described him as "the son who had to make nice" but also was outraged by the tone and apparent intent of the article itself. In an open letter to *Forbes* Publisher Steve Forbes, he wrote, "I was looking forward to seeing the story on our company in the current issue of your magazine very much — I'd made myself and my executive team generously available since we have long admired *Forbes'* deregulatory sensibility and support of entrepreneurs. We believed both helped to make *Forbes* the best choice to carry an exclusive — and truthful — look at our company at this important time. I have to say I was deeply disappointed. The story sensationalized a straightforward succession discussion, got basic facts incorrect [despite the good efforts of my corporate communications department, working with your fact checkers], and most disturbingly, took an unnecessarily mean-spirited and snide tone about my father.... I expected something better from *Forbes*."

The seeds of this new attitude were sown some 18 months earlier when Radio division CEO John Hogan had hired a corporate reputation specialist, Lisa Dollinger, who had served in a similar capacity at Capstar in the late '90s before that company merged into AMFM and eventually was acquired by Clear Channel. Dollinger had spent the previous three years running her own successful public relations firm in Austin, and was instantly intrigued when Hogan called and asked if she wanted to leap from the frying pan back into the fire. "When John called me I felt a mixture of elation and dread, because I knew what a huge job it would be to rectify public perception of the company," she recalls. "When I came to work for Clear Channel I was fully focused on going back to the basics and determining exactly what the facts were." To this end, she booked herself an extensive "listening tour" so she could speak with people at all levels within the company — managers, program directors, business managers, receptionists, and on-air personalities — and outside of it. "I first wanted to feel the pains of integration in order to understand what this company was, and where it was going," she explains. Dollinger then embarked on a mission to meet with as many general and trade reporters as possible to ascertain their perceptions of Clear Channel in order to understand the origin and depth of the negativity.

"I really was surprised at the level of hostility, bias, and preconceived notions about the company," she says. "There were so many perceptions that were not based on any kind of factual information at all. Many reporters believed things, or had personal biases, because they had read all these stories that had been written for years by detractors, while the company had remained silent. Lowry, Mark, and Randall Mays all thought this nonsense that they were reading on the Internet would go away because it was so outrageously false that no one would believe it. They really thought that the facts would speak for themselves, and they didn't want to engage in any kind of public hand-to-hand combat."

Dollinger says that the facts clearly did not speak for themselves, largely because the nature of the Internet often favors insinuation over fact. "The Web allows anybody to express their opinions, whether they are based in fact or not, and people tend to believe what they read," she says. "So if a company such as Clear Channel does not answer accusations, and take a stand against erroneous coverage then people believe what they hear or read as fact."

With this understanding in mind, Dollinger took it upon herself to contact any and all journalists who covered the radio industry and let them know there now was a media point-person within Clear Channel. "We let them know there was someone to talk to at the company," she explains. "I wanted them to know that if they were going to write a story about our company, I expected them to call us and we would provide them with whatever they needed. But this media tour turned out to be a continual education process. The first time that I sat down with a lot of these reporters there was open hostility, and not much open-mindedness."

Dollinger says she approached each reporter by asking, in a non-confrontational manner, what they had heard about Clear Channel without trying to dispel any preconceived notions. "I just opened up the belly of the beast, and said that I would answer every question they asked, and if I didn't know the answer, I would find it," she explains.

The result? "Most people were shocked," Dollinger recalls. "They were stunned at the disparity between what they had heard and what the reality was, and after those meetings we started to build relationships and trust. We didn't expect people just to take our word for things, and some media outlets frankly had their guns raised and aimed. Of course, I understand that this is a large company doing business on the airwaves, so there's a lot of emotion involved. There also was a presumption that big media was bad, and I completely understand people's fears and concerns."

Still, the negative press was out there, and correcting a long-ignored public perception of Clear Channel's activities during consolidation was much like trying to un-boil an egg — particularly when the news media that were so critical of the company also were in competition with it for ad dollars. Within the company's San Antonio offices, there was a mixed feeling of relief that some of the long-standing misperceptions finally were being answered, even while some of the old stories continue to be repeated via the online ether. While the rectification process is ongoing, Dollinger says she senses that a turning point may have been reached. "My focus here has been to help people understand that what we do as a company, first and foremost, is serve the communities and the people in those communities. It's not only the right thing to do; it's the key to our doing well." Now serving in the role of chief communications officer at Clear Channel, Dollinger observes that "a company is not a logo, a board of directors, or some slogan. A company is a marriage of people, and it's the people who define what that company is. With Clear Channel it hurt me to see them painted with a brush that so unfairly misrepresented them — and the radio industry itself."

To Clear Channel co-founder Red McCombs, the negative press was predictable and almost inevitable. "The reason we got so much bad press to me was very simple," he says. "First, we were so much better than the other companies in the radio business. Some of our competitors did a good job of making us look like bad guys, which we weren't. Also, people who were concerned about public policy suddenly realized that on any given day, half the people in the U.S. might be listening to a Clear Channel radio station. That's quite a huge audience, and nothing like that had ever happened before. Rather than admit that they were getting beat in the marketplace, it made them feel better to say, 'I got beat because these guys are just gorillas and I'm just a little guy.' The fact is, all of our stations are little guys, too. We run 1,200 stations about the same as someone else would run one or two. They're all individual stations. We've had to prove again and again that we're primarily committed to the communities in which we operate, and people are starting to accept it."

"It was a very tough time for Mark and Randall and especially Dad," oldest daughter Kathryn Mays Johnson says. "A few years ago there were these articles that came out about Dad that were devastating. Prior to 2003, people would ask to come in so they could write a story, and we'd give them access to everything. Then they'd write things that weren't even part of the conversation."

"I never thought of Clear Channel being this sledgehammer that was flattening the rest of the industry," says *Radio & Records* Publisher and CEO Erica Farber. "They did inject a new sense of accountability, but accountability is always scary when you're not accustomed to it. People are bound to criticize that, but at least they had the fortitude to try something new rather than do nothing. At the start of consolidation no one knew what was going to work, so they were trailblazers in that regard."

"When they stop going after you, it's over," adds Donald Trump, on-air personality for Clear Channel's Premiere Radio Networks, himself the target of considerable media criticism. "They go after you because they're jealous, they go after you because they're envious, they go after you because they can't do it themselves. That defines the critics of the Mays family and Clear Channel: they're jealous, they're envious, and they know they can't do it themselves."

CHAPTER SEVEN

THE INCIDENT
IN MINOT

PERHAPS THE MOST STUNNING EXAMPLE OF MISINFORMATION SPREAD ABOUT Clear Channel, shortly after its consolidation binge, involved an incident in Minot, North Dakota.

Located almost in the center of the North American continent, Minot, North Dakota, truly is the image of the American heartland. Situated at the crossroads of U.S. Routes 2, 52, and 83, just 55 miles directly south of the Canadian border, this city of 36,000 was founded in 1887 when the Great Northern Railroad was carved out of the vast prairie of north-central America. Known as the "magic city" because of an explosive period of growth during the first half of the 20th century, Minot is the seat of Ward County and home to Minot Air Force Base, which in turn is home to the 5th Bomb Wing, one of two B-52H Stratofortress bomber bases in the U.S. Recognized as a regional center of commerce, education, health care, and finance, Minot also is home to a large plant that provides much of the pasta consumed in cities up and down the east coast.

Because of its centralized location and its proximity to all parts north, Minot serves as a central transportation hub not only for the state of North Dakota, but also Montana and the Canadian provinces of Saskatchewan and Manitoba. The city supports a number of major trucking firms, is home to a modern international airport, and falls directly on the major lines of three independent railroads.

A searing cold was pushing down from the arctic in the early morning hours of January 18, 2002, when a Canadian Pacific Railroad train came roaring through Minot. As one witness later would describe it, "It was one of those dark nights where you looked at the lights and it seemed as if there was crystal in the air, with sort of a mystical, foggy look to it. It was not snowing at the time, but there was snow on the ground — and it was cold. *Very cold.*"

The train was a long one — 112 cars in all — and as it neared Minot on the western edge of town early that morning it suddenly derailed, causing 31 cars to come off the tracks. An explosion followed almost instantly, and five tank cars carrying liquid anhydrous ammonia ruptured, discharging a poisonous cloud of gas into the night air. Anhydrous ammonia is a widely used farm fertilizer that is described as a hydroscopic compound, which means that it seeks water from whatever source is closest — including the human body. Any exposed sources of moisture — including eyes, lungs, and skin — are at the most risk because of their high moisture content.

At the time of the crash on that January morning, the temperature in Minot was recorded at six degrees below zero. The chemical was being transported in pressurized tank cars, but when the liquid escaped it immediately turned into gas which, because of the extreme cold, did not evaporate as quickly as it would have had the accident happened during a warmer time of the year. Additionally, the relative humidity at the time of the crash was 78 percent, which meant that the moisture in the frigid air quickly bonded with the anhydrous ammonia.

A cloud of poisonous gas quickly formed in the area surrounding the train derailment, and Minot residents living in and near the vicinity awoke in the middle of the night to burning eyes and a painful, fiery feeling in their lungs. As the white cloud spread along the edge of town, those who didn't hide in their bathrooms or their basements tried to contact the city's emergency services to see what had happened — and to get help for them and their loved ones. Three hundred people were injured and one died that night.

In an action that would trigger a new focus in Washington, DC, about the state of the country's emergency preparedness, a police dispatcher picked up the Emergency Broadcast System telephone and called the local EBS radio station to alert whoever was on duty that night about the disaster.

The problem? The Emergency Broadcast System had been shut down seven years prior by the U.S. government, replaced by the fully automated Emergency Alert System, in which special automated equipment is used by the National Weather Service, local police, and other agencies to break into a broadcast to directly alert citizens about emergency situations. The NWS has been interrupting Minot radio broadcasts successfully for years using the equipment. It later would be discovered that the EAS equipment delivered to the Minot police department had never been installed and was not being used by the local authorities.

Minot police chief Fred Draovitch later complained that no one at the station answered at the EBS number. He believed, at what arguably could be considered the city's most dire moment, that the local radio station that was assigned to communicate emergency information to the community to which it was licensed to serve, was silent.

The Minot police chief was wrong.

Rick Stensby, who has lived in Minot for 30 years, currently serves as general manager of the city's six Clear Channel radio stations, including KCJB-AM (the community's primary Emergency Alert System station), KRRZ-AM, KYYX-FM, KIZZ-FM, KZPR-FM, and KMXA-FM. According to Stensby, not only was a live board operator working at the primary EAS station that night, with the alert system fully functional, but the entire six-station cluster was instrumental in communicating news of the derailment to the city of Minot despite the police department's inability to activate the federally mandated emergency system.

Shortly after the train derailed, Stensby says he was awakened by a phone call from his mother, who was living in the area that had been engulfed by the cloud of anhydrous ammonia. "She was in the path of the gas as it went through the city," he recalls. "She said she had called the police department, but the woman who answered the phone said she didn't know what my mother was talking about. Then, as the dispatcher was asking questions, she said she had to go because all the lines had just lit up." Concerned for the safety of his mother, who was in her bathroom trying to escape the cloud of gas and take care of the burning sensation in her eyes, Stensby told her that that he would drive down and pick her up.

"Toward the end of the conversation I opened my sliding glass doors and I could hear the civil defense sirens start up," Stensby recalls. "It was really kind of freaky because it was dead quiet outside. Then, all of a sudden, I heard these sirens and a recorded voice saying there was an emergency, and everyone should stay in their houses." Immediately after he hung up the phone rang again. This time the person on the other end of the line was Alison Bostow, operations director at Clear Channel's Minot radio stations, who coincidentally lived just a few blocks from Stensby's stricken mother. "She let me know that she was in her basement, and that she was in contact with Don May, our news director, as well as Gerry Michaels, our radio station board operator, who had been calling her because he'd been getting swamped with phone calls. The station lines were all filled with people asking what the hell was going on. Michaels, who had been a full-time employee of the station for over 20 years — long before Clear Channel purchased it — was at the station and had been trying to call the police, but the phone lines there were all busy."

At that point, Stensby says, News Director Don May contacted several individual police officers via cell phone, and was able to piece together enough information about the accident, which the station then was able to broadcast over the air. Meanwhile, Stensby tried to drive down to the section of town where both his mother and Alison Bostow lived but, he says, "I couldn't get anywhere near the area. The air was so thick with this anhydrous gas that you couldn't see, much less breathe, so I had to leave my mother in her bathroom for the entire night. Her eyes and face were burned. I was able to get her out in the morning, around 8:00. Alison wasn't able to get out of her house, either, but she was on the phone to our announcers and our sales-people, getting them to come in to the station to answer phones, man the other stations, and get out the news and information as we received it."

After Stensby realized he wouldn't be able to help his mother, he drove to the building that at the time housed three of Clear Channel's six stations. "When I walked in, I was so happy to see that I had a full house of employees on the phone, answering calls and doing the best they could," he says. Later that morning the gas cloud dissipated and Stensby's mother and Alison Bostow were able to leave their homes, along with the other Minot residents who had suffered through the night.

"That should have been the end of it," observes Stensby, who had served as general manager of three of the six Clear Channel stations since 1991. "But then, a day or so later, the *Minot Daily News* ran that article in which the chief of police said that they had called the radio station's Emergency Broadcast System telephone, but that nobody answered it. And I believe that within the article it was suggested that there was no one at the radio station, nobody to answer the phone. Chief Draovitch said that he was going to try to fix the problem by giving the radio station employees pagers so the police department could contact our announcers immediately if there was an emergency."

SEVERAL DAYS LATER THE *MINOT DAILY NEWS* DIRECTLY POINTED AN ACCUSA-tory finger at the station, KCJB-AM 910, for failing to fulfill its EBS duties. The fact that the station was one of six in Minot owned by Clear Channel thrust the story into the national spotlight. Not because of the injuries, but because a radio company that was viewed as overly bloated by the spoils of deregulation had apparently failed in its mission to serve the residents of its community of license. In the ensuing months a num-ber of advocacy groups — including Project Censored, *The Nation,* and the Campaign for Press and Broadcasting Freedoms — repeated the mantra that Minot, North Dakota, was a perfect example of all that was wrong with radio deregulation. In fact, North Dakota Democratic senator Byron Dorgan repeatedly pointed to the Minot incident during subsequent hear-ings on media consolidation, identifying Clear Channel as the primary cul-prit that cold morning in 2002. "The question is, 'Where does this stop?'" the *New York Times* quoted him in a March 29, 2003, article about the derail-ment, more than a year after the gas spill occurred.

The news media — and all the websites, interest groups, and politi-cians that latched on to the story — were severely misinformed. The pre-vailing story — the one in which the Minot police department tried in vain to contact the Emergency Broadcast System station — turns out to be nothing more than a cover-up for the police department's own failures. What struck Stensby was that Minot's chief of police didn't seem to realize that the Emergency Broadcasting System had been replaced in the mid-1990s by the fully automated Emergency Alert System. "I called the chief and said, 'I'm just wondering if you're up to date. The EBS phone that you say you were calling the station on was disconnected when this new system came in.' In fact, that unit was disconnected several years before the sta-tions were acquired by Clear Channel in 2001. The phone still hung on the wall out at that old facility that the previous owners owned, but it was obsolete." Stensby also contacted the *Minot Daily News* — with which the radio stations are highly competitive for local advertising dollars — and informed the editor of the inaccuracy of the paper's reporting.

When Stensby further pressed Chief Draovitch about the obsolete Emergency Broadcast System, the police chief conceded privately that he was aware of the newer EAS process but had not yet implemented it. As Stensby recalls, "He told me, 'I think I know what you're talking about, Rick. We have it in a box on a desk here.' The simple fact was that they had never hooked up the new system. They didn't even know how, or even if, it worked."

Stensby explained to Draovitch that the EAS is activated by throwing a switch, which allows the police department or any other emergency response organization to cut into whatever programming is being broadcast on the air and pre-empt it with an emergency message.

"Whoever throws that switch has complete control of the broadcast," says Stensby today. "Even though we always have an announcer at the station, there doesn't have to be one for the EAS to work. We have gone around and around in circles on this, but the point is, there was a live announcer in those studios of KCJB, the primary alert station. There always is, 24 hours a day, seven days a week. This was the case before Clear Channel owned the stations and after they bought them. But the EAS system doesn't require an announcer at the station; it's set up to be operated by whoever needs to use it."

When Stensby offered to help the police department install its EAS system — which was still in a box — Chief Draovitch said he'd prefer to keep using the old EBS system. "I explained to him that we have no choice," Stensby says. "This was federally mandated to the radio stations, and we're federally licensed. So at that point, he said, 'Any help you can provide would be greatly appreciated.'"

Alan Brace, an engineer from Clear Channel's Minneapolis cluster, then came to Minot and worked with the company's regional engineer, Brian Funk, to install the new EAS equipment at police headquarters. That's when it was discovered that someone at the police station had, indeed, taken the device out of the box several years earlier.

"They did hook it up, but my engineer found out that someone at the police department had changed a crystal in the radio at the police department," Stensby explains. "That means that even if it had been hooked up that night, it would not have talked to our receiver. The police at one time had tried to twist that story around to make it out that that's why they couldn't call, but the point is, they changed the crystal. And then they put it back in the box."

The two engineers got the EAS system up and running, but all was not yet running smoothly. "We still have to call and remind the police when their regularly scheduled tests are coming up," Stensby says. "They still forget to do it. And since then, they've kept insisting that it was the radio station's equipment that didn't work. That is a total lie. Not only did ours work — not only do we have all the test logs — but ours has been used a lot. Just before the accident it had been used by the National Weather Service for cold weather and blizzard advisories. The system worked; it has always worked."

What Stensby says is shocking to him is that "to cover their asses, the police lied and blamed the people who helped them set their system up. All the chief would have had to do is say, after the disaster, 'After that night, thank goodness for cell phones. My people were able to get in contact with the radio station people and vice versa. We were able to get the message out. But through this experience we also learned that we were not up and functioning on our EAS system. Thanks to the good people at Clear Channel in Minot; they provided engineers at no charge, and they have everything working. So now we won't have to just count on cell phones the next time.' That would have been it."

But, of course, that was *not* it. The "incident in Minot" erupted into a national issue and a number of federal legislators and regulators jumped on it. At a time when many private, public, and political factions were eager to seize on any event that might convince Congress to try to squeeze ownership rules back into the tube, Minot was seen as a perfect demonizing issue of why Clear Channel or any other group shouldn't own so many stations.

Today, several years after the train derailment, the incident still hovers just as that cloud of poisonous gas hovered over Minot on that cold January morning. In fact, Chief Draovitch continued to blame the Clear Channel stations until late 2005 when — after Stensby publicly called him out on the issue — he agreed to initiate an internal investigation on the incident and why communications broke down. According to Stensby, the investigation never materialized, and Draovitch resigned in June 2006 after 38 years with the Minot Police Department.

"For our detractors and certain politicians, the Minot misrepresentation was a very convenient vehicle for people who didn't like consolidation," says Clear Channel's Chief Communications Officer Lisa Dollinger. "We do business there, our employees live there, our radio stations work with the community, and there was nothing to be gained from our getting into some national stand-off with the local police chief in Minot."

"Everybody now knows exactly what happened in Minot," says Mark Mays. "I've even spoken with Senator Dorgan about it. He has tried to use that incident as part of his political agenda. I told him that if you look at Minot before consolidation versus after consolidation, there now are twice as many formats on the air as there were before. People in Minot love radio much more after consolidation because there are more formats, more choices, and better radio. He finally had to concede that he has never received a call or a letter from a constituent who has complained about radio in Minot."

As for the derailment itself, Canadian Pacific admitted liability in the accident. Over one hundred civil lawsuits were filed by the 300-plus individuals who were treated for burns and breathing problems, and a handful of them thus far have been settled out of court. The remaining cases are still pending.

MINOT IS NOT THE ONLY OCCASION IN WHICH THE EMERGENCY ALERT SYSTEM was improperly activated. An eerily similar incident occurred on January 7, 2005, when a Norfolk Southern freight train with 42 cars collided with a locomotive pulling two cars in Graniteville, South Carolina. The crash occurred outside an Avondale Mills textile plant at 2:40 a.m. causing 14 cars to derail.

According to Peter N. Frommer, director of the Aiken, South Carolina Department of Public Safety, the Norfolk train was heading northbound on the main track when it accidentally veered toward a side spur, colliding head-on with a stationary locomotive attached to two cars. The collision, which took place at 2:40 a.m., caused 14 railroad cars — four of which were tank cars filled with deadly chlorine gas — to derail upon impact. One of the tank cars was cut completely in half, causing 90 tons of gas to be released almost instantly. A large gash was torn in the side of a second car, causing chlorine to leak from it for approximately three days, until repair crews could construct a patch to cover the hole. The remaining two tank cars containing chlorine lay scattered and damaged in the wreckage. The Department of Health and Environmental Control later reported that local hospitals treated more than 200 people, and a mandated evacuation displaced some 5,400 of the town's 7,000 residents.

In an article published by the Commission on Accreditation for Law Enforcement Agencies, Frommer says that "most townspeople were asleep when the sound of the collision and the strange smell of the chlorine gas reached their homes. Getting residents to safety would be a challenge for many hours to follow. Within minutes of the crash, 911 operators received hundreds of calls for help from frantic people suffocating by poisonous gas."

Emergency responders rushed to the scene of the collision, but found themselves encumbered along the way by numerous trucks and other vehicles crowded with scared residents, many of whom were suffering from respiratory distress. "From phone calls and radio communications, incident commanders quickly realized some of the people fleeing the gas in the darkness did not realize the location of the accident and were blindly running into the contaminated area instead of away from it," Frommer observes. Emergency personnel elected to send a reverse 911 message that instructed residents to turn off their heating systems, place wet blankets around doors and windows, and to remain in their homes. "Incident commanders also realized immediately that the media would play a big role in getting proper instructions to the residents," Frommer notes. "The media were instructed to report directly to the staging area to begin live newscasts to provide information on the accident and proper instructions in an effort to evacuate residents of Graniteville and the surrounding areas, and to address the necessary safety precautions."

While the Emergency Alert System was activated by the National Weather Service, it did not alert residents in the vicinity of the derailment until two hours after the fact. As M. Marian Mustoe reported in the January 18, 2006, issue of *Radio World Online,* "Although the local primary stations were monitoring their assigned NWS sources, the actuation was sent to other surrounding NWS transmitters. The activation had to be rerouted to trigger the EAS decoders across the state line in Augusta, Georgia, at local primary stations WBBQ-FM and WYZA-FM," both of which are owned by Clear Channel. "Conversely, it was these radio stations that covered the event with live news immediately following the event and hours before the arrival of the official activation of the EAS. NWS Radio did provide a public alert but could not act as a news outlet."

"Clear Channel employees in Georgia and South Carolina went above and beyond the call of duty that day to step in when it became clear that local authorities were not successful in activating the EAS system to alert citizens of the dangerous conditions," observes Clear Channel Radio Senior Vice President of Engineering Steve Davis. Speaking at the National Alliance of State Broadcasters Associations' 2006 National Summit on EAS and Emergency Communications in Alexandria, Virginia, Davis noted that, "For those who aren't familiar with radio engineering jargon, 'activated' refers to when a third-party automatically interrupts a radio station's signal remotely. It's a hallmark of the Emergency Alert System. The National Weather Service is the most frequent user of this feature, for things like tornado warnings. But all local and federal authorities have the ability to do this, as well. In the case of Graniteville, Clear Channel subsequently collaborated with the National Weather Service in Columbia, South Carolina, and the local emergency management office in Augusta, Georgia, to determine that no station was activated properly."

While it remains unclear exactly how the local authorities attempted to activate the EAS, "The South Carolina primary station, WCOS-FM, and the secondary station, WLJK-TV, were not activated by the local authorities, even though the EAS equipment at those stations was working properly at the time of the accident," Davis noted. "We receive test results monthly from both stations, so we know the stations' systems were fully operational. It was determined later that the local authorities did not properly operate the EAS equipment in their possession, nor did they verify that the attempt to send alerts was received by the public. That day, Clear Channel's local engineers manually activated their own stations, helping to avert possible public contact with the dangerous chemicals."

Davis summed it up to the NASBA's national summit this way: "It bears repeating that success depends on three things: One, that the federal agencies overseeing the nation's EAS ensure the equipment at local law enforcement facilities is operational and that local law enforcement and emergency personnel are properly trained in its use and EAS procedures; two, that local broadcasters ensure that their equipment is operational and that their staff is properly trained; and three, that there is a healthy dialogue and collaboration among local authorities and broadcasters. That means that if there are individuals who cannot perform in this manner, those individuals are replaced with individuals who can. We must all accept our collective and interwoven responsibility as first responders."

CHAPTER EIGHT

A MATTER
OF INDECENCY

BLAME IT ON A WARDROBE MALFUNCTION OR SIMPLY A RISQUÉ DANCE NUMBER that stepped too close to the edge of good taste, Janet Jackson's momentary uncloaking during her Super Bowl XXXVIII halftime show in 2004 generated a firestorm of anti-indecency rhetoric that quickly turned into a political hot potato in an equally hot election year. And Clear Channel would be among the companies brought before Congressional panels in Washington to account for its broadcasts.

Despite the fact that Jackson's brief exposure occurred on television, federal regulators and legislators quickly pounced on what they perceived as a steadily growing thrust toward indecent programming on the radio. As noted previously, federal law bars over-the-air radio and television stations from airing references to sexual and excretory functions between 6:00 a.m. and 10:00 p.m., when children may be tuning in. Specifically, the FCC defines broadcast indecency as "language or material that, in context, depicts or describes, in terms patently offensive as measured by contemporary community standards for the broadcast medium, sexual or excretory organs or activities." The rules do not apply to subscription cable and satellite channels, or to satellite radio.

Then-FCC Chairman Michael Powell was part of that stunned Super Bowl audience and was not amused — or titillated — by what he had witnessed during the halftime show, which was produced by Viacom's MTV. Within a seven-week period immediately following the February 1 event, both the House of Representatives and the Senate drafted and passed measures detailing punitive measures ostensibly designed to curtail further broadcasts of indecent material on radio and television. Specifically, the House overwhelmingly approved (on a 391-22 vote) legislation that would substantially increase the maximum fine for a broadcast license-holder from $27,500 to $500,000, while the fine for a performer who engaged in indecent programming would jump from $11,000 to $500,000. Similarly, the Senate weighed in with a bill that would raise licensee fines to $500,000 as well as order the FCC to look at ways to protect children from violence on television — plus put on hold sweeping media ownership changes that the Commission adopted in June of the previous year.

Many First Amendment proponents vehemently argued at the time that any such legislation would undermine free speech rights and would send a chilling message about the government's interpretation of the First Amendment. "Such legislation ... represents an unconstitutional threat to free speech and would have an unnecessary chilling effect on artistic freedom," American Federation of Television and Radio Artists President John Connolly and National Executive Director Greg Hessinger wrote in a letter sent to House and Senate members. "It is important to note that the FCC has never fined an individual performer or announcer; therefore this legislation represents a fundamental shift with significant ramifications."

The two AFTRA executives went on to say that the legislation "cuts to the very heart of one of our nation's core values — free speech — and does so in the face of mounting evidence that the American public does not favor legislative intervention. They understand that free speech is fundamentally threatened when standards are vague and penalties excessive, as in the case of this bill. The fines contemplated by the bill could easily bankrupt individual artists and announcers."

Of course, "indecency" has been a thorn in the side of radio and television broadcasters for many years, long before Howard Stern elected to entertain the male 18–34 year-old audience with talk of sex, sex, and more sex. Both chastised and lauded for his unique talent for grabbing and holding the attention of his 8.5 million over-the-air listeners with a daily dose of coarse humor and frank discussion about all things sexual, Stern had been cited — and fined — by the FCC on numerous occasions. Over the years Stern consistently has maintained that, while his show might be considered offensive by some people, everyone has the right to turn the dial if they don't like what he has to say.

Congress appears to disagree. On February 12, just 11 days after the 2004 Super Bowl, members of the House Telecommunications Committee grilled former Viacom Chief Operating Officer Mel Karmazin for more than two hours, blasting him for a halftime show that was alternately described as "raunchy" and "disgusting." Rep. Heather Wilson, a Republican from New Mexico, personally rebuked him, charging, "You knew what you were doing ... you knew that shock and indecency create a buzz that moves market share and lines your pockets."

According to Viacom-owned CBS News, which reported the story that night on the evening news, some lawmakers questioned whether the problem of broadcast indecency was confined to the television networks, or if violations of the rules possibly were related to recently relaxed media ownership laws. These same legislators also criticized the FCC for disregarding the issue of broadcast indecency for years, levying fines that were seen as little more than "slaps on the wrists." As Massachusetts Democrat Edward Markey observed, "It is increasingly clear the paltry fines the FCC assesses have become nothing more than a joke." He noted that in 2003 the FCC received over 240,000 complaints about 375 different programs, but only three notices of liability were issued.

"Karmazin ticked off a lot of members of the committee," says Clear Channel Chief Legal Counsel Andrew Levin. "Many people believed he wasn't apologetic or contrite enough. But he was caught between a rock and a hard place. He didn't want to admit any liability, because that would have caused him legal problems, yet at the same time he had to try to come off like he believed it was the wrong thing to do. Then Heather Wilson started talking about her children, and said she was almost in tears about how her young son had seen what happened at the Super Bowl. Then she started in on Karmazin about the Opie and Anthony stunt at St. Patrick's Cathedral, referring to the now-infamous 2002 incident in which the controversial on-air duo aired a "play-by-play" broadcast of two listeners engaging in sexual intercourse in church. Even though Karmazin had fired them for that, she asked him point-blank whether he believed that broadcast was indecent. Again, how could he say 'yes,' because the FCC was ready to fine him. So he had to say 'no.' And she lashed out at him and said, 'The problem in America is CEOs like you who sit in your board rooms and offices and are totally out of touch, and this is clearly indecent programming as far as I'm concerned. You just don't know what you're talking about.'"

In an ironic twist, CBS Radio rehired Opie and Anthony in the spring of 2006 to replace former Van Halen front man David Lee Roth, who had been signed to do mornings after Howard Stern bolted for the safe harbor of satellite radio.

Following the hearing, many committee members were so unimpressed with Karmazin's performance, Levin says, that the subcommittee scheduled another hearing on indecency. "[Clear Channel Radio CEO] John Hogan was asked to testify at that hearing, and the day before that hearing he met with a lot of the committee members so he would have a sense of what they were like," Levin says. "When we got back to the office that evening we received a fax of a transcript of a Howard Stern show from that morning that contained a healthy amount of really vulgar, disgusting language that was clearly indecent."

It was at that point that Hogan decided to suspend Howard Stern from the six Clear Channel stations on which his program aired. "Further, he decided we would ask Infinity, which distributed the show, for assurances that in the future Stern would conform to the existing indecency laws," Levin says. "We announced the decision that night, and the next morning at the hearing Heather Wilson and others congratulated John for doing what he did, even though it was at a significant cost to Clear Channel."

"Clear Channel drew a line in the sand with regard to protecting our listeners from indecent content and Howard Stern's show blew right through it," Hogan later commented in a corporate statement. "It was vulgar, offensive, and insulting, not just to women and African Americans but to anyone with a sense of common decency." Hogan reiterated that the Howard Stern show would not air on the company's stations until it adhered to acceptable broadcasting standards, which the program ostensibly never did before the shock jock jumped to Sirius Satellite Radio in January 2006.

The Stern incident occurred at roughly the same time that the FCC had levied a $715,000 fine against Clear Channel morning show personality Todd "Bubba The Love Sponge" Clem for nine alleged violations that, the FCC said, "involved graphic and explicit sexual material and was designed to pander to, titillate, and shock listeners." In his testimony before the House subcommittee, Hogan opened his remarks by saying, "I'm embarrassed. I've read the transcript of a Clear Channel radio show featuring the personality known as Bubba the Love Sponge. As a broadcaster, as a CEO, and as a parent of a nine-year-old girl, I am ashamed to be in any way associated with those words. They are tasteless, they are vulgar, and they should not, do not, and will not, represent what Clear Channel is about."

The following week, when Clear Channel announced it would not contest the "Bubba" fine, Hogan said, "We fully accept our responsibility for airing inappropriate content and accept the consequences. Our company simply does not want to be associated with indecency. We know we can deliver great radio without compromising our integrity as broadcasters." Clem also was summarily fired.

During his House testimony, Hogan explained that Clear Channel had developed a new "Responsible Broadcasting Initiative," which consists of five separate components designed to ensure that all of the company's on-air personalities refrain from stepping over the indecency line. The first element of the initiative involved company-wide training, with the intention of educating all employees about the company's values, its mission, and its sense of corporate responsibility. If that training failed to clearly define what is and is not acceptable, the second component was designed to take effect if Clear Channel was issued a Notice of Apparent Liability for a specific broadcast. At that point, the offending DJ automatically would be suspended, and all those involved with the incident would undergo "remedial training" on the FCC's indecency regulations, and convince station management that they understand where the Commission draws the line. That DJ's broadcasts also would be put on a time delay system so that a program monitor would have the ability to interrupt a broadcast if its content crosses "the line."

Further, if the FCC's Notice of Apparent Liability was adjudicated and Clear Channel was found to have aired an indecent program, the third component would kick in and the offending DJ would be terminated without delay. There would be no appeals and no intermediate steps. The fourth part of the initiative involved air personalities' contracts, which now stipulated that they shared financial responsibility if they uttered indecent material on the air. "While this in no way absolves us of our legal responsibilities as licensees, we hope that it will act as a deterrent to airing material that crosses the line," Hogan told the House subcommittee.

The fifth component pledged ongoing involvement with other broadcast, cable, and satellite companies and their respective industries to develop an industry-wide response to indecency and violence. "In our view, industry-developed guidelines will be as effective as government-imposed regulations without running afoul of First Amendment protections that we all respect," Hogan said. "As a company, our success has always been based on our decentralized management approach. We have over 900 program directors in local markets across the country making decisions about what gets aired based on the preferences of the communities in which they live. Localism is at the heart and soul of our industry and of Clear Channel, and localism requires local control."

Just six weeks later, Clear Channel exercised the first component of the initiative by terminating Larry Wachs and Eric Von Haessler, a.k.a. "The Regular Guys" on WKLS-FM in Atlanta. "In line with our zero-tolerance policy and after conducting a thorough investigation of a March 19 broadcast on WKLS-FM, we have decided we will no longer broadcast 'The Regular Guys,'" Clear Channel Vice President Pat McDonnell said in a statement. The stunt for which the duo got fired was staged in an attempt to mock the Federal Communications Commission's crackdown on indecency. Wachs and Von Haessler had taped a porn star discussing certain sexual practices, then played the recording backward over the air. The prank went south when they accidentally left a microphone on and listeners heard explicit sexual talk during a Honda commercial. The popular duo subsequently was rehired and received additional sensitivity training regarding indecent programming, intentional or otherwise. That training may or may not have worked, since the duo again was dismissed in October 2006 for activities that Atlanta Market Manager Chuck Deskins said amounted to "inappropriate conduct affecting fellow employees."

The "Regular Guys'" 2004 suspension occurred the day after Clear Channel received notice that the FCC was planning to levy a $495,000 fine against the company for 18 violations the Commission said were committed on Howard Stern's show. The FCC's fine stemmed from the complaint of a listener in Fort Lauderdale who had alerted the Commission about a program that included discussion of sex accompanied by sounds of flatulence. The FCC imposed the maximum fine of $27,500 for each of 18 violations on six Clear Channel stations: WBGG in Fort Lauderdale; WTKS-FM in Cocoa Beach, Fla.; WTFX-FM in Louisville, Ky.; KIOZ in San Diego; WNVE in Honeoye Falls, N.Y.; and WSDS-FM in Pittsburgh. The FCC fined each station for two specific incidents during a single program, the first time it ever had done so.

Not long afterward, Clear Channel was hit by another FCC fine, this time a $247,500 levy against "Elliot (Segal) In The Morning" for a March 2003 live on-air interview with an unidentified woman who discussed adult-film star Ron Jeremy. According to the FCC, the program — broadcast on stations in Washington, Richmond, and Bethany Beach, Delaware — "contained graphic and explicit references to sexual activities, including repeated discussion of oral sex, group sex, masturbation, and the sexual performance of a porn legend."

It was against this backdrop that Infinity Broadcasting and Howard Stern's own company, One Twelve Inc., sued Clear Channel in June 2004 for breach of contract. Claiming that the company violated the terms of its agreement in six U.S. markets in which Stern's show was canceled, the plaintiffs sought more than $10 million in damages; both parties also claimed that Clear Channel owed them license fees. Meanwhile, Stern announced that Infinity had added his show to nine more of its own stations, including in five of the six markets where Clear Channel had stopped airing the program. "This will teach the FCC a lesson that we will fight back," Stern said in a live broadcast press conference — otherwise known as his morning show.

The following month Clear Channel returned fire, filing a countersuit against Infinity and One Twelve, also charging breach of contract and claiming more than $3 million in damages. In its suit, Clear Channel countered that it had every right to drop the program, since certain segments were not in compliance with federal law and FCC regulations, as Clear Channel says was required by the contracts between the parties. Those contracts also stipulated that Clear Channel could not alter the show in any way, meaning the company was powerless to delete unlawful content before it aired.

"The radio show was pulled because Mr. Stern and Infinity refused to assure us that future programs would conform to the law," Andrew Levin observed in a statement issued at the time. "That was a key term in the agreement, and we gave them every opportunity to make good on their word before we permanently retired the show. We simply weren't willing to put the future of our radio station licenses in the hands of Mr. Stern or Infinity. Fortunately, our contract doesn't require us to do that."

On his program, Stern insisted that Clear Channel's purported ties to the Bush administration were behind the company's decision to remove him from the air. Indeed, he predicted at one point his show would be totally off the air by summer 2004. "The plug is about to be pulled on me. I'm saying my goodbyes now. There's nothing you can do about it. Vote George Bush out of office — that's all I ask. Remember me when you go to the voting booth. I just want to do fart jokes and have stripper chicks in here." Stern's prediction proved to be off the mark, as he remained on terrestrial radio until December 2005, when he made his move to satellite radio.

In fact, Stern for months continued to insist that the real reason Clear Channel dropped him was because this was a political hot button in a super-charged election year. Once a Bush supporter, Stern had vocally criticized the president for invading Iraq; he also repeatedly was disparaging of FCC Chairman Powell.

On February 24, 2005, all parties agreed to drop their lawsuits. "We are pleased to resolve this contractual dispute with Howard Stern without further legal expense and delay," Andrew Levin said in a statement. "Today, Clear Channel stations are entertaining listeners without being indecent, and we intend to keep it that way."

Clear Channel also remained concerned about the growing disparity in federal government regulations concerning media content as it is delivered over competing platforms. "Congress and the FCC should be troubled that the current law unwittingly creates a safe haven for indecent programming on other media platforms, including satellite radio," Levin said in a statement. "Unfortunately these outlets are fast becoming the wild west for sexually explicit programming. The law needs to catch up to technology, or our children will be the ultimate victims."

After lengthy negotiations, in early June 2004 — at about the same time that Infinity and Howard Stern filed their lawsuits — Clear Channel reached an agreement with the FCC to pay more than $1.7 million in penalties to satisfy all outstanding fines and complaints relating to broadcasts of allegedly indecent material on its radio stations. Under the terms of the agreement, Clear Channel said it would make a "voluntary contribution" of $1,750,000 to the U.S. Treasury, while the FCC would "vacate existing fines and terminate current investigations and complaints" against Clear Channel. In addition to the one-time payment, Clear Channel agreed to enforce its Responsible Broadcasting Initiative for at least three years, and establish a strong disciplinary plan for any employee who violates Commission rules in the future.

"It was a tough negotiation, but a fair resolution," Andrew Levin says. "We didn't agree that all the complaints were legally indecent, but some clearly crossed the line and for those we have taken full responsibility. No broadcaster has taken stronger steps to ensure its broadcasts comply with the law and we intend to keep it that way."

"The settlement allows Clear Channel to close the chapter on indecency and move forward with our business," John Hogan commented at the time. "This has been a complicated and controversial issue but it has also proven that we can provide compelling, entertaining, and informative programming without being indecent."

Of course, even that settlement was not without its own controversy. On June 10, 2004, the Parents Television Council announced its opposition to the settlement, insisting that hundreds of indecency complaints had been filed against Clear Channel. Calling the $1.75 million fine a mere drop in the bucket, the PTC complained that "not only are the public's complaints being summarily dismissed without a hearing, but any complaint filed over programming that aired prior to June 8 is also to be rejected, sight unseen."

While conceding that "Clear Channel Communications has made sincere and productive steps toward enforcing commonsense broadcast decency standards," PTC President Brent Bozell nevertheless was disappointed. "We understand that given the recent positive actions of Clear Channel, an olive branch could have been extended by the FCC. Instead they handed Clear Channel the entire tree."

In retrospect, Clear Channel CEO Mark Mays says, "When we took Howard Stern off the air, it was the first time ever in the history of this company that we dictated down to any of our markets. We told those programmers not only what they could run, but what they couldn't run. That was a change from how we always had left everything up to local control, but the indecency battle was heating up and it created a challenge for us." Despite some critics' charges that Clear Channel was caving in to government censorship when First Amendment rights were at stake, Mays insists it was the only proper decision the company could make. "Our shareholders don't want us to not have FCC licensing," he explains. "It becomes a very short business cycle if you have nothing from which to generate cash flow. Legally, we didn't have a choice. It was a tough decision in that we've always had an environment where we would tell our managers, 'You program the stations however you want to — we're not going to tell you what you can or can't run.' We had told them that, while we may not like or agree with Howard, if they wanted to put him on their station, it was their market decision."

Both houses of Congress have written and rewritten legislation that would raise the stakes for broadcasters and performers who were found to have engaged in indecent broadcasts. Following earlier attempts in 2004 to legislate penalties for on-air indecency, the House of Representatives in early 2005 passed a bill that raised the maximum fine of $32,500 for a violation of its indecency standards to $500,000, and would also permit the FCC to increase the fine on performers who "commit indecent acts" from $11,000 to $500,000. The proposal also mandated that the station's license be revoked after a broadcaster's third offense. At the same time, key senators introduced legislation that would raise the maximum FCC fine to $325,000, with a cap of $3 million in fines per day per broadcaster.

Neither piece of legislation was enacted by the 109th Congress, but Rep. Fred Upton (R-MI) reintroduced indecency legislation in early 2006 that again, because of the November election, was expected to achieve traction by both political parties. Four months later, in May 2006, the U.S. Senate passed the Broadcast Decency Enforcement Act, the House approved it without change, and President Bush signed it into law on June 15.

As the owner of more than 1,000 radio stations, Clear Channel has the greatest odds of running afoul of the new indecency legislation and thus has become increasingly vigilant about its "zero tolerance policy toward indecency." "We watch it all the time," Andrew Levin says. "We train, we retrain, and we train some more, but there still are complaints that come in from the public. The FCC now has taken the position that they're going to investigate every complaint, so as soon as they get one about Clear Channel we get a letter that we have to respond to. We have to investigate the facts of that complaint, put the response in writing, then hope that the FCC sees it our way and decides it was not a violation. So far we've been fortunate that the complaints that have come in have largely been unfounded."

BELOW: *Lowry Mays during his high school football years in Highland Park.* OPPOSITE TOP: *Lowry at age three, photographed with older sister JoAnn at their house in Houston, where the Mays family lived before moving to Dallas.* OPPOSITE BOTTOM: *Lowry Mays enrolled at Texas A&M University as a petroleum engineering student, but he also was involved with the ROTC program that brought him three post-graduate years with the U.S. Air Force. Those years would be instrumental in shaping the course of his personal and professional life.*

PREVIOUS: *After graduating from Texas A&M, Lowry Mays was stationed at Brooks Air Force Base in San Antonio where, as a second lieutenant and petroleum officer, he met Peggy Pitman. Shortly afterwards he was relocated to Taiwan to oversee construction of an oil pipeline, but he returned to Texas the following summer to marry Peggy. This photo was taken on their wedding day — July 31, 1959 — shortly before he escorted her back across the Pacific so he could finish his tour of duty.* OPPOSITE: *Lowry Mays broadcasting from the WOAI studios in San Antonio, Texas.* ABOVE: *After purchasing KEEZ-FM in San Antonio in 1972, Lowry Mays served as president of parent company San Antonio Broadcasting. He also stayed with his investment banking firm for several more years until WOAI-AM began seeing some positive cash flow.*

OPPOSITE TOP: Randall, Kathy, Lowry and Mark Mays. OPPOSITE BOTTOM: This annual holiday celebration brought together 26 members of the Mays family, including Lowry and Peggy Mays; Randall, Mark, Kathy, and Linda, and their spouses; plus 16 grandchildren. ABOVE: Lowry Mays photographed with son Mark in the early 1970s, around the time that Lowry and Red McCombs co-signed the note on KEEZ-FM in San Antonio.

750,000 Shares

CLEAR CHANNEL COMMUNICATIONS, INC.

Common Stock

Prior to this offering, there has been no public market for the Common Stock of the Company. See "Underwriting" for information relating to the method of determining the initial public offering price.

THESE SECURITIES HAVE NOT BEEN APPROVED OR DISAPPROVED BY THE SECURITIES AND EXCHANGE COMMISSION NOR HAS THE COMMISSION PASSED UPON THE ACCURACY OR ADEQUACY OF THIS PROSPECTUS. ANY REPRESENTATION TO THE CONTRARY IS A CRIMINAL OFFENSE.

	Price to Public	Underwriting Discounts and Commissions(1)	Proceeds to Company(2)
Per Share	$10.00	$0.75	$9.25
Total Minimum	$7,500,000	$562,500	$6,937,500
Total Maximum(3)	$8,400,000	$630,000	$7,770,000

(1) See "Underwriting."

(2) Before deducting expenses payable by the Company, estimated at approximately $285,000.

(3) Assuming full exercise of the 30-day option granted by the Company to the Underwriters to purchase, on the same terms, up to an additional 90,000 shares of Common Stock to cover any over-allotments. See "Underwriting."

The shares of Common Stock are offered by the several Underwriters when, as and if issued by the Company and accepted by the Underwriters and subject to their right to reject orders in whole or in part. It is expected that delivery of the shares will be made in New York, New York, on or about April 27, 1984.

Blyth Eastman Paine Webber
INCORPORATED

Schneider, Bernet & Hickman, Inc.

The date of this Prospectus is April 19, 1984.

OPPOSITE TOP: *This photo, taken at WOAI-AM's studios in San Antonio, appeared on the cover of Clear Channel's first Annual Report for 1984. Kathy Mays is seated at left, being interviewed by Carl Wigglesworth and Mary Denman. Seen through the window in the rear is long-time agriculture man, Bill McReynolds, who worked for WOAI for over 50 years. OPPOSITE BOTTOM: In 1988 the Clear Channel board of directors consisted of (l-r) Alan Feld, partner in Akin, Gump, Strauss, Hauer, and Feld; Red McCombs; Lowry Mays; Ted Strauss, chairman and CEO of First City Bank of Dallas; and John Williams, regional vice president of Thomson McKinnon Securities, Inc. ABOVE: Clear Channel's initial public offering of 750,000 shares of stock in April 1984.*

OPPOSITE TOP: *Lowry Mays at WOAI.* OPPOSITE BOTTOM: *Lowry Mays surrounded by his family after they were named "Giants of Broadcasting" by the Library of American Broadcasting.* TOP: *Lowry Mays and Red McCombs receiving an award from the American Academy of Achievement.* ABOVE: *Lowry Mays in the early days of Clear Channel.*

OPPOSITE TOP: *Lowry Mays during a light moment at an industry meeting in Washington, DC.* OPPOSITE BOTTOM: *Lowry and Mark at Mark's graduation from high school.* ABOVE: *Lowry behind the wheel of his old T Willy Jeep, similar to the one he drove while supervising the construction of the oil pipeline in Taiwan.*

ABOVE: *Lowry Mays served as treasurer of one of Sen. Lloyd Bentsen's (D-TX) campaigns. Here he's pictured (far right) with Bentsen (second from left).* OPPOSITE TOP: *Lowry Mays with former CBS News anchor Walter Cronkite.* OPPOSITE BOTTOM: *Lowry Mays (second from right) taking a break from a round of golf in Sun Valley, Idaho, with broadcasting colleagues (l-r) Jim May, who served as executive vice president of government relations at NAB; former Fisher Broadcasting CEO Ben Tucker; and Eddie Fritts, former president and CEO of the National Association of Broadcasters.*

OPPOSITE TOP: Clear Channel Outdoor launches its first indoor digital billboard network reaching elite business travelers through LED displays in Chicago O'Hare International Airport. OPPOSITE BOTTOM AND ABOVE: Clear Channel Spectacolor billboards, wallscapes and rooftop signage in New York City's Times Square.

OPPOSITE TOP AND BOTTOM: This Clear Channel billboard and donation drive are part of the company's $65 million, cross-divisional relief effort in support of communities affected by the 2005 hurricane season. TOP: Randall Mays accepts an award from the National MS Society in recognition of the company's nationwide commitment and support. ABOVE: In 2006, Clear Channel Radio's News/Talk KLVI 560 AM was honored with the prestigious Crystal Award for community service from the National Association of Broadcasters. Pictured during one of their many community service activities from left to right are: Dana Melancon, KLVI Weather Reporter, Al Caldwell, legendary KLVI Morning Personality (a Marconi Winner), Dr. Dan Ford of the Salvation Army and a donor to the Katrina Relief Fund. FOLLOWING: Mark Mays, chief executive officer; Lowry Mays, chairman of the board; and Randall Mays, president and chief financial officer.

CHAPTER NINE

THE DAY THE MUSIC DIED (... OR NOT)

ALMOST FROM ITS VERY INCEPTION IN 1920, COMMERCIAL RADIO HAS NURTURED the love affair that the American public has had with music. In its very earliest years, the industry served up an audio palette of vaudevillians who sang and danced their way into the hearts of a small but loyal audience that was just beginning to understand how this new electronic medium could fill their living rooms with laughter, joy, and awe. Until the advent of radio, most of this entertainment could only be enjoyed at the local opera house, concert hall, or maybe a band pavilion in the town square on a Sunday afternoon. This began to change, however, as America very quickly became obsessed with that new piece of furniture with a speaker and a tuning dial.

Two years into radio's infancy, in 1922, WSB-AM in Atlanta broadcast what at the time was considered the first country music ever to be played on the radio, and just five years later the Grand Ole Opry broadcast its first radio show in Nashville. In the early '30s the Metropolitan Opera in New York aired an entire opera over the radio, and one year later a young broadcaster named Ed Sullivan introduced his first music acts on CBS Radio. Since then musical entertainment — both live and pre-recorded — has become a mainstay on radio stations from coast to coast. As the late thriller writer Trevanian noted in his semi-autobiographical novel *The Crazyladies Of Pearl Street,* "I used to stand before our Emerson for hours, one foot hooked behind the other, my eyes defocused, thoughtlessly tearing up little bits of paper as my imagination battened on the radio as an unending flow of ambrosia, food for the mind and the soul that sustained you when you needed support, exercised you when your emotions or intellect were flabby, and cosseted you when you needed rest and escape." The signal that emanated from the large single speaker of that old Emerson or from the tinny AM speakers in the dashboard of the family Ford served up a rich smorgasbord for the ears, capturing all who listened, and in the years leading up to and following World War II radio helped the U.S. come of age.

Of course, this scenario changed dramatically in the early 1950s when radio was forced to adapt to the media revolution that resulted from the widespread introduction of television. Where families once gathered 'round to listen to (and stare at) that console radio that provided them with a lifeline to a world outside their homes, the square picture tube of the Philco or Zenith TV set now took its place. Television in short order absorbed virtually all the entertainment programming that radio spawned, leaving radio to reinvent itself or suffer the plight of the buggy whip.

Fortunately, the music industry was experiencing some changes of its own, as the record labels were experimenting with singles-based records that had large holes in the middle and spun at 45 revolutions per minute. These "45s," as well as the recently released 33-1/3 RPM "long playing" albums, made contemporary music accessible to millions of consumers, many of them teenagers and young adults. As radio struggled to find its own niche in the post-TV world, a natural relationship emerged whereby the music companies used radio to market their product, and radio used the pre-recorded music to fill adequately a void that television wouldn't be able to adequately fill until MTV was introduced in the early 1980s.

While this depiction of events might sound elementary, it encapsulates the comfortable partnership that the radio and record industries have enjoyed since the early 1950s. It also lays the groundwork for the vast explosion of music radio stations that was to come in the 1970s and '80s, as the music that was being created and sold began to splinter from such basic genres as pop and country and R&B into album rock, progressive rock, adult contemporary, and then later into such sub-genres as urban, disco, techno-pop, and alternative. Consumers were becoming increasingly discerning in their collective taste, and both the radio companies and record labels were willing to accommodate them with new artists and musical styles. As a result, radio formats flourished and record sales soared.

When deregulation begat consolidation in the late 1990s, the forces of change raised the hackles of many individuals and organizations whose purpose was allied closely with maintaining the *status quo*. Similarly, as radio groups began to play musical chairs with radio formats, shifting them around to create "platform synergies" within specific markets, many of the people whose lives and livelihoods depended on providing an ever-expanding universe of music product began to worry that radio's interests no longer were aligned with theirs.

Individuals and groups that stood to be most affected by this process — whether real or not — began to raise their voices in protest of what they called the "dumbing-down" of radio programming. Virtually all large radio companies were condemned for an alleged lack of musical diversity and, because Clear Channel was the largest of these, it drew the lion's share of criticism.

In truth, Clear Channel has introduced more new artists and more new songs to radio than any other radio company. Nevertheless, no organization has taken consolidation — and Clear Channel — to task more than the Future of Music Coalition, a self-described "not-for-profit collaboration between members of the music, technology, public policy, and intellectual property law communities." A 147-page report issued by the group on November 18, 2002, that has been cited, copied, and/or posted on numerous Internet websites and blogs, makes several sweeping claims, including statements that "format consolidation leads to fewer gatekeepers.... A small number of companies control what music is played on specific formats ... [and] overwhelming consolidation of these formats deprives citizens the opportunity to hear a wide range of music."

While conceding that, from 1996 to 2000, format variety — "the average number of formats available in each geographic market" — increased in both large and small markets, the organization claimed that "considerable format overlap" existed and amounted to "massive missed opportunities for format variety, which might in turn enhance programming diversity." Other groups, including the Center for Digital Democracy, quickly piled on once the report was published to demonize radio in general and Clear Channel in particular.

While the 147-page FMC study is impressive in its scope and its dedication to musicians' issues, it appears to miss one major issue: As a medium that is charged with serving the public interest, radio companies at all times have sought to broadcast programming that will attract the greatest number of listeners possible. While some artists who write and perform in micro-niche genres would dearly love to attract airplay in order to boost their fan base, both the radio and recording industries over the last 50 years have functioned largely within a "hit record" mindset. While the record labels can be credited — or blamed, depending on one's point of view — with creating a marketplace in which a few artists appeal to a vast majority of consumers, the fact remains that many record buyers gravitate toward those artists who have broad appeal within their demographic.

It's no accident, therefore, that most radio stations identify themselves by the type of music they play, and tend to play the records that listeners like to hear most often. Over the years, as musical tastes have become more sophisticated, these musical tastes have generated more specific genres (in radio they're represented on-air as formats), which then break down into sub-genres. Thirty years ago, a country station played virtually all brands of music that were coming out of Nashville, but today a country-formatted station might play classic country (Hank Williams and Merle Haggard), contemporary country (Brooks and Dunn and Tim McGraw), a more cutting-edge form of country (Gretchen Wilson and Rascal Flatts), or Americana (Alison Krauss and Nickel Creek) — but generally not all four. Similarly, Top 40 music can be broken down into rhythmic Top 40 and pop Top 40. The same distinctions can be made for urban, adult contemporary, rock, and even oldies.

These format specifications were developed by radio programmers over the years as both the music and audience tastes changed. In the 1950s, when radio was struggling to overcome the challenges posed by television, the advent of 45 rpm records and jukeboxes proved to be a major force in the formation and evolution of music radio. As the oft-repeated legend goes, a pair of radio pioneers — Todd Storz and Bill Stewart — were in a bar in Omaha, Nebraska, in the early 1950s when they discovered — several cocktails into what turned out to be a long evening — that other patrons had been playing the same few songs over and over again on the jukebox. Stewart later took his "discovery" to another radio pioneer, Gordon McClendon, who in 1947 had built the studios for KLIF-AM in the basement of the Cliff Towers Hotel in Dallas. He convinced McClendon that this jukebox activity reflected consumer taste in music, and they subsequently embarked on a mission to research sales activity in Dallas record stores.

McClendon and Storz began developing playlists that primarily were dominated by those newer songs that were more popular, while relegating other records to "B" lists and "recurrents" — those that had already worn out their hit status but were still popular when played less often.

While this "origin of the Top 40 species" has been questioned in recent years (and may have been predated by a university research project conducted in the 1950s), it is indicative of how radio had to transform itself from what had been the American family's primary entertainment medium into a new source of entertainment, at roughly the same time that recording companies were churning out volumes of music product, trying to see what would stick. Country music was hugely popular at the time, and so were records that at one time fit the mold of "black" or "dance" music. Again, enterprising disc jockeys detected a burgeoning enthusiasm for these types of records and within a short time the Top 40 era had begun. Cleveland DJ Alan Freed is credited with coining the term "rock and roll" in the mid-'50s in an attempt to put a popular spin on it, and more than 50 years later the genre is still very much alive and well.

As Top 40 matured and artists began experimenting with various musical styles, the music began to edge outside the format's traditional lines. Bill Haley's Comets and Frankie Valli ran headlong into the Beatles and the Stones and the Doors and Led Zeppelin, much at the same time that the radio industry discovered the higher fidelity of the FM band. Radio programmers who were tired of spinning Herman's Hermits and the Archies found that the songs that were identified by record labels as hits often weren't as popular with listeners as the "album cuts" that could be found further toward the center of a record — and further away from the more broadly defined taste of American pop music listeners.

Thus, "album-oriented rock" was born, and as music radio fragmented in the 1970s and '80s, various versions developed in almost parallel universes. Meanwhile, members of the "sock hop generation" discovered such artists as Bread and the Carpenters and Anne Murray, giving way to adult contemporary, a term that another music industry legend, Bill Gavin, is credited with having coined in 1973.

Meanwhile, artists outside the commercial mainstream continued to produce records in distinct, but not as widely consumed, music styles. Jazz, R&B, and bluegrass sold a fraction of the number of records as the major musical acts, and dedicated record companies — often smaller labels or imprints at the larger labels — continued to service this consumer segment. Later these micro-genres would include techno-pop, Euro-dance, new age, and smooth jazz, but only the latter ever gained enough consumer traction to create a viable radio format.

Understandably, the dedicated musicians who continue to write and perform within these small musical genres tend to blame both the radio and record industries for pigeon-holing them to the point where album sales and airplay are almost nonexistent. Nevertheless, in a world where consumers increasingly exert more choice over virtually all aspects of their lives, artists who appeal to a small fraction of the public will receive an equally small amount of radio airplay.

Today, a consolidated radio market is very much like a shopping mall. At each end of the mall one tends to find an anchor store — the popular, heritage retailer whose wide range of goods attracts a broad consumer base. Situated between these two stores is a variety of other retail outlets, selling everything from clothing to records to video games to shoes. Certainly, certain products found in some of these stores are somewhat similar; for instance, in any mall in the U.S. one can probably find 10 or 15 clothing stores, three or four shoe stores, a bookstore, a record store, and maybe a half dozen fast food restaurants. What you probably will not see, unless you walk the halls of a dying mall whose owner is scrambling to fill leases any possible way, is a specialty store selling only dragonfly figurines or tarot cards. Certainly, there is a consumer marketplace for such items, but neither enterprise likely would succeed if it were tucked between Old Navy and American Eagle Outfitters.

While this comparison may oversimplify the situation, it illustrates that not every distinct musical genre can be accommodated with the limited number of licensed stations in each market. Of course, it could be argued that a city like New York, which is penetrated by at least 72 commercial and public radio stations, might be able to have enough advertising to support one that plays an Americana format with a bluegrass edge. However, of those stations, only 25 regularly achieve an audience share of 1.0 or better in the Arbitron ratings (listeners 12-plus, Monday-through-Sunday). These stations are owned by a total of 10 radio groups, all of which have the objective of serving a distinct segment of the audience while turning a profit. While the artistic community might be grateful if at least one of these companies took a leap of faith and played records from lesser-known musicians, it is almost certain that the resulting loss of audience would drop that station into the "less-than-one-share" radio hinterlands.

The FMC's contention that format "overlap" and "redundancy" have increased because of consolidation is unfounded. As former NAB president and CEO Eddie Fritts told The Media Institute in an address on April 23, 2003, "The plain fact is that because of deregulation, local radio stations are more competitive with other media. And it is because of deregulation that consumers have a wider array of formats from which to choose. From hip-hop to gospel, from all-sports to all-children's stations, radio format diversity has exploded."

Fritts pointed out that, prior to 1996, there were fewer than 400 Spanish-language radio stations in the U.S., vs. 630 (in 2003). "Fifteen years ago in Washington, DC, there was one foreign language radio station. Today, there are 12. In my book, that's diversity." Fritts cited separate polls conducted by The Mellman Group and Zogby International, each of which showed that Americans "give high marks to local radio stations for providing news, information, and entertainment programming that they value. And all free of charge." Fritts went on to say that a study conducted by Arbitron showed that 79 percent of Americans believe they get more or the same amount of programming choice as they did five years ago.

Ultimately, it all comes down to supply and demand: If the consumer demands it, the radio companies will supply it. "Why wouldn't a station try to play those songs that people really want to hear?" says Clear Channel's Randall Mays. "What a concept! Now, I can understand that there are people who don't like Top 40 and they therefore say radio is not diverse enough. To me that's just crazy. The definition of Top 40 is we play the 40 most popular songs. These are the 40 songs people want to hear the most."

"There is a reason there aren't any Zydeco formats outside the state of Louisiana," adds John Hogan. "Not enough people want to listen to them. The fact is, the number of formats available today is significantly larger than it was pre-Telecom. In 1996 there were approximately 35 formats on the air. Today, there are more than 80. There are more distinct artists and songs on the radio today than there were four or five years ago. Think about it: It's in Clear Channel's best interest to give the listeners what they want to hear. If we do that, they'll keep coming back."

There's very little question that over the past 50 years radio programming has fragmented considerably in order to serve an increasingly diverse audience. More and more genres are represented on radio station playlists, and over the last 10 years the number of formats — notwithstanding some natural overlap — has more than doubled, according to the

National Association of Broadcasters. Further, a February 2006 Mediabase report shows that the number of unique songs played by radio stations more than doubled between 2001 and 2005. Specifically, a total of 71,111 individual songs were played by U.S. radio stations in 2001; that number increased to 77,404 in 2002, 87,271 in 2003, 121,213 in 2004, and 144,673 in 2005. In 2001 Clear Channel played 41,478 unique songs, 44,190 in 2002, 48,435 in 2003, 58,197 in 2004, and 70,808 in 2005. Similarly, in 2001 U.S. radio stations played records from 12,657 unique artists, a number that almost doubled to 23,570 artists in 2005. (For the record, Mediabase is a division of Clear Channel-owned Premiere Radio Networks, and monitors radio playlists of some 1,800 stations in 175 U.S. and Canadian markets, 24 hours a day, seven days a week. Data collected through its monitoring process is available to radio stations, research firms, record labels, and radio trade publications that maintain radio airplay charts.)

Rich Meyer, president of Mediabase, notes that these raw "unique song" numbers account for all versions produced and distributed by record labels, including live performances, special dance mixes, and format remixes. For example, Santana, Santana featuring Rob Thomas, Santana featuring Michele Branch, and Santana featuring Steven Tyler all are considered to be unique artists. Still, the clear explosion in the number of unique songs over the last five years indicates that the creation and availability of new music is only increasing.

Despite the Mediabase evidence to the contrary, the FMC report spurred considerable dialogue in Washington, with some lawmakers buying into the notion that consolidation severely limited musicians' access to the radio airwaves. Following the presentation of the report at the FMC's annual policy summit, Wisconsin Democratic Senator Russell Feingold suggested that deregulation led to a flurry of bad music and "pay-for-play" schemes that made it impossible for independent artists to get airplay. "If you don't have the money to play in the system, you are shut out," he said. "You've got to pay to play."

PAY FOR PLAY

Virtually every major broadcasting company that has operated in the radio industry over the last 50 years has been scrutinized at some point for the alleged practice of accepting compensation in return for adding a record to its playlist.

In the early days of music radio the practice of "payola" was said to have begun with disc jockeys who selected their own music and theoretically could be persuaded to play a record if the label or promoter chipped in a little "sweetener" to make the deal mutually beneficial. As the industry matured and music playlists increasingly were determined by the station's music director and program director, record promoters refocused their efforts on these individuals and stations that had the ability to "break" a record.

While few individuals ever have been indicted and/or prosecuted for engaging in "pay for play," sporadic efforts have been made to rein it in. Legendary Cleveland DJ Alan Freed was convicted in 1960 for taking money in exchange for radio airplay, but until recently very little progress had been made in identifying those men and women who received compensation (usually money, but sometimes, allegedly, drugs, sexual favors, or other assorted "door prizes").

In 1986 an NBC Nightly News report produced by Brian Ross initiated a federal probe of payola, resulting in a 56-count indictment against veteran independent promoter Joe Isgro. The case eventually was dismissed "with prejudice" for "outrageous government misconduct" after the presiding judge ruled that prosecutors had tried to hide contradictory testimony. (In 2000 Isgro pleaded guilty to conspiracy and extortion charges for running a loan-sharking operation in Beverly Hills.)

More recently, New York Attorney General Eliot Spitzer launched his own investigation into payola. First focusing on the record labels, in 2005 he negotiated cash settlements with Sony BMG Music Entertainment and Warner Music Group, both of which agreed to stop the practice of using promoters to pay for radio airplay. Sony BMG agreed to a $10 million fine, while Warner Music Group agreed to pay $5 million; in May 2006 Universal Music Group also agreed to pay $12 million to settle similar charges.

Early in 2006 Spitzer extended his investigation to radio, issuing subpoenas to nine of the country's largest radio groups, including Clear Channel, which he said provided air time in exchange for record company payoffs. "A lot of the major songs have been implicated in this and it showed how pervasive the payola infrastructure had become," Spitzer told the Associated Press on February 9, 2006. "Probably many of the songs that were beneficiaries of the payola scheme would have succeeded without it, but certainly payola became part of the promotional structure and was integral to the game to get songs to the top. Major artists, major songs were sent up the charts through improper payments to buy spins on the air that translated into sales." Two Clear Channel program directors implicated in Spitzer's initial investigation were dismissed.

"We take this issue very seriously and our policy is clear: If you engage in pay-for-play, you cannot work for Clear Channel," John Hogan said in a statement at the time. "We believe the vast majority of our programmers are doing a terrific job, fully within the law." Although Clear Channel severed its ties with independent record promoters in 2003, Hogan said that the company would take whatever steps were necessary to ensure that any such behavior does not occur again.

Following up on Spitzer's investigation, the FCC in April 2006 launched its own probe of payola, focusing specifically on Clear Channel, CBS Radio, Entercom, and Citadel Broadcasting.

"Our policy couldn't be clearer," Clear Channel Chief Legal Officer Andrew Levin said following the announcement. "We have zero tolerance for pay-for-play. Any employee who violates that policy faces disciplinary action up to and including dismissal."

Any company that doesn't pay heed to Elliot Spitzer does so at their own peril, Levin says. "To comply with his ongoing investigation we have been asked for, and turned over, a lot of documents during the period that he was investigating the record labels. We don't believe that there's anything in those documents that implicates the company. We've gone back and looked at all of the e-mails, we sent our forensic auditors out to interview folks, and we found — after several months and dozens of interviews — two individuals we believed engaged in illegal activity for their own personal gain. That clearly was against company policy and clearly against the law, and we fired them as soon as we found out."

In its most basic definition, payola is simply the process of playing a record for consideration — money or items of value — without informing the audience or the Internal Revenue Service. Spitzer's charges appear to have extended that definition to include the violation of consumer protection statutes that prohibit deceptive business practices, specifically accepting money in exchange for airplay that conceivably could affect a song's position on music industry record charts.

In the past, independent record promoters reportedly served as a conduit between the music label and the radio station, financially compensating stations (or their personnel) in exchange for data about spins (how many times a record got played) and "adds" (whether a record was added to a station's playlist). Cash payments were logged as station income and were reported as such to the IRS, but individual abuses still occasionally occurred.

The best way to stop the independent promotion system altogether was for the labels to stop paying the promoters, Clear Channel's Andrew Levin observes. "We're not talking a lot of money in the grand scheme of things," he says.

So in April 2003 John Hogan and Mark Mays decided to cut off all relationships with independent promoters.

"The labels were not really that upset, but the independent promoters were very upset," Levin adds. "Anecdotally, the labels may have been concerned that our decision could affect them because they had this lingering perception that independent promotion actually had some impact on what was played, so if one label stopped doing it, it was like unilateral disarmament. They thought it would put them at a disadvantage. But because we stopped taking the indie money across the board, I don't think the labels were all that upset."

Of course, for a company that owns some 1,005 radio stations, maintaining a watchful eye on each of the men and women who keep those stations running is next to impossible. "You're always going to have a few bad apples, especially in a company this large," Levin says. "We have 900 program directors — that's a tremendous number of employees. I'm sure fast-food chains have people who put their hand in the till. No matter what you do, no matter how many policies you put into place or how many affidavits you require employees to sign, or how many hidden cameras that fast-food chain puts in behind the counters to make sure their employees aren't stealing from them, you're always going to have people who do the wrong thing. All you really can do is monitor and enforce your rules consistently and regularly, and that's what we try to do."

THAT'S ENTERTAINMENT

The 2000 acquisition of SFX Entertainment and the attempt to synergize it with Clear Channel's Radio division almost instantly raised cries of foul play among many of the nation's independent concert producers and promoters, as well as program directors at competing radio stations.

SFX Entertainment was founded in the 1990s by Robert Sillerman, who previously had owned and sold a number of profitable radio stations, earning him a reputation within the industry as a dealmaker extraordinaire. A consummate entrepreneur, Sillerman recognized the value in consolidating the national concert and promotion business much the same way the radio industry was consolidating. By the time Clear Channel purchased the company, SFX owned 16 amphitheaters and 120 concert venues throughout the U.S.. Sillerman had attempted to grow his operational revenue by demonstrating to various companies how they could expand their branding potential by advertising at concerts and other musical performances. But it was only after Clear Channel paired the recently acquired company with its Radio division that ad dollars expanded almost exponentially.

"When we first looked at SFX we thought it was definitely a content play," Mark Mays recalls. "Our perspective was that we had live content with which we could develop synergies by developing additional content to push through our distribution network. We thought that the ability to promote new and different events and drive that by using our unsold airtime would be a big attraction."

After the merger, a number of artists voiced their concerns that Clear Channel was exerting undue control over ticket prices, venues, and promotional appearances. Such artists as Steve Miller, Neil Young, and Britney Spears claimed that they either were pressured to play in Clear Channel venues, perform at promotion concerts for Clear Channel radio stations, or were penalized with reduced airplay for not playing by Clear Channel's rules. In a well-publicized conflict, Spears — through her manager — insisted that Clear Channel stations gave her records fewer "spins" when she did not tour with Clear Channel than when she did work with the company.

"We actually showed her that when we were promoting her tour, we spun her records a lot less than when we didn't have her tour," says Mark Mays, who maintains that there was no connection between records that got played on Clear Channel radio stations and what producers, promoters, or venues those artists chose to use. "The reason for the airplay discrepancy was that she had a good album when she wasn't touring with us, and a lesser album when she was touring with us. So it was a false accusation."

In fact, for the four years covering 2000 through 2003, Clear Channel played Spears' records consistently, representing 34 percent, 33 percent, 33 percent, and 36 percent of total U.S. airplay, respectively. That turns out to be more than the company's "fair share" — at the time, Clear Channel owned less than 10 percent of all the radio stations in the U.S.

Fingers also were pointed at Clear Channel for what some critics viewed as strong-arm corporate tactics. Most notably, Denver promoter Nobody

In Particular Presents Inc. filed a lawsuit in 2001 alleging that Clear Channel tried to monopolize the promotions business in Colorado by withholding airplay from musicians who booked shows through other promoters. Clear Channel vehemently denied the allegations, and in April 2004 NIPP released internal Clear Channel e-mails quoting company officials as wanting to "crush" competitors, as well as seemingly threatening record labels and artists. The judge in the case, Edward Nottingham, tossed out several of NIPP's claims, including the allegation that the company's stronghold in Denver's radio and rock concert market constituted an illegal monopoly. The judge said that Clear Channel's radio power, coupled with its nearly 51 percent share of the rock concert market, is "impressive, [but] it is not monopolistic." The trial had been set for August 2004, but both sides settled out of court in June. Details of the settlement were not disclosed, although it was widely reported in the press that no money changed hands.

"Clear Channel admitted no wrongdoing in connection with the lawsuit, but we are pleased to get the matter behind us," Andrew Levin said at the time. "NIPP and Clear Channel can now get back to what we each do best — providing great music to the people of Denver."

"This was a long and difficult battle, and we are very happy with this agreement," NIPP founder Doug Kauffman said in a statement.

"Ultimately, there is no connection between what got played on Clear Channel stations and what concert tours or venues were chosen by artists," Mark Mays maintains. "It is crucial for us to have good relationships with artists, but even more important, we must have outstanding relationships with our audiences," he says. "There isn't an artist or a tour or a concert out there that is valuable enough to disrupt the relationship we have with our radio listeners and ticket buyers."

Whatever real or perceived pressures Clear Channel might have exerted on the radio and entertainment industries, the company's influence over the concert business now is a moot point. On December 21, 2005, the company effectively spun the division off into its own independent company called Live Nation. "We realized that these two divisions didn't work as well together as we would have wanted," says Mark Mays. "The local managers worked with the radio guys, but not nearly to the same extent that the radio sales managers would work together, or the programming guys would work together. It was a difficult task to try to get them to work across divisional lines, much more so than we anticipated.

"There's no question there was a lot of backlash from that acquisition," Mays continues. "The regulators and the music industry both were telling us we were controlling the whole industry. Internally we couldn't get anybody to work together, and then the Wall Street guys said, 'That business isn't synergistic at all with your business.'"

The more Clear Channel examined the scenario, Mays says, the more he and other key executives began to wonder if there was some merit to some of this talk. "We began to realize that it was probably right down the middle of all of them. Were we moving markets? Absolutely not. Did it work better than Wall Street thought it did? Yes. But we got ourselves in this box, and we saw we weren't winning at all with this structure."

Thus, while the company still believed strongly in the upside of the Entertainment division, the decision was made to spin it off. "Those who liked the business and wanted to participate in the upside could hold on to their stock, while those who didn't could monetize it," Mays says. "The regulators could say, 'Great — now they're not part of that business,' and all the music industry people could say, 'Oh, thank God.' I find it kind of ironic in a way, because for years a lot of artists were always asking how we could make it easier for them to use radio stations to promote their concerts. Now they won't be able to do that."

Of course, radio's primary responsibility is to its listeners, not the musical artists whose records get played — or don't. "It is not our job or our goal to break new music just for the sake of breaking new music," says John Hogan. "An entire other industry does that. Now, about 250 of our radio stations are formatically aligned with breaking new music, and in those instances, we're very focused on making sure that we stay ahead of the curve. On those stations we're looking for the 'Next Big Thing,' whether it's in country, rap, or rock. That leaves 750 stations where we're playing what hundreds of thousands — if not millions — of people have told us through phone calls and research they want to hear."

FEAR AND LOATHING OF VOICETRACKING

In today's post-consolidation radio world, many critics and anti-deregulation activists continue to hammer the industry for minimizing the needs of the local community in favor of the corporate bottom line. The perception is that there is a preponderance of "canned" content that's created in central programming hubs and distributed to a regional network of radio stations, thus eliminating local jobs, local flavor, and locally produced content. The assumption is that a radio company could eliminate a number of costly airshifts by importing four-hour programming segments voiced by professional DJs in other markets, or even at different company-owned stations in the same market. Usually, due to advances in technology, these "cyberjocks" could voice and produce a program in a fraction of the time required by an in-studio personality doing the broadcast in "real time." As programmers and local air personalities were displaced by programming that originated "out-of-market," it became a popular intramural sport to hammer any company that engaged in this programming practice, which has come to be known as "voicetracking."

Contrary to considerable public folklore, the use of voicetracking literally predates deregulation and consolidation by decades. Discounting the golden age of radio, when radio stations employed a generous mix of local and remote broadcasters, one form of voicetracking or another has been used frequently throughout the medium's "music era," roughly described as that five-decade period ranging from the mid-'50s to the present.

As more and more music came to be played by more and more radio stations, financial pressures and a sometimes-shallow talent pool led many radio companies to use programming supplied by syndication companies. These automated programming systems usually provided either a combination of music and prerecorded announcements or just the music, allowing a local disk jockey to voice his or her airshift and then stamp time signals on the audio tape so the music playback system knew when to cut to the "live" voice and then cut back to the next song.

Later, as the FM band began to take hold and the number of music-formatted radio stations on the air began to stretch finances even thinner, these same syndication companies — and some new networks — converted from distributing programming via reel-to-reel tape to newer, more efficient satellite feeds. Same concept, different method. Instead of using the U.S. Postal Service to rush programming to stations, it was transmitted directly to satellite dishes located at the station's studio or transmitter site. Today, radio companies use both satellite and high-speed broadband Internet technology to distribute a wide range of programming to their stations.

As John Hogan explains, "If we can take 'A' talent in Dayton and either put them on more dayparts on their current stations in Dayton, or put them on additional stations in Dayton, or put them on additional stations around Dayton, and give listeners in any of those examples a better experience, that's a positive. Sure, that means that the mediocre 'C-' or 'D+'

on-air host gets displaced, and they're not going to feel very good about it. But at the end of the day, we have put better content on the air."

In fact, Clear Channel's use of voicetracking reached its peak several years ago, and currently "talent importation" — that is, using voiced elements created in another market — accounts for just nine percent of the company's on-air content, with most of these dayparts occurring in overnight shifts. Another eight percent originates in the same market in which it is broadcast, but is "time-shifted" to another daypart or co-owned radio station.

"It never seemed to be an issue with the listener, and it still isn't," says Clear Channel's Tom Owens. "Most of this criticism is coming from people who were displaced, but remember — criticism with a vested interest is just a sales pitch without a disclaimer."

Owens says that today's voicetracking is much more sophisticated and locally oriented than any of its pre-consolidation incarnations. "Each day the imported talent receives direction from the local market program director," he explains. "They are provided local content, contests, weather, and news, and provide same-day content specifically targeted to that single station's audience and provided by the single station's local programming leadership."

Still, many critics fantasize that Clear Channel's San Antonio headquarters contains a programming hub, with a cadre of national programmers sitting around a table deciding which records will be played on the company's stations that week. Then the centralized broadcasting hub kicks in, with dozens of studios cranked up to full power as national DJs transmit their shows to scores of stations around the country. While this certainly describes the way both Sirius and XM program their hundred-plus channels in New York and Washington, respectively, nothing could be farther from the truth for Clear Channel — or most other terrestrial radio groups, for that matter.

The fact is, Clear Channel employs over 900 program directors who oversee programming operations at its 1,005 U.S. radio stations. As with all other areas of management and operations, these men and women are responsible for their own "stores" completely independent of each other. While they do share audience research data, each station is programmed locally in order to appeal to the tastes and sensitivities of each specific market. "There are no mass-market formulas or generic templates," says Tom Owens. "Every market situation tends to be unique and must be individually assessed on its own merits."

CHAPTER TEN

INSIDE THE BELTWAY: WASHINGTON AND POLITICS

AT THE START OF 2003, DURING THE WEEKS IMMEDIATELY PRECEDING THE U.S. invasion of Iraq, a series of radio station events calling for support of American troops garnered almost instant attention in the media. At roughly the same time that Natalie Maines made her now-infamous comments about being ashamed of a fellow Texan (see Chapter 6), conservative talk show host Glenn Beck had begun to make appearances across the U.S. at independently staged "Rallies For America." These rallies attracted thousands of supporters, and later were characterized by Clear Channel's detractors as driven by a pro-Bush agenda. While some reporters characterized them as pro-war rallies, others defined them as a show of support for the young men and women who soon would be going to war.

The rallies actually were organized by stations belonging to a number of radio groups, including Viacom's Infinity Broadcasting, Cox Radio, Federated Media, and Susquehanna Broadcasting. One of the rallies was organized independently by a 16-year-old girl. Included in this group of organizers were the local management teams of 13 stations owned by Clear Channel (at the time, the company owned more than 1,200 stations).

Despite the facts, Paul Krugman of the *New York Times* wrote a column on March 26, 2003, that singled out Clear Channel, accusing it of orchestrating "most" of the rallies from its corporate headquarters and repeated many of the most salacious allegations from the Salon.com article series. The title of the article was "Clear Channel Has Ties to Bush." Dozens of similarly themed stories began appearing in newspapers and on television news broadcasts around the country.

Once again, an action that began at the local level almost instantly made a giant faith-based leap to what was perceived as part of Clear Channel's political corporate agenda. The fact remained, however, that the Clear Channel stations that did participate in these rallies did so at the urging of their listeners, who repeatedly called or e-mailed their local stations to voice their support for the concept.

Based in New York, Glenn Beck has made a name for himself by championing a number of socio-political causes, often in severely non-traditional ways. In this case, however, he insists that the idea for the "support-the-troops" rallies originated not with him, but with a talk show host named Daryl Ankarlo at Susquehanna Media's KLIF-AM in Dallas. "It was a rainy Wednesday in February and Daryl, whose son was in the Marines, had called me because my show airs on his station," he recalls. "He told me they were planning a rally to support the troops, and they were going to invite listeners to come out and participate. I was interested in what he was doing, and asked him to please call me after the rally and tell me how it went."

Beck says that the turnout for the event surprised even him. "Daryl called me that night and said, 'Glenn, there were like a thousand people there. Despite the rain and the cold all these people turned out.'" Beck immediately realized that the rally had struck a chord with the audience, and invited Ankarlo to call his nationally syndicated show the next day to discuss the experience. "He did, and again he explained that a thousand people showed up in the rain," Beck continues. "Now, I've been in radio long enough to know that people often fudge the numbers, but Daryl insisted that a thousand folks really were there."

As soon as Ankarlo was off the air Beck decided he wanted to become involved with the rallies, but he suspected that very few program directors would want to take on the task. "I knew that 80 percent of them would say, 'No, we can't do that, nobody will come,'" he says. "They'd have a billion reasons not to do it. So instead of suggesting it to the programmers I turned it over to my listeners. On my show I said, 'This is a fantastic idea, and other people should do them. If you want to do one in your town, you should call your radio stations and tell them.'"

By the end of his show that day Beck had amassed a stack of e-mails and phone messages from dozens of program directors, many of whom complained that his callers had overloaded their stations' phones all day. "It was obvious we had hit a nerve," Beck says. "The audience was interested, the timing was right, and a great number of people wanted to show support for the troops. I started getting calls from program directors who said they wanted me to come in and be part of these rallies, but I said that because of time constraints I could only do a few of them. So I hand-picked the ones I could attend, and specifically chose only those stations that were not putting politicians on the stage. I insisted that they not make this about George Bush or other politicians; it had to be about supporting the troops."

Beck, who has earned a reputation for being a bit of a maverick talk show host, says he had a personal motivation for wanting to become involved in the rallies. "In the 1980s I worked with a guy who was a Vietnam veteran, and his life was such a wreck because, when he got back, people dismissed his service," Beck explains. "He was proud of what he had done, and I remember at the time promising myself that if we, as a nation, ever again chose to go to war, I couldn't be a part of a process that demonized these guys. I can't imagine going to war and shooting people, and the games that would play in your head. It would be important to get some reinforcement that people knew it was for a good reason, and they supported it. That's why I felt passionately about it. In almost every speech I did, I asked Vietnam veterans to stand up so I could officially welcome them home and thank them for their service. It was all about the troops, and not about George W. Bush."

That Clear Channel became so closely connected with the rallies — and subsequently was chastised for ostensibly drumming up support for President Bush and the looming war in Iraq — is ludicrous, Beck insists. "The Clear Channel connection was laughable, and the way the media jumped on it was frustrating. They got so much wrong, and that was my first taste of how irresponsible the quote-unquote 'responsible journalists' are. No one ever made a phone call to me, and they never asked for the facts. What made it even more frustrating was that I never spoke directly to anybody at Clear Channel, except for the people in Corporate Communications, because at some point they had to get involved since the company was getting so hammered."

Though imaginary, the Clear Channel war rally/White House line was an easy one for the company's critics to draw. Given the Mays family's friendship with former President George H.W. Bush and an amicable relationship with the current president, it was a seemingly short leap of faith to label the pro-troop rallies as a subtle effort on Clear Channel's part to build public sentiment for a war whose support was far from unanimous. Such a conclusion, however, is the same specious and hollow "guilt-by-association" argument that was used by former Senator Joe McCarthy of Wisconsin until CBS journalist Edward R. Murrow shut him down.

Beck found the exchange of venomous rhetoric more and more troubling. "I've known Mark Mays for a long time," he says. "He negotiated my first contract at Clear Channel. I know all the players at the company. They're from Texas and, while I've never talked to them about their politics, I suspect I know what they are. But I also know that the company is not driven by a political agenda, so what I can't understand is how this company can be perceived as being tied so heavily to the Bush White House. While it's true that the company syndicates Rush Limbaugh and Dr. Laura, this is the same company that had Bubba The Love Sponge and Howard Stern on the air in the same markets." Clear Channel also became the largest broadcaster of Air America programming, and remained so even after that network's declaration of bankruptcy in 2006.

While certain factions of the media incorrectly portray Clear Channel as a top-down company that issues corporate mandates to its local stations, nothing could be further from the truth, Beck says. "To be honest, they are so locally controlled that they would never dream of telling a station to make this decision or that decision."

Beck recalls the time a number of years ago when he was program director of three Clear Channel stations in Connecticut and had learned that Mark Mays was coming to town for a visit. "I had this whole pitch ready for him, explaining exactly what I wanted to do with each of the stations. About halfway through my pitch Mark's eyes just glazed over, and I could tell he didn't give a flying crap. I could have told him that I was planning on playing Nazi polka music, and he would have said exactly what he did, which was, 'Are you going to meet your bottom line?' I answered, 'Yeah, I think so.' At which point he said, 'Glenn, you do whatever you want. We're here to support you, so if you believe that's the right thing, do it.' That shook me to the core."

STRANGE BEDFELLOWS

The atmosphere that Andrew Levin encountered when he opened Clear

Channel's Washington legal office in December of 2002 was tense. Even though the Rallies For America uproar was still several weeks in the future, Levin says, "There was this prevailing notion that Clear Channel was an evil empire, that big was bad, and that the ownership of 1,200 radio stations was a blight against public policy. Clear Channel didn't really have any Washington representation up until that point. We had some outside firms that were lobbying on our behalf, but we didn't really have a dedicated office. The company realized that it needed to have some people on the ground in D.C. to educate folks on the Hill and at the FCC about what we were doing, and why having more radio stations in a particular market was actually beneficial, not just to the company and to the industry as a whole, but also to the listener."

One month after Clear Channel opened the Washington office, Arizona Senator John McCain began to take an aggressive stand against further relaxation of media ownership rules for radio and television. "A lot of public interest groups were beating the drum, saying that consolidation had run amok and that it was bad for the public," Levin observes. "My view was that it wasn't really media consolidation that a lot of these groups were fighting against; it was another agenda altogether. Remember, this was right after the 2002 election, and a lot of groups at that time existed for the sole purpose of trying to elect a Democratic presidential candidate."

Levin, himself a registered Democrat, says he is not a conspiracy theorist, but insists that a number of advocacy groups were pursuing a hidden agenda — and media ownership was one way to galvanize their collective base. "They painted the Bush administration as getting too cozy with the media industry, trying to control the airwaves," he explains. "Clear Channel was a fantastic target because Lowry Mays was known to be an acquaintance, if not a friend, of 'Bush One.' These groups used that friendship as a way to bootstrap some kind of cozy relationship with the current Bush administration, which frankly didn't exist, and doesn't to this day."

The image of a cozy relationship — real or not — made for good reading in the press and on the Internet. By tying a conservative Lowry Mays to the Bush family, pointing out that Clear Channel owned over 1,200 radio stations and linking the syndication of Rush Limbaugh and Glenn Beck, the concept of a right-wing conspiracy infiltrating the radio airwaves began to take flight.

"Meanwhile, it was quite clear that Senator McCain was contemplating a future run for the presidency," Levin continues. "He's always contemplating a run. He had been trying to put on a new face for several years, and he was doing a pretty good job of being a populist Republican — a bit different from the rest. So he wanted to take on the media consolidation issue that was getting a lot of publicity."

To that end, in January 2003, McCain called Lowry Mays before the Senate Commerce Committee hearing on media consolidating. "We went through many days of preparation," Levin says. "That gave us the opportunity to really get ourselves focused on what the facts were, how we were going to educate people better, and what our messaging was going to be. We met with Senator McCain the day before the hearing, and we quickly realized that it was not going to be the friendliest of hearings."

It wasn't.

In prepared text delivered at the beginning of his testimony, Lowry Mays noted that, "While radio may have changed in many ways over my three decades in the business, the key lessons I learned from that first San Antonio radio station still apply today. Stations must serve the needs and interests of their local communities, listeners, and advertisers alike. Radio is inherently a local medium and always will be. That means Clear Channel — along with nearly 4,000 other owners of radio stations in the U.S. — must continually strive to serve our local communities in the best ways we can."

Noting that some critics of consolidation claim that the commitment to local listeners has been lost as a result of deregulation, Lowry Mays insisted that nothing could be further from the truth. "Listeners want to hear a variety of music, news, local affairs, and other entertainment programming that appeals to their individual tastes," he stated. "And in today's multimedia world, those listeners are very discerning. If they don't like what they hear, they will turn the dial, burn a CD, or download an MP3 recording that is more to their taste. It's that simple, and that's risky to our financial health. That's why Clear Channel will always be in tune with what local listeners want to hear. One tired song, a commercial that lasts too long, or a failure to provide timely news, weather, or traffic, and the listener is gone. After all, radio is the only business I know of where you can lose a customer with the push of a button at 60 miles per hour."

"Lowry did a fantastic job and made some very key points," Levin recalls. "And the entire experience really got us focused on what the issues were, what the facts were, and how we were going to educate people in Washington better."

Lowry Mays' assessment was that McCain asked some pretty tough questions — over and over again. "He kept trying to grind me down, repeatedly asking me whether we were going to expand the company any more," Mays recalls. "He obviously thought we were too damned big as it was, and he kept saying, 'Are you going to acquire any more radio stations?' And I would answer that if we had the opportunity and they were good investments, we might do that. And he would say, "I'm going to ask you again — would you do that?" Finally I said, "Well, I just don't know."

McCain wasn't the only tenacious lawmaker in the hearing room, as North Dakota Senator Byron Dorgan was equally strident in his questioning. "Dorgan was pretty tough, because the Minot incident had happened the previous year," Lowry Mays says. "He felt we owned too many stations in his state."

Equal-opportunity Senate grilling aside, the purported Mays-Bush connection made for great fodder through the summer of 2003. In fact, during the early days of the Iraq war, when the Pentagon released its deck of cards identifying the 55 most-wanted members of Saddam Hussein's regime, a separate deck of "War Party Playing Cards" surfaced, depicting politicians and friends of the Bush administration. Lowry Mays was one of them, although he admittedly was just about the lowest in the deck — the two of clubs. While the FBI took the matter seriously, Mays just shakes his head with dismay at how a long-term friendship with the president and his family can be misconstrued to such a degree.

"I met George Bush 41 when I was on the Board of Regents at Texas A&M and we got his library there," Lowry says with a shrug of his broad shoulders. "I have been very close to him ever since then. I was a big supporter of his library, and he just turned out to be a personal friend. And when George Bush 43 was governor I supported him and got to know him. I'm on the board of Laura Bush's foundation, so I know the family extremely well. But I don't use that for political gain for me, the family, or the company."

What few people realize about Lowry Mays is that he was a born-and-raised Democrat. "As so many people were in Texas back in the '60s, I was fairly active in the Democratic party," he says. "I really didn't move from being a Democrat to Republican; it's like [Georgia Democratic Senator] Zell Miller said, 'I didn't leave the party, the party left me.' I was appointed to the Board of Regents at A&M by a Democratic governor, Mark White. In fact, I'm the only person in the history of Texas to be appointed to that post by a Democratic governor and a Republican governor. Certainly, I have been very active in politics, but it hasn't always been on the Republican side of the aisle."

Among Lowry Mays' many close friends are Bob Strauss, former chairman of the Democratic National Committee and ambassador to Russia; his brother Ted serves on the Clear Channel board of directors. "Of course, former Democratic governors Mark White and Dolph Briscoe are still very good friends, as well," he says.

Whatever Clear Channel's critics choose to believe about the Mays family or the company itself, Lowry is adamant about the lack of a connection between what goes on in San Antonio and at 1600 Pennsylvania Avenue in Washington. "None of our relationships with the Bushes has anything to do with what we program on our radio stations," he steadfastly maintains.

Clear Channel's Radio division isn't the only target of political scrutiny; the company's Outdoor division came under similar fire during the summer of 2004 for refusing to allow a self-proclaimed private group of wives of prominent California businessmen to display a billboard with an image of a bomb during the Republican National Convention in New York. Berkeley, California-based Project Billboard orginally had contracted with the company under the name "Liberty Festival Foundation," and the company was led to believe that the display would be used to promote some sort of live-entertainment event.

But when the artwork arrived, it depicted a red, white, and blue bomb, accompanied by the slogan, "Democracy Is Best Taught by Example, Not by War." The billboard was scheduled to be in place from August 2 through Election Day on November 2.

The Outdoor division refused to display the billboard, objecting to its "bomb imagery" in a post-9/11 New York, but not its message. "We have no political agenda," Clear Channel Outdoor CEO Paul Meyer said at the time, noting that the Marriott Marquis, on whose building the billboard is located, also objected to the advertisement. The Marriott is one of only a few landlords that reserve the right to approve all copy. "It's not the message; it was the imagery. In the city of New York, at the current time, bomb imagery is inappropriate," Meyer said.

"The billboard was meant to be provocative," Deborah Rappaport, director of Project Billboard, told *The Washington Post* on July 13, 2004. "Our intent is to increase the amount and level of discourse on one of the most important issues facing the nation."

Clear Channel Spectacolor, which actually had arranged the lease for the rejected billboard, said in a company statement that its contract with the landlord prohibits political advertising on its property. Further, Spectacolor CEO Michael Forte insisted that the division was not aware when the contract was signed that the ad would contain political content. Once it was clear that the ad contained political content, the division was obligated to reject it, the company statement said.

Paul Meyer completely supported Forte's decision. "Times Square has periodic bomb scares and drills with the police and bomb-sniffing dogs, and Michael decided that no type of bomb imagery was appropriate," he explains.

Meyer remembers the entire incident as "an unbelievable set-up. We told the client that we would work on the copy with them, as long as we could come up with something other than bomb imagery," he says. "On Friday of that week we offered copy that replaced the bomb image with a dove, but by the following Monday they had filed a lawsuit. They got tremendous publicity from the whole incident."

While Meyer insists that Clear Channel in no way was unambiguous in its challenge that its objection was with the bomb imagery, not the political message, he does concede that the company has conservative business standards in the Outdoor division where billboards are visible 24/7.

"We are totally apolitical, and I don't care if it's Democrats or Republicans or anti-war or pro-war. As long as the copy meets our standards, we will put it up. But we're a highly regulated business, and some of our greatest strengths also are some of our biggest risks. The consumer can't avoid us. You can't say to your kids, 'You can't watch that billboard.' That billboard is up, so we have people from age 6 to 106 looking at it. We have a responsibility to police that copy, because if we don't the government will."

Eventually, in a negotiated agreement with Project Billboard, Clear Channel offered the group two separate billboards: one that wraps around the Condé Nast building at 42nd Street and Broadway, and a second vertical display on the side of the W Hotel at Broadway and 47th Street. That sign included a running electronic ticker illustrating how much the United States is spending on the war in Iraq. According to the *New York Times,* the cost of the two billboards was $402,471, compared with $388,644 for the rejected display at the Marriott.

A company statement released after the billboard controversy was resolved, and posted on its website, notes that "Politics plays absolutely no role in reviewing ad copy. In fact, Clear Channel Outdoor actively works with groups across the political spectrum to help them reach their target audiences. That said, we reserve the right to reject any copy that would be offensive to a local community."

Even prior to the Rallies for America, politics was perceived to have merged with Clear Channel's programming shortly after the September 11, 2001, terrorist attacks on the World Trade Center in New York and the Pentagon in Washington. Within days of the tragedy word began circulating that the company had issued a list of songs that its radio stations were forbidden from playing on the air. Depending on the media report (and they are many and varied) this list included anything from Elton John's *Bennie and the Jets* to John Lennon's *Imagine* to all songs performed by the rock group Rage Against The Machine. Some songs ostensibly were included on the list because they contained references to such things as planes, flying, falling, or death in their titles, while others simply referred to objects or sentiments that could remind listeners of aspects of human mortality. Some media accounts put the list at 150 individual songs covering a wide range of artists, topics, emotions, and musical genres.

In fact, there was no corporate list either compiled or distributed by Clear Channel. "This is one of the many myths about the company," says Tom Owens. "There never was a nationally-distributed '9/11 safe list.' The real story is that Jack Evans, who was overseeing the company's West Coast operations at the time, began circulating a list of songs that he felt some of his regional stations should be aware of in light of the attack. In concept it was not unreasonable; NBC, Fox, CBS, MTV, and other entertainment outlets considered similar sensitivities to current events in their programming choices right after the tragedy." Such movies as *Collateral Damage* and *Bad Company* were delayed for months because of lingering sensitivities to their collective subject matter, and even late-night television tread lightly on the topics of death and terrorism.

In any event, there was no ban on playing any of the songs, and Owens says that by the time he became aware that a compendium of questionable songs was developing, the "list" had reached a limited number of stations, at which point he discontinued it immediately.

While some stations initially did exercise caution when compiling their post-9/11 playlists, many other Clear Channel stations made a point of playing songs that reportedly were included on an *ad hoc* "list" that by now could be found in various forms on the Internet — and many of them actually increased airplay of these recordings in part to create greater awareness of the tragedy.

To many of the company's critics, the dots connected by Glenn Beck's appearances at the Rallies For America, Howard Stern's condemnation of Clear Channel, the (now-debunked) Dixie Chicks ban, and the Mays connection to Bush 41 delineate a political conspiracy between San Antonio and 1600 Pennsylvania Avenue. Extreme theorists also point to the connection between Tom and Steve Hicks and current president George W. Bush, who benefited handsomely when Tom Hicks purchased the Texas Rangers in 1998, delivering a $15 million profit to the then-governor of Texas. Shortly thereafter the Hicks brothers sold their radio company, AMFM, to Clear Channel for $24 billion.

It's preposterous to think that any single media entity has control of what people see or hear," concludes Randall Mays. "It could have been possible thirty or forty years ago, but because there are so many other places to get the news throughout the day, it's impossible for any one entity to have that kind of influence. This whole perception of our company's power is totally distorted. We simply have advocacy groups that were so opposed to media concentration that they created stories to promote their beliefs."

POLITICAL TALK RADIO

There's a pervasive perception that talk radio in America has leaned considerably right of center over the past two decades. The successes of such talk show hosts as Rush Limbaugh, Sean Hannity, Glenn Beck, Michael Savage, Laura Ingraham, and even Dr. Laura Schlessinger have fed this perception. Millions of listeners each week tune religiously to radio programs (and personalities) that promote conservative American values and devoutly faith-based viewpoints, while castigating those who embrace decidedly more liberal positions, wide-ranging religious beliefs, and/or alternative lifestyles.

The fact is, radio hasn't always been that way. In the days prior to Rush Limbaugh's talk radio renaissance in Sacramento in 1988, there arguably were more nationally recognized liberal voices on the radio than conservative. Such stations as KABC Los Angeles, WOR New York, WGN Chicago, and KOA in Denver all had enormous audiences primarily because of programming that attracted listeners from the left side of the dial.

Then a former rock and roll disk jockey with a stridently (some might say obnoxious) right-wing point of view hit talk radio, and almost single-handedly rescued the AM band from a near-death experience.

"If anything, until Rush Limbaugh came along, liberals had a near lock on being funny and entertaining about politics," says former Air America Radio President Gary Krantz. "But they were comedians such as George Carlin and Robert Klein, or the cast of *Saturday Night Live*. Beginning in 1988 Rush ushered in the concept that talk hosts can be advocates. After him, the proliferation of conservative talkers grew because radio tends to clone, not counter-program. Until Air America, specifically Al Franken, Randi Rhodes, and Janeane Garafalo, there were few who could cross over to the other side of the aisle successfully, after several previous attempts at 'liberal talk' that did not succeed."

"The radio industry describes Rush Limbaugh's success as overnight, but it wasn't," says Clear Channel's top talk programmer Gabe Hobbs. "It took about three years for him to catch on, but within that time frame he became a gigantic hit — the biggest thing to hit the airwaves since Walter Winchell."

Within months, dozens — possibly hundreds — of Rush wannabes also took to the air, effectively careening the political talk radio format to the right. "A lot of managers looked at what Rush was doing and said, 'Holy cow, that's the formula,'" Hobbs recalls. "And they started hiring guys who could take a conservative stance. Now, most of them weren't any good, and certainly none of them was as entertaining as Rush."

"Conservative talk radio has worked very well because, for a long time, there were very few places where a person with a conservative mindset could go and find a mirror that would help them recognize and explain their political beliefs," adds Kraig Kitchin, former president of Premiere Radio Networks. "Talk radio is one of the few places — in addition to magazines like the *National Review* and the *Washington Times* — that really mirror the thinking of a lot of people who were conservative."

"The great ones make it look easy, but it's not about political ideology," observes John Hogan. "It's about their ability to connect with an audience. It's about their ability to put in the time, the energy, the effort, and the passion to be interesting and compelling, every single day of the week. It's a mistake to think that somebody can come in and, simply because they have a political position, be as successful as someone who has polished his or her on-air presentation. That's a mistake that the progressive people have made, as well as other conservative folks who have wanted to get into radio."

Most talk programmers still say an answer to why talk radio veered right remains elusive — though it is clear that the political left did not respond to Rush's inroads. Certainly, there were attempts, with such personalities as former New York Governor Mario Cuomo and Texas Representative Jim Hightower. But other than some steadfast liberal constituents who loyally tuned in every day to hear the left jab at the right, these hosts gained little traction on radio.

Critics who suggest that talk stations should follow Rush Limbaugh or Michael Savage with Al Franken or Ed Schultz in order to balance the programming lack an understanding of basic radio programming. Just as Top 40, country, or jazz listeners tune in to a specific station to hear a particular genre of music, talk radio listeners tune in to their favorite station because they know what they will get. The primary objective of any radio programmer is to build the station's ratings, and that is done by attracting and keeping an audience for a long period of time.

Ratings generally are measured two ways: "cume" listening, or the raw number of individuals who listen to a station during a certain period; and average quarter hour (AQH) listening, roughly defined as the percentage of overall radio listeners who are tuned in to a specific station during any fifteen-minute period. The way to boost a station's AQH is to expand its "time spent listening," meaning the amount of time a person listens to that station during a given day.

This is why stations that lean toward a political talk format generally broadcast one kind of programming. A station that carries a complete conservative slate of such hosts as Rush Limbaugh, Michael Savage, Laura Ingraham, and Sean Hannity is much more likely to deliver greater "time spent listening" than a station that chases listeners who don't want to hear a program that offends their political or social sensibilities. Thus, Ed Schultz would stand a good chance of driving Rush Limbaugh listeners right into a straightjacket, just as Michael Savage would probably send Al Franken listeners in search of a hot, cleansing shower.

The lack of liberal/progressive talk programming on the radio so concerned North Dakota Senator Byron Dorgan that he invited Lowry Mays to Washington to speak to the Democratic caucus about starting a liberal talk radio network. "I told him that it just wouldn't work," Lowry recalls. "I explained that liberals had been tried on the radio, but people just don't listen. He said that they 'listen to Rush Limbaugh and the bag of lies he tells every day.' Well, it turns out that we had two hosts — one in North Dakota, Ed Schultz, and Randi Rhodes in West Palm Beach — and I said to Senator Dorgan, 'We'll try to find them a spot.'"

Lowry says he had a similar conversation with Air America, which was convinced that because Clear Channel owned over 1,200 radio stations he could put a progressive format on wherever he decided to. "I had to explain that our local managers run those stations, not me," he says. "I'm not going to tell them how to program. But instead of listening to what I was saying, a lot of people assumed that I wouldn't put that programming on the air because I had some sort of agenda to support Bush. They even called me the father of conservative talk radio."

"Prior to 2004 I had been trying to figure out how to do a left-of-center talk radio, or as we now call it, progressive talk radio," says Clear Channel's Hobbs. "Then Air America came along twenty-four hours, seven days a week, and suddenly I saw something I could use as a backbone for a new kind of talk radio station."

"Clear Channel has been extremely supportive," says Gary Krantz. "They were among the early adopters of the format. In every single case they have preceded the format switch with solid research to identify the audience hole, and Gabe Hobbs has identified a very simple formula that says that if a market has an NPR affiliate, a college or university, and is a state capital, the likelihood of a successful progressive talk format is very high."

Clear Channel now has a couple dozen progressive stations on the air, some of which have done sufficiently well, but not all have yet to pull the same audience numbers that long-time conservative stations enjoy. Many stations that Clear Channel converted to progressive talk were doing so poorly before the format switch that they can't help but perform better. Still, because of the widespread perception that Clear Channel is inherently conservative, Hobbs frequently is asked whether he personally is "red" or "blue." "What I tell them is that when it comes to radio, I'm green," he laughs.

CHAPTER ELEVEN

THE STORM OF THE CENTURY

ON THE MORNING OF AUGUST 24, 2005, A TROPICAL SYSTEM THAT HAD BEEN lingering around the Bahamas began to pick up enough strength to be given a name: Tropical Storm Katrina. The following day, after churning around in the Atlantic, Katrina set her sights west toward southern Florida, initially with only minimal Category 1 hurricane-force winds. Millions of weather-weary Floridians braced themselves for yet another storm, but the National Hurricane Center suggested that the most they should expect was a lot of rain and some gale-force winds. At that point, as storm shutters were being nailed up and tarp-covered roofs were being tied down, there was no real hint that Katrina soon would become a monster.

Katrina tracked to the west overnight and crossed the state of Florida in just six hours. By midnight of August 26, the weather system had nearly doubled in size and the strong tropospheric ridge that so far had kept the hurricane on a west-southwestwardly track began to shift eastward, causing the hurricane to turn northwest the next day, August 28. At that point Katrina strengthened from a low-end Category 3 hurricane to a Category 5 in less than 12 hours, reaching an intensity of 169 mph by midday. The storm attained its peak intensity of 174 mph that evening when it was about 170 nautical miles southeast of the mouth of the Mississippi.

During the evening, Katrina's eyewall contracted and an outer ring of convection consolidated, causing the storm to lose strength. Early the following morning, August 29, Katrina turned to the north and made landfall near the town of Buras in southern Louisiana as a strong Category 3 hurricane with maximum sustained winds of 127 mph. The storm continued to barrel inland on a path that took it almost directly over the city of New Orleans. Despite its rapid weakening, "Katrina was an extraordinarily powerful and deadly hurricane that carved a wide swath of catastrophic damage and inflicted large loss of life," according to an NHC summary prepared by Richard D. Knabb, Jamie R. Rhome, and Daniel P. Brown and released on December 20, 2005. "It was the costliest and one of the five deadliest hurricanes to ever strike the United States. The damage and loss of life inflicted by this massive hurricane in Louisiana and Mississippi were staggering, with significant effects extending into the Florida panhandle, Georgia, and Alabama. Considering the scope of its impacts, Katrina was one of the most devastating natural disasters in United States history."

By now the sights and sounds of the devastation that Hurricane Katrina turned loose on the Gulf Coast area are familiar to most Americans. Sewage-tainted flood waters two stories deep. Decaying bodies in the streets. Refugees standing on rooftops hoping to be rescued by passing boats or helicopters. Rescue workers waiting for authorities and supplies that inexcusably were late to arrive. Angry finger-pointing and blame-storming while politicians were staging photo ops and backpedaling. But back in the early hours and days of this disaster, it is well-documented that virtually the only positive response to come out of this mess was that of local radio broadcasters. Even as studios were flooding, power lines were snapping, and transmitters were popping like gunfire, a dedicated coalition of broadcasters illustrated radio's reciprocal bond with the local communities it serves. From helping to save families stranded in their homes, to providing accurate accounts of the devastation, to serving as a mouthpiece for government officials solving problems or lambasting others for their ineffectiveness, an ad hoc group of broadcasters formed by Clear Channel and Entercom singularly served the residents of southern Louisiana and outlying areas of the Gulf Coast. These usually competitive radio groups both were hard-hit, losing their respective signals within hours of the storm's arrival, but an overwhelming commitment to their collective listeners induced the two rivals to join forces and work together during the days and weeks to come.

Collectively known as the United Radio Broadcasters of New Orleans, this "broadcast cooperative" worked against great odds to broadcast news and information to a widespread audience that had lost just about everything — except hope. The makeshift signal broadcast by URBNO provided the only communications link that many individuals — victims and first responders alike — had with the outside world. With electricity non-existent, phones down, shortwave communications failing, and all other media dark, radio was up and running.

Central to this dedicated group of men and women — some of whom had lost their entire homes — was Dick Lewis, market manager for Clear Channel's Baton Rouge stations and regional vice president overseeing the company's New Orleans, Shreveport, Alexandria, and Biloxi operations. "When I think back about the Katrina experience, it was the people who made the difference. I was privileged to be with some really good, dedicated, smart and talented people. I saw the difference between average and exceptional. When the real test came, our folks were ready and able to perform. They did so at the highest level of professionalism. It was awesome. I am very proud of them and of what radio accomplished."

Lewis was more prepared than most to deal with a storm as destructive as Katrina. Many years earlier, at age eight, he and his family were driving through northeast Oklahoma when they encountered a powerful tornado, up close and personal. Lewis recalls, "When I am asked how I got into radio I always remember the time WKY radio was the only sanity in the world. I was about eight years old. I grew up in Oklahoma's tornado alley. My mom, younger brother and I were in the Woodward area heading home to Paul's Valley when the sky turned inky black in the middle of the afternoon. Soon the only thing you could see was a dull glow from the headlights and then the noise started, a low roar moving our way. My mom thought she might have to stop on the railroad tracks, so we were looking for a train's headlights. The train never came. Instead, the car bounced like a basketball. The roar was deafening. In that panic, when fear filled the car, the only sanity was WKY radio telling us where the storm was, where it was moving and most important to me, how fast it was moving. That day I remember thinking, 'Gosh, I would like to be in radio some day. I would like to be the voice of sanity.' At 13, I started my radio career at KVLH in Paul's Valley."

That life choice took Lewis on a circuitous route to Baton Rouge, where he was positioned not only to experience Katrina's wrath firsthand, but also more than prepared to deal with the almost total devastation that followed in its wake. Lewis said, "Damage to Baton Rouge was minimal beyond fallen trees and branches. The downed trees and limbs took power lines with them, so virtually all of the city was without power for a period of time. Thankfully, Clear Channel is committed to being prepared for the worst. As soon as power was lost at the studio, the transmitter generators fired up. Dedicated generators allow us to continue to serve the community. While it sounds like everything ran smoothly, that wasn't the case. We had the needed equipment, but even with all of our preparedness plans, nothing ever prepared us for Katrina. For instance, we never envisioned a situation that took the studio, STL, and central hub out of action for weeks and months. We were forced to evacuate our facility to keep our employees safe. We had to create a new plan, based on the horrific reality of the situation at hand."

Certainly, Lewis was not alone in his commitment and dedication to the people of southern Louisiana. In fact the United Radio Broadcasters of New Orleans was the combined brainchild of Clear Channel Vice President of News Programming Gabe Hobbs and his counterpart, Ken Beck, Vice President of News/Talk Sports at Entercom, a radio and television broadcasting company based in Bala Cynwyd, Pennsylvania. When it became obvious that the rising water in New Orleans would quickly force an evacuation of both companies' studios, Beck and Hobbs worked out a temporary "broadcast merger" in two quick phone calls. "Right after the storm had passed, Ken gave me a call at home and said, "Is there something we should be doing together?"' Hobbs says. "And I told him, 'Funny you should ask, because I was just kicking around this idea of United Radio Broadcasters of New Orleans, where we all pool our resources — engineering, programming, sticks, whatever we have — and produce one information stream.' The idea was to put it on AM, FM, the Internet, and offer it free of charge to anyone who wanted it."

Both programmers saw the concept as a "no-brainer," so a plan was put in motion to bring certain elements of both companies together. Since both groups evacuated their New Orleans facilities and some station employees had yet to be located, it was decided that the team would move into Clear Channel's Baton Rouge studios, creating a pool of reporters who would work in concert to deliver the news around the clock. Entercom provided WWL emergency programming, coupled with its news and emergency response experience in the New Orleans market, while Clear Channel offered Baton Rouge studio space for the entire operation.

"We've had a lot of practice over the last year alone, with six or seven major storms coming ashore," Hobbs observes. "FEMA should come watch what we do. We have standby parts and transmitters and fuel trucks all poised in hub markets like Atlanta and Tampa, ready to drive in as the storm abates. We had studios and facilities in Baton Rouge, and we had a helicopter, an amphibious vehicle, and some other assets to get engineers in and out of some transmitter sites."

In the early days of the disaster, the combined news product was being transmitted to three area radio stations: WWL, WSMB, and WLMG. "Clear Channel and Entercom staffers worked side by side under pretty cramped conditions," Ken Beck recounts. "Staffers who could not live at home or nearby were housed in RVs parked around the building." He says that many employees initially had lost touch with their families, and worked even while they had no word on whether their spouses, children, and parents were safe. "Staffs from both companies bore this well and were dedicated to getting these critical broadcasts out to the New Orleans and Gulf Coast areas," he notes.

Still, it was Clear Channel's Lewis who kept the joint broadcasting effort up and running, particularly in the early days of Katrina's widespread destruction. When it became apparent that all the disaster plans that were established in the calm before the storm weren't going to work, alternative arrangements to remain on the air had to be developed quickly. Lewis says that it was apparent on Sunday, the day before Katrina made landfall, that Clear Channel likely would lose its New Orleans facility. "We never envisioned a plan that did not depend on the main studio hub. Sunday midday as the storm began to move in, we discovered we didn't have full control over all of our New Orleans stations. Normally, you would call an engineer and they would flip the right switch, work their magic, and it would all function properly. However, there was no one in the New Orleans studios. To protect our people I issued an evacuation order at 10 that morning, so the physical plant was empty. The next best thing was to get an engineer to the studio so Richard Perry, chief engineer of our Baton Rouge stations, and I climbed in my Hummer and headed to New Orleans. That was not my best idea. About halfway to New Orleans, wind gusts were strong enough to blow the Hummer across the road. Our best option was to get to safety and figure a different way to control the stations."

That's when things quit functioning. "Nothing or at least very little of what we expected to happen actually happened," Lewis recounts. "I can still hear the words of Troy Langham, Clear Channel corporate engineering SVP: 'Don't depend on systems and equipment to work when you need them to if you don't use them regularly.' At this point we knew all of our plans were toast. In order to stay on the air, serve the community, provide lifesaving information that only radio can provide, we would have to improvise on the fly. All of the best intentions won't do much good unless you have the equipment and the great minds. Thankfully, Clear Channel is well stocked with both." As the storm edged in over southern Louisiana, Lewis had to turn off the stations, which is an abomination to any career radio broadcaster. And as the stations went dark, he and his staff immediately tried to figure out how to get them back on as quickly as possible after the storm blew through. Of course, at that point no one really had any clear realization of just how extensive the damage would be, nor of the scope of the subsequent evacuation. Lewis says, "In the early hours of the storm, we had all seven stations on the air but only controlled the audio source on five of them. It is difficult for a broadcaster to decide to turn off a perfectly good transmitter, but that is what we decided to do until we could get a dedicated audio tram to the transmitter. This was the beginning of improvisation."

"I chartered a helicopter and for the next few days we transported engineers and equipment to the sites. What made Katrina different from New Orleans was our conditions actually got worse after the storm passed. The usual scenario is that you hunker down for the few hours for the storm and then it is over and you go about doing the repairs. Once Katrina passed New Orleans, instead of the expected improvement in the situation, the levees broke, the flood came, and instead of breathing a sigh of relief, people were challenged for their very survival. And the only information going into the city was coming from radio. We had to make it work."

Lewis says that the only way he could broadcast without using the New Orleans studios was to realign the satellite dishes, but in order to get a data stream to those dishes, he needed something he didn't have. About 2 o'clock the following morning, Lewis and an engineer were discussing their few options, when Lewis suggested using DirecTV dishes. They were small and could be transported to the transmitter site, which by then was well under water. For the next twelve hours, between 2:00 a.m. and 2:00 p.m., Lewis and his engineering crew constructed an entirely new delivery system that streamed the broadcast signal via the Internet to an uplink in Cheyenne, Wyoming. The signal was then transmitted to DirecTV's satellite in geosynchronous orbit, and bounced back down to dish antennas that meanwhile had been installed at the transmitter site. Lewis credits lack of sleep and a crisis-based thought process for coming up with a concept that was well outside the box. "What is the saying about necessity being the mother of invention? We had working transmitters but no distribution network. At one point we were daisy-chaining the audio from WFMF in Baton Rouge to 104.1 in Vacherie, then picking up the signal on a transistor radio with nothing but a Sure microphone wired as the audio input at 93.3. It worked but it was not reliable or dependable. In the wee hours of the morning [seems like a lot of the best ideas surfaced in the late night and early morning hours], Troy Langham and I were trying to figure out a way to get satellite down links at the transmitter sites. Our only means of transportation was helicopter, so getting a 10-foot dish was out of the question. I asked Troy about DirecTV. The dishes are small, the equipment package is light, so why couldn't we wire them into the transmitters, I thought? Troy said if I could get the dishes to the site he would find a way to get the audio to them. Troy knew somebody who knew somebody, and by two o'clock the next afternoon we were operational. The United Radio Broadcasters of New Orleans signal originated from the Clear Channel studio in Baton Rouge and was put on a dedicated broadband circuit to a DirecTV uplink in Cheyenne, Wyoming, then back to our transmitters. It worked. It was robust. It saved lives. Keep in mind that time was the enemy. With every passing minute, the flood waters grew deeper. Uncertainty abounded. No one knew what would happen next".

As night fell over New Orleans, residents began to understand the full extent of what had happened to their beloved city. Lewis says, "New Orleans was a city without any electrical power. Think about it: The fourth largest city in America dark at night. No lights, no hum from the air conditioner, no television or Internet. And for many, no hope except what we put on the radio. Radio may be taken for granted during good times, but in times of disaster, radio is your only lifeline. In the Clear Channel studio in Baton Rouge, the engineers in one night built a studio suite for United Radio. We invited Entercom to join us in Baton Rouge. Their New Orleans studio was damaged beyond use. In fact, many Entercom employees were stranded in their studios. We used the Clear Channel helicopter to rescue them and carry them to safety. So during a crisis of Biblical proportion, the front line reporters and responders had to live through it and care for their families, friends, and homes, all the while being responsible and professional in order to carry out lifesaving duties for the community at large. What a time — I saw the best and the worst in people."

As the concept of the United Radio Broadcasters of New Orleans was put into motion, Clear Channel rushed in engineers with tons of equipment. "Clear Channel moved fast to bring in enough equipment to start five radio stations—supplies, material, exceptionally talented manpower from engineers and IT pros, to fuel haulers, reporters and on-air hosts," Lewis says. "They brought in multiple spares of everything you could think of. Our parking lot in Baton Rouge was filled with 18-wheelers, vehicles filled with supplies, station vans, all-terrain vehicles, you name it; it looked like something out of an episode of M*A*S*H. WJBO, Clear Channel's news/talk station in Baton Rouge, has a studio, and we were in the process of building a new studio and control room. The new studio and control room were nowhere near completion, and none of the wiring had been installed, but from five o'clock that night until three the next morning, we constructed that studio and built the framework for United Radio Broadcasters of New Orleans. We were on the air at three o'clock Wednesday morning."

Lewis recalls, "I remember working for Dynamic Broadcasting years ago before consolidation. A hurricane hit our station in Corpus Christi. The company didn't have the money to cope. So there was no assistance. Instead, the company had to shut down Corpus Christi's operations, close the news department, and fire lots of folks just to keep the door open. Thankfully, that isn't the case today. Before Katrina's winds were completely gone, Clear Channel had supplies and replacement parts and people arriving in Baton Rouge. I mentioned that Baton Rouge didn't have power, so one of the great sights was a refrigerated 18-wheeler Clear Channel brought in, loaded with milk, ice, water, food, things you couldn't get in Baton Rouge. The next truck had dozens and dozens of small generators. These were loaned out to anyone who needed them."

"Our facilities in Baton Rouge became sort of a tent city, with all the motor homes and trucks and food," says Clear Channel Executive Vice-President of Distribution Development Jeff Littlejohn. "We had planned this through real trials, and we had gone through several hurricanes in Florida the year before. We watch these hurricanes and try to guess where they're going to go, and then we stage all our equipment and supplies in Jackson, Atlanta, Charlotte, and Houston. So as soon as the storm went through and the roads were open, we were able to get in there and start establishing our radio stations."

As the make-shift broadcasting unit went on the air, it was critical not only to team up a Clear Channel reporter with an Entercom reporter, but also to have at least one person from New Orleans broadcasting at all times. Lewis says, "National television got a lot wrong in the early days of the storm. For example, CNN would show footage of a fire and it would be mislabeled because they didn't have detailed information," Lewis recalls. "That coverage was not local. Our people were local, and we were the primary source of news. If it happened in Louisiana, it was likely reported by United Radio, and was disseminated to other news sources out of our stations in Baton Rouge. This was a life-and-death mission for us, and our engineers in particular went through nine kinds of hell to keep the stations up and running. This was a joint effort of Clear Channel and Entercom and it saved lives and sustained hope for many when there was little hope to be found."

That combined effort initially lasted two weeks before both companies began to peel radio stations away and return to regular programming. Part of this was due to technical reasons, since both companies developed the ability to generate and carry independent program streams, and part of it was that URBNO knew that people inside New Orleans needed some entertainment relief in addition to a steady stream of news and information. About three weeks after Katrina the combined group was down to one Entercom AM, and a Clear Channel AM and FM. The following week the remaining stations returned to their usual on-air content.

On a corporate level, both Clear Channel Radio CEO John Hogan and Entercom CEO David Field were completely behind the plan from the start, to the point where Hobbs and Beck were told not to worry about the financial aspects of the "merger." "That meant that when Ken and I would talk we didn't have to get into any of this 'we'll pay for this if you pay for that,'" Gabe Hobbs said at the time. "We just did it, and those guys could work out who pays for it. That took the pressure off right away."

To Lewis, the experience of pulling together such a disparate band of broadcasters, many of whom had lost everything they owned, was one that speaks to the true nature of radio and its commitment to community service. "It has forever changed me and my thinking. The world is captivated by the Internet, by satellite radio, the iPod and other new technologies. All of these have a place, but it is a fair-weather place. Disaster is a local event. It's local homes and families, cities, towns and streets with names only a local person can know. In these times when the power is out, the TV is dark, satellite radio is babbling inane trivia, and computer monitors are blank and Internet streams silent, local radio is the one and only lifeline you can depend on. How fortunate I am to be part of a company that fully appreciates the enormous responsibility we have to our communities."

"This was one of the easiest calls I've ever had to make," Hobbs observes, speaking of the joint decision with Entercom to form URBNO. "The interesting thing is, before consolidation, the only thing that would have been on the air was silence. It physically would not have been possible to bring these kinds of resources together. Entercom was able to fly in news people from all of their other markets, and we have a triage crew that works specifically for hurricanes. We have massive stores of fuel, spare antennas, satellite dishes, and trucks that we were able to bring in and make this run smoothly. It just wouldn't make economic sense for a small company that owns eight or ten stations to own fuel depots in the Southeast in case of a hurricane, or to own a fleet of trucks, or to have a warehouse full of spare satellite dishes or antennas. But we have lots of resources, plus we have perhaps the best plan in the nation for doing this sort of thing. No one can come close to matching the resources that we can bring to bear."

Don't even try suggesting to Hobbs that radio news coverage has diminished under industry consolidation. With approximately 200 news stations in 156 markets within the Clear Channel sphere, Hobbs says that the company's ability to respond to emergencies and provide relevant data to listeners has never been stronger. Certainly, critics will trot out statistics that suggest that news coverage of local community issues has tapered off over the years, and there is some evidence to support this fact. But as Hobbs points out, most of that decrease came years earlier when the FCC eliminated a number of previous regulations related to news and public affairs programming.

"A number of uneducated observers blame consolidation for the decrease in radio news, and that's hogwash," Hobbs says. "They don't realize that the FCC began to deregulate in the early '80s, and dropped the rule that said a certain percentage of programming had to be information and public affairs. It was at that point that FM music stations began to jettison their news departments. This was fifteen years before the Telecom Act was passed. All of a sudden, Top 40 stations and rock stations stopped doing news, or they began to merely just offer a couple of minutes of headlines during morning drive."

In fact, Hobbs says that consolidation has allowed Clear Channel — and some other radio companies — actually to provide more extensive coverage of local news than prior to deregulation. "Frankly, the bigger we have gotten, the better we have become at providing news and information," he observes. "The quantity and quality of our news product has increased with the size of the company, to the point where we've outgrown mainstream networks. We have a larger infrastructure than they do, and in fact we provide them with a good amount of coverage." One example of this came on the morning of February 1, 2003, when the space shuttle Columbia broke up upon re-entry into Texas. "That was a Saturday morning, and because we own stations all across the states of Texas, Louisiana, and Florida we had reporters in the debris field within minutes. We had a reporter at the Johnson Space Center in Houston, we had a reporter at the Kennedy Space Center in Cape Canaveral, and we had anchor desks in Houston and Tampa feeding this information out."

Clear Channel's primary network news affiliate at the time was ABC Radio Networks, but because that company had no reporters in the field until later in the day, Hobbs says that what the network fed Saturday morning into early afternoon was Clear Channel's coverage. "We were ABC that day, until they could get their people in place, and even after that, they still relied heavily on us," he notes.

Clear Channel's newsgathering operations are set up very much the same as the programming departments at its music stations, Hobbs says. Each news/talk station has its own news department, and the news directors at each of these stations answer to their local program directors who, in turn, report to regional programmers. "We do have a national news operation in Chicago, but it has no oversight authority over local programming," he explains. "They exist merely to provide assets and to coordinate coverage between markets on those stories whose interest extends beyond the local market." One of the earliest stories that this national network covered was the news that professional golfer Paine Stewart's private jet was flying hundreds of miles off course and likely was going to crash. "We knew about this ahead of time, so we called our station in Bismarck and told them to get someone in a car, have them start driving south, and we'd tell them when and where the plane went down." As tragic as this story turned out to be, it exemplifies the on-the-spot commitment of Clear Channel's post-consolidation news organization.

Hobbs insists that another advantage of consolidation is the ability to bring news-gathering resources to smaller markets that wouldn't otherwise have access. "Take Toledo, Ohio, for example," he says. "We have a twenty-four hour, seven-day-a-week live news operation there. Now, we import some of our news product from Columbus, primarily the late-night, overnight, and weekend newscasts. But we also have news reporters on the ground in Toledo who feed the Columbus hub. For the first time in history, Toledo has a 24/7 news operation, something they never had before consolidation because the economics just didn't make sense." Hobbs stresses that, contrary to what some critics maintain, local news in Toledo — and other Clear Channel markets — is just that: local. "We're not importing the news from Los Angeles," he says. "It's coming from Columbus, and they're working with the local reporters whom we employ in Toledo. Some are newspaper reporters, and some are in television, so our local stations have access to a live local newscast — not a network newscast — around the clock."

CHAPTER TWELVE

SERVICE TO THE COMMUNITY

IN 2005 U.S. RADIO AND TELEVISION COMPANIES CONTRIBUTED MORE THAN $10.3 billion, both in financial contributions and on-air promotional time. If there is a local cause or charity, usually a radio station is right there, doing whatever it can to provide support, either on the air or on the ground. As Clear Channel's Chief Communications Officer Lisa Dollinger says, "The goal of radio is to super-serve listeners. That's our responsibility, and if we can deliver those listeners, we can attract advertisers and help drive their businesses. A lot of people take radio for granted and don't fully appreciate the function of radio stations in local communities. From serving communities during disasters, to raising funds, to raising awareness, and providing all sorts of volunteerism — radio does so many great things for local communities. Most of the time radio people do what they do but they never say a word about it. There are so many great stories — not just at Clear Channel, but through-out the radio industry — of what local stations are doing to help their com-munities, and that's a message that can sometimes get lost in translation."

The aftermath of Hurricane Katrina probably provides the best glimpse of radio's — and Clear Channel's — commitment to the local communities they serve. The communication lifeline provided by the United Radio Broadcasters of New Orleans already has been recounted (please see

Chapter 11), but the radio industry's commitment to provide assistance to those who were most severely affected by the storm extended for months after the disaster. As soon as the flood waters began streaming into New Orleans' 9th ward, many radio companies and their stations initiated on-air pleas for their listeners to pitch in and help. During this period Clear Channel coordinated a cross-divisional program designed to take advantage of the company's massive size and reach. In the two months following the hurricane, the program generated more than $65 million, with funds coming from employee donations, benefit concerts and relief drives, radiothons and telethons asking for critical supplies including food, water and clothing collected by Clear Channel radio and television stations. Additionally, there were celebrity public service announcements recorded by and aired on most Clear Channel radio and television stations across the country, and billboard space encouraging support of the American Red Cross and Clear Channel's website, StormAid.com.

"What happened in the aftermath of Katrina shows the power and the passion of our people," observes Dollinger. "It also shows what a consolidated media company such as Clear Channel can do for communities and people during times of great peril. The $65 million we raised went to the Red Cross, the Salvation Army, Habitat for Humanity, and various other local relief organizations. Whether it was food, water, diapers, or clothes, many of our stations actually drove trucks down to affected areas to deliver these goods."

Dollinger insists that the resources that Clear Channel was able to marshal and to apply to those communities in a very quick and efficient manner could never have been done prior to consolidation. "The word 'hero' is thrown around far too casually these days, but these individuals within the company — especially our engineers, who were on the front lines — were truly heroic," she says. "They risked their own lives to ensure that diesel fuel got to the affected areas so the generators could keep running and the stations could keep people informed. When nothing else worked — when the television didn't work and the Internet didn't work — radio was a vital link to the community. We had disk jockeys who were talking to people in New Orleans who were trying to get out of their homes to get onto their roofs, and those DJs never in a million years thought they would have to tell them how to climb out the window onto their roof, or how to unhinge the front door and use it as a life raft." In order to keep its emergency generators working, even when FEMA showed its inadequacies, Clear Channel was able to tap into diesel fuel reserves that were stored by the Outdoor division in Florida and deliver it to Biloxi or Baton Rouge. The Outdoor division even sent used advertising "vinyls" to affected areas so people could use them as temporary roofing materials.

Speaking before the Progress and Freedom Foundation in October 2005, Mark Mays noted that "the past five weeks have given us enormous clarity on free radio's vital role in our local communities. Radio was, literally, the lifeline to thousands who were trapped in the flood waters along the Gulf Coast. It was free radio professionals who opened impassible roads and waded through life-threatening waters to restore broadcasts. It was free radio that dispatched rescue workers to people trying to escape rising water by climbing onto their roofs. It was free radio that delivered life-saving information from local authorities to citizens, including where to get water and food and ice. And it was free radio that put aside corporate affiliations to combine resources and staffs to create an unprecedented 24/7 joint broadcast that saved peoples' lives. When the electricity didn't work, when television didn't work, when the Internet didn't work, when pay radio didn't work, free radio worked."

Also in 2005, Clear Channel stations donated airtime valued at $160 million in support of The Advertising Council's many and varied public service advertising campaigns — the largest contribution of advertising time and space from any media company in the organization's history. "Clear Channel has set an example for the radio, outdoor and television industries in terms of planning support and running campaigns that are important and relevant to their audiences," said Peggy Conlon, president and chief executive officer of The Advertising Council. "The company's ongoing commitment to our organization and our messages is an indication of how Clear Channel values its relationship with its audiences and embraces public service."

"Providing resources to extend the reach of the important messages communicated through the Ad Council's PSAs is a social obligation that Clear Channel embraces," adds Mark Mays. "It is an example of how the company's local business model works to support communities. We are proud to be furthering our collaborative public service efforts with the Ad Council and hope to motivate Americans to take action."

While virtually all of Clear Channel's local businesses are heavily involved in specific causes and charitable groups, the company has no corporate dictate governing which organizations they should support. "The very foundation of our business model for radio, television, and outdoor rests on local connections and local community service," Dollinger observes. "Becoming an integral part of the local market through service is critical to maintaining that connection, and our people do that by staying in close touch with the community in which they live and work and send their children to school everyday. As a result they become intimately aware of the local communities' needs, so if there is a need for a children's wing in the local hospital, they step up and take a leadership role in filling that need."

Radio stations, and the people who work there, are ingrained with the notion of local service, and they often are the first in the market to swing into action, raising funds and awareness, recruiting volunteers — whatever is necessary to serve the unique needs of that community. As a result, Dollinger says, "Community service within Clear Channel is not just something we do because it's good business, which it is, but it is at the very heart of who we are as a company. With radio being the local business it is, we have to know who our listeners are. We have to know what their needs are, and we have to be able to connect with them and give them what they want every day of the week. We usually do this with our programming so they become raving fanatics for our local brands, and to keep them coming back each and every day to listen to those stations. That, in turn, provides a compelling product for our advertisers, which is how we sustain the business. But it all begins and ends with that local connectivity."

Ironically, the various services provided by radio stations often go almost unnoticed within those communities because the employees involved either don't trumpet their efforts, or because local media outlets — specifically television stations and newspapers — prefer not to draw attention to their local competition. As a result, if a station raises $100,000 for Hurricane Katrina victims, that relief effort usually goes unnoticed except possibly for a brief mention in a trade publication or at a local Rotary dinner. "Unfortunately in this day and age it's not enough just to do good work; you have to tell people about it," Dollinger points out. "Radio's history is rich with community service, and radio people have a real passion for what they do. So over the last few years we've tried to open up the lines of communication between our stations and our outdoor businesses, and let them identify for us what causes and charitable organizations they are doing the most for."

To help draw attention to the many organizations with which Clear Channel businesses work on a local market level, the company began a program known as Clear Channel Local Spirit. The purpose of this program, Dollinger says, is to offer information on and resources from those organizations, via the company's websites and the employee intranet. "We have a mechanism called the PSA Highway, where we allow any 401(c)3 nonprofit organization to post or upload its public service announcements," she says. "This way our media properties can have full access to those and use them as appropriate in their communities. This also allows us and the individual organizations to see what they and our properties have done."

Case in point: St. Jude's Children's Hospital, which over the years was cognizant of Clear Channel's fundraising efforts on the local level, but had never been able to provide a full accounting of the resources, funds, and free airtime that the company's stations had provided every year. "St. Jude's was aware that our individual radio stations and media businesses were doing incredible things for them each year, in terms of raising funds, providing PSAs and promotional time, and conducting telethons, radiothons, and special events," Dollinger says. "But at the corporate level we didn't know what that number looked like. They helped us aggregate it, and it was an amazing number, $7.7 million; in fact, it was so much more than they had ever seen from an organization that they awarded us with St. Jude's first ever recognition medal."

Similarly, the National Multiple Sclerosis Society in 2006 recognized Clear Channel for all the work the company has done to raise awareness and generate funds for research. "Our Outdoor division and radio and television stations all devoted millions of dollars in airtime and board space to promote a campaign called 'The Face of MS,'" Dollinger says. "We not only gave them a voice through our media properties, but our Creative Services Group worked with them to help create better, more effective, more compelling radio spots. Meanwhile, the creative people within our Outdoor division helped them make the most effective use of the medium." Other organizations for which Clear Channel has provided resources, airtime, volunteers, and creative assistance include the American Heart Association, the March of Dimes, Habitat for Humanity, the Salvation Army, the Red Cross, and UNICEF.

Additionally, the company's relief fund website, StormAid.com, has been used to raise money for relief efforts for victims of the 2005 tsunami in southeast Asia as well as victims of Hurricanes Katrina and Rita. "We actually were honored by the U.S. Library of Congress for that website," Dollinger notes. "While we still have billboards asking people to go to StormAid.com to donate to the Red Cross, it all comes down to the community. Our local managers make all the decisions about what organizations they're going to raise money for. We recognize that, and the important thing for us at the corporate level is to provide resources and support for those activities and those organizations in need. That said, in 2005 alone, Clear Channel's total philanthropic contributions totaled over $1 billion."

THE MAYS FAMILY

Of course, no company is any stronger than its cornerstone, and in the case of Clear Channel one need look no farther than Lowry Mays. As the original "accidental broadcaster," Mays is best known for taking one under-powered and under-funded San Antonio FM station and turning that enterprise into the world's largest radio broadcasting company. At the peak of Clear Channel's acquisition activity he was putting in 60-80 hour work weeks, shaping legislative and regulatory policy, and using his business acumen to amass the largest group of radio stations and billboards in the world. Still, throughout this frenetic period, he managed to find enough hours in the day to relax on his 2,000-acre ranch north of San Antonio and unwind with his wife and family among his longhorn cattle, zebra, and African bongos — a species of antelope recognized by its large curving horns and striped hides. He also found the time — along with his wife, Peggy — to remain active within the San Antonio community, working both with local charitable causes as well as other endeavors in the state of Texas and throughout the U.S. As noted previously, he has served as past chairman of the Texas A&M University board of regents, is the past chairman of the United Way of San Antonio, and has held a leadership role at numerous other civic organizations.

Lowry Mays' connection with Texas A&M extends back to when he was an undergraduate there, and he says he was profoundly honored when former Texas Democratic Governor Mark White appointed him to the university's board of regents in 1986. He subsequently was reappointed, and later served as the chairman of the board, a position he relinquished several years ago. "I'm no longer chairman, but I'm still on the board and will be for another couple of years," says Mays, who — as previously noted — graduated from the university in 1957 with a degree in petroleum engineering.

In recognition of Lowry's extensive commitment to the university, Texas A&M's business school in 1997 formally was named the Lowry Mays College & Graduate School of Business in his honor. This was after Mays provided the school with $15 million to be used to enhance the programs of the college of business and provide career opportunities for Texas A&M business graduates. "This historic day is made possible through the philanthropy of a great Texas Aggie and my personal friend," Texas A&M President Ray Bowen said at the dedication ceremony. "Your generosity challenges us to move to higher levels of excellence."

"There are few times when you can point to a single day that ensures a stamp on the future, and this is such a day," A&M System Regent Robert Allen of Houston added. "Texas A&M's business school will proudly and forever bear the name of this industry giant."

Lowry Mays also sits on the board of the M.D. Anderson Cancer Center in Houston, an institution that Clear Channel founding partner Red McCombs also holds near and dear. "We committed to give them significant support for research because I think they saved my life 25 years ago," says Mays, who was diagnosed with a melanoma cancer similar to that which took the life of his first cousin, Jerry Mays, who played with the Kansas City Chiefs when they won their two Super Bowls in the 1960s. Lowry says that because of the outstanding attention and care that he received while undergoing cancer surgery, he agreed to serve on the center's board of regents. As a gesture of his gratitude and philanthropy, he and Peggy donated $20 million to the center in 2005.

In addition to the cancer center, most of Peggy Mays' interest now is focused on several local organizations. "She's on the boards of the two large art museums here and the board of the National Wildlife Museum" Lowry says. "We're both on the board of the Autry National Center, which formerly was known as the Autry Museum of Western Heritage, and she's very interested in the art world and cultural things, and we support those institutions through our foundations."

The Mays' reach throughout the San Antonio community is both extensive and time-honored, dating back at least to the early years of Clear Channel. Chief among these is the United Way of San Antonio, for which Lowry Mays served as chairman of the board in 1995. The organization's president, Howard Nolan, says he first became acquainted with the Mays family in 1977 when he moved to the city to head up the organization's local chapter. "At that time Peggy was the day-to-day operating head of the volunteer center, and I would see her constantly, because we were in the same building together," he recalls. "It was through Peggy that I had an opportunity to meet Lowry, and together we got him involved in many aspects of the United Way. By the time he was named the chairman of the board, he was grounded in our philosophy and what was happening with the United Way of San Antonio."

Nolan says that Lowry first served as general campaign chair for the organization, helping to continue a succession of increasingly successful fundraising campaigns. "He was a major part of the leadership that made that possible," he says. "Even though he was traveling all over the world and building his company, he always had time to make those key calls, in addition to being very generous with his own personal wealth. Lowry is no different today than he was some 30 years ago in the way he relates to you or other people. Of course, 30 years ago he certainly didn't have the financial resources or the position he has now, but he's still the same individual who was willing to roll up his sleeves to make this organization and a lot of other organizations in San Antonio what they are today. His stature has not changed as an individual in this community."

Mark, Randall, and Kathy Mays have continued the family involvement within the United Way, each of them active in various roles. "They all have this strong sense of giving back that their parents set for them," Nolan says. "Mark is on our executive board, Randall is on some very key committees, and Kathy is involved with our women's leadership council. It wasn't just one generation; this has been passed down to the next generation, and I'm certain that it will be passed down to the next one, as well."

Ditto the San Antonio Zoo. Owned and operated by the San Antonio Zoological Society, the zoo was founded in 1914 by Colonel George Brackenridge, founder of the *San Antonio Express-News*. Brackenridge collected an assortment of buffalo, elk, deer, monkeys, lions, and bears on land he had deeded to the city in what now is known as Brackenridge Park, and since then the zoo has grown to the point that it now is home to more than 3,800 animals embodying some 750 species. As with most civic or charitable organizations, the zoo relies heavily on numerous volunteers and private and corporate donors to keep it running. To this end, Lowry and Peggy Mays have contributed substantial time and dollars to help the zoo attract the 850,000 visitors who walk through its gates annually.

"Lowry always has been very supportive of the zoo from a monetary standpoint as well as a time and energy standpoint," says Steve McCusky, the zoo's executive director. "He's always offered to do whatever he could, either within the company or within the family. He's somebody I personally could call and say, 'Lowry, here's what we need, and here's how you can help.' He served as a member of the society's board, and was a committee chair for our most recent capital campaign. With the money that Lowry helped raise, we've been able to break ground on our Africa Live exhibit, which is the biggest endeavor we've ever undertaken. He came out to the ground-breaking ceremony in a wheelchair and spoke about his memories of the zoo, how involved he's been with it over the years."

Perhaps the greatest local beneficiary of the Mays family largesse and community involvement is the YMCA of Greater San Antonio. Founded in 1876, the organization originally provided lodging, food, reading rooms, and recreation to cowboys, railroad employees, and men and boys looking for work in the city. In the late 1800s the YMCA founded a Ladies' Auxiliary, and in 1907 the organization moved into its first permanent building in downtown San Antonio. Today the organization consists of 12 separate facilities serving over 67,000 members and program participants in 10 South Texas counties, and relies on some 4,600 program volunteers and 278 policy volunteers to meet community needs.

No individual or family is more involved with the San Antonio YMCA than Lowry Mays and his sons. "Lowry has served on the board of directors and currently is on the president's advisory council," says Baron Herdelin-Doherty, the organization's president and CEO. "They are very involved not only in donating money and offering their time, but also in using the facilities." In fact, the family has grown so committed to the YMCA that one of the 12 area facilities is named in their honor. "The Mays Family YMCA is a really large program center," Herdelin-Doherty says. "It has a number of sports fields and batting cages, and they gave us the seed money to build a facility on that property this year. This is our biggest sports complex serving over 8,000 children annually in youth football, baseball, T-ball, soccer, and basketball. The entire family has been super-supportive of the Y. The Mays boys played sports here as kids, and their kids are playing YMCA sports now. You could say it's a generational situation for their family."

As it does in most communities it serves, Clear Channel also contributes thousands of dollars annually to help various programs within the San Antonio YMCA. "Every year the company gives us approximately $60,000 worth of billboards and radio spots to promote our annual 'Y Partners' campaign," Herdelin-Doherty says. "This programs provides scholarships for families that can't afford a sports membership. Every year we raise almost $1 million annually to provide those scholarships, and Clear Channel donates the airtime and billboard space to help us do that."

Likewise, the San Antonio Museum of Art has been a major focal point of the Mays family philanthropy, primarily through efforts spearheaded by Peggy Mays. Best described as containing an encyclopedic collection of artwork, the museum — which was founded in 1981 — has four fully endowed curatorships covering Asian art, Latin American art, modern contemporary, and western antiquities. "We're brash and new and we've grown enormously fast," says Marion Oettinger, the museum's director. "Over the years the Mays have been very generous to us, particularly Peggy, who is a very active member of the board. Most recently she took on the tremendous task of heading up the committee that oversaw the construction of the new Asian wing, a 15,000 square-foot gallery featuring art from Japan, Korea, China, India, Vietnam. She is on our collections committee, the executive committee, and the trustee management committee, and she's heavily involved in our long-term planning." The Mays family also made a significant donation to the museum, resulting in an endowed gallery in their name.

Oettinger says the entire Mays family not only is intimately involved with the museum, but conveys a sense of dedication and commitment in all aspects of their charitable involvement. "These are people who interact with their environment," he observes. "You can tell when they've been in the room, because it feels different. They change the chemistry of a space. They've had many blessings and good fortune in their lives, but they've worked very hard for everything — and they feel a responsibility and opportunity to give back. That's why they have been so involved in so many community projects. They continue to lend their names to causes and organizations in which they believe strongly, and of course they give of their fortune, their time, and their reputation."

To that end, the entire Mays family was honored in March 2006 by the Lone Star Chapter of the National Multiple Sclerosis Society, recognizing their support in fighting the debilitating disease. The board of trustees presented the Mays family with the Society's Hope Award at a dinner that also served as a fundraiser for the organization. "We are pleased to honor such a generous and supportive family with the Hope Award this year," Lone Star Chapter President Mark Neagli said at the presentation. "The Mays family members exemplify conscientious and thoughtful community leadership."

As noted earlier, this leadership began many years ago, long before Clear Channel Communications was conceived. Kathryn Mays recalls her parents not only participating in, but chairing virtually every sort of community service project or event in the city of San Antonio. "I remember one in particular, an event for Southwest Foundation Forum for Biomedical Research," she says. "The theme for the fundraiser was the Wizard of Oz. My sister Linda was Dorothy. We placed menus at the tables, and it was a family event. Throughout our lives we saw them giving back to the community — Dad headed up the United Way, and he was always involved with the Chamber of Commerce, not only helping the city to develop, but also serving as a resource behind the city."

Lowry says his philosophy of life is simple: "You should be able to give back more than you take out," he explains. "That's the reason I do things in the business community. I've been the president of the San Antonio Chamber of Commerce and chairman of the United Way campaign. I've held every leadership position there is in San Antonio, and that's a way to give back to the community."

That's a side that few broadcasters get to see outside South Texas, one that Clear Channel Radio President John Hogan says he was unaware of until he relocated to corporate headquarters. "Before I actually knew Lowry personally, I admired him as a broadcaster," he says. "He built the business as it is today, and now that I know him as more than just the chairman of Clear Channel, I can say that he genuinely is a good man. His family is incredibly important to him, and the company truly is an extension of his family. Also, having spent some time now in San Antonio, I've learned that he has a strong sense of giving back. He kept this company in San Antonio, which was a very powerful statement. This isn't a natural home for a media company, and he's had numerous opportunities to move to other places, but he's kept it here because he loves San Antonio. He has given back to the community in a lot of very public ways, but also some private ways. As the company has gotten bigger his ability to do that has grown, and now there's a foundation that helps administer those things. But those things he cares about, he cares about deeply, and he's committed to them one hundred percent."

While some philanthropists seek to generate headlines with their generosity, Lowry Mays tends to do it in a committed but low-key fashion, Hogan observes. "He does it quietly," he says. "There's no political motivation for it. He doesn't do things because it looks good, sounds good, or positions himself or the company well. He does what he does because he believes in Texas A&M, he believes in the YMCA, he believes in the other causes that he has supported. That's a very genuine, sincere, thoughtful approach."

RED AND CHARLINE MCCOMBS

A strong sense of civic responsibility also is ingrained in Clear Channel's co-founder, Red McCombs, who was raised in the West Texas dust bowl during the Depression. "When I was growing up my Dad worked six days a week," he recalls, speaking in his office at McCombs Plaza on the outskirts of San Antonio. "He would come home on Saturday night with his pay envelope, which would have $24.75 cash in it. My mother would put the envelope on the kitchen table and take out $2.50, which she would put in another envelope for the First Baptist Church. Giving and sharing was something I grew up with; it was just part of life. This was the middle of the Depression and a lot of people who were experiencing hard times traveled through our little town on their way west. My mother always had food for them, and she always had a place for them to stay, even if it was just a quilt on the yard in front of the house. We always helped people, and we always shared with them."

Now that McCombs' wealth can be measured in the ten-figure range (in 2006 *Forbes* estimated his personal worth at $1.2 billion), he and his wife Charline have the wherewithal to expand on the charity that Red's folks extended to those Depression-era men and women whose fortunes were less secure. "Giving back has always been a natural thing for me, but it never got any recognition until it got up there with a lot of zeroes," he grins. "Charline and I have shared our resources all our lives; that's never really changed. And now that we have a lot more resources we have a lot more to share." The McCombs Foundation, chartered in 1981, makes an average of 300 gifts every year to various organizations that fund cancer research, youth activities, sports, religion, and leadership. The Foundation also gives college scholarships to the children of the employees of McCombs' various business enterprises. While most of these donations tend to be in the $5,000 range, some have extended well into seven or eight digits. For example, between 1996 and 2000, the Foundation pledged more than $7 million to Southwestern University for construction of a student center, a dormitory, and other facilities, and in 1999 $1 million was donated for the creation of the Charline McCombs Empire Theater for the performing arts.

"This little theater in downtown San Antonio had run out of money," Red recalls. "They were restoring it, and it had a lot of support from the community, but there were a lot of cost overruns. So that $1 million was very significant in what they were able to do." The following year, the McCombs Foundation contributed $50 million to the University of Texas at Austin to establish the Red McCombs School of Business.

"When we make a gift of substantial money we like to make it where we know it's going to make a difference," McCombs says. Case in point: As a life-long sports fanatic, McCombs says he didn't realize until recently that women's college athletics lacked significant funding. "I was ignorant of that fact," he admits. "But when I became aware of this discrepancy, I gave $5 million to the University of Texas' women's athletics department to build a new softball field. I didn't know at the time that it was the biggest gift that had ever been given to women's athletics in the U.S., but I did know that it would make a difference."

Red and Charline McCombs made another difference when the McCombs Foundation, in 2005, pledged $30 million to the M.D. Anderson Cancer Center at the University of Texas. The gift was designed to help launch a long-term research initiative at the Center, and when completed in 2008, the Red and Charline McCombs Institute for the Early Detection and Treatment of Cancer will house a number of existing and new programs, including the Cancer Metastasis Research Center, the Center for Immunology Research, the Kleberg Center for Molecular Markers, and the Proton Therapy Center. Two other research facilities — the Center for Advanced Biomedical Imaging Research and the Center for Targeted Therapy — are scheduled for completion by 2008. The M.D. Anderson center says that the Proton Therapy Center will offer direct patient care, and clinical research with patients will be carried out there and in the Center for Advanced Biomedical Imaging. In the other centers, new diagnostic tests and therapies will be developed and then will be introduced to patients. The emphasis will be on early detection and prevention research, which will lead to treatments for individual patients that are more effective and less invasive. "I am convinced that this institute will be very much involved in eradicating cancer," McCombs says.

A self-confessed sports fanatic — he is the former owner of the San Antonio Spurs, the Denver Nuggets, and the Minnesota Vikings — McCombs says that he has had what can best be described as a life full of opportunity and success. Nothing thrills him more than having been able to walk into the owners' box in the Metrodome in Minneapolis or watch his team defeat the New York Knicks at Madison Square Garden. Well, nothing except maybe being able to give away much of the fortune he has amassed in the years since he bought that first Class B baseball team in Corpus Christi. "We enjoy the giving very much," McCombs says with a look of distinct pride. "There was never any plan that we would leave a big estate for someone to wrestle over. We've been fortunate, we've made a lot of money, we've given a lot of money away — and if I'm fortunate enough to make some more money, we'll give even more away."

CHAPTER THIRTEEN

ALL IN
THE FAMILY

WITH A MARKET CAP OF APPROXIMATELY $17 BILLION, CLEAR CHANNEL HAS earned its designation as one of the largest media companies in the world. But when a company grows that large in such a short time, upsetting traditional business practices within the industries in which it operates, many people tend to see it just for its size, its power, its influence, and what is perceived as its many faults. It's easy for critics and detractors to take aim at a company they perceive to be devoid of spirit or soul, and a host of individuals have made a pastime — and in a few cases a cottage industry — of such an endeavor. But strip away the bricks and mortar, the P&Ls, the quarterly reports, the boardrooms, and the hyperbole, and you're left with very real men and women who have made the company what it is. The Mays family is very much the backbone and the heart of Clear Channel, and all them — mother and father, brothers and sisters, nieces and nephews, sons and daughters — are as fiercely dedicated to the company as they are committed to one another.

Clear Channel is an entity that represents the quintessential American dream. Neither Lowry Mays nor Red McCombs bought that first radio station in San Antonio with the notion of building a billion-dollar company; in fact, as we now know, they weren't all that excited to buy that stand-alone FM at all. But buy it they did, and over the ensuing years the company expanded from that one under-performing property in South Texas to the corporate giant it is today. Along the way, Lowry Mays and his family diligently worked to improve every facet of the company's operations, engineered ownership and regulatory changes that they and the industry could take advantage of, and produced the programming that would attract listeners — and, by proxy, advertising clients. When financial opportunities presented themselves, they expanded into other synergistic industries, all the while keeping a close eye on the bottom line.

In a paradoxical world where individuals, communities, and countries rely on business for employment, goods, and services, *big business* in some sectors has become synonymous with malevolence. By extrapolation, those who engage in and prosper from big business are painted with deep, dark hues like some sort of corporate noir wherein great evil lurks in the hearts of its executive board room. Granted, some corporations in recent years have been found to be run by executives whose sloth, greed, and clear disregard for the law blinded them to the proprieties of business. During the first few years of this decade, the morning papers were teeming with images of perp-walking chief executives and financial officers with their suit jackets pulled over their heads in an effort to shield their faces from the cameras. But Lowry Mays — the entire Mays family, in fact — cannot be included among these ranks. Certainly, their deliberate business sense and entrepreneurial spirit have led them to make lots of money. And their willingness to take calculated risks has allowed them to create opportunities that other corporate leaders would, and did, consider far too chancy, or impractical. But a strong sense of ethics and even stronger family ties have given the Mays family a healthy perspective of responsibility and trust that has kept Clear Channel vigorous and prosperous during good economic times and bad, despite the caustic barbs and criticisms that continuously are hurled in its direction.

Perhaps it is this strong sense of family and trusting Texas naiveté that prevented the Mays family from anticipating or understanding the political acrimony that was aimed at Clear Channel until consolidation was well into the late innings. "We clearly were not foreseeing any of this negativity," says Mark Mays. "We did a very poor job at being proactive. When we started getting bad press, around 2001 or 2002, we were not very sophisticated in our PR efforts. We were naïve enough to think that people actually told the truth, and actually researched things. But what we were quickly finding out was that people are going to put any spin on it that they want to, without regard to the truth."

Anyone with the time or inclination to look past the near-ubiquitous Internet postings and blogs will find that, with Clear Channel, what you see is pretty much what you get. The Lowry, Mark, and Randall triumvirate keeps the company operating within a sound fiduciary environment, while constantly ensuring that its functions are significantly decentralized. It all goes back to those "peanut stands on the prairie": as long as those stands continue to produce revenue and drive cash flow, the local managers are left to create and sell what the local markets will bear. That's the way Lowry Mays set up the company with that first station in 1972, and nothing has changed in the years since then.

"Whatever venom the critics hurl at Clear Channel and all its perceived trespasses, it's difficult to find anyone who doesn't respect and admire Lowry Mays," says New York real estate maven and billionaire Donald Trump, who has hosted a radio show distributed by the company's Premiere Radio Networks. "He should be commended for his entrepreneurial spirit, his acute business sense, his drive to succeed, and what can only be described as a heartfelt commitment to his family. The entire Mays family is extraordinary, not only in the business that they know best, which is the radio business, but because they are extraordinary entrepreneurs. The combination of entrepreneurship, imagination, and just pure genius is what built Clear Channel. And that's the Mays family — all of those ingredients. They've built something in their industry that can never be duplicated."

Closer to home within the broadcasting industry, former NAB President/CEO Eddie Fritts says he considers Lowry Mays not only a pioneer broadcaster, but a close friend and colleague. "I've known Lowry for a long time," he notes. "I've played golf with him, I've gone hunting with him, and we've gone on fishing trips together. And I can say, without a doubt, that Lowry is a fine role model. He's a great example at what success in America can be. Lowry has been a great leader, and he's set a strong example for his entire family, as well. If you think about it, going back to that first radio station Lowry bought because it was in financial trouble, to the company they operate today, they literally have cast the mold for this industry and how it will continue to operate for the foreseeable future."

Bill Stakelin, CEO of Regent Broadcasting and former chairman of the NAB board of directors, is equally reverential of Lowry's business acumen and his contribution to the radio industry. "Lowry is probably one of the most intellectual and honest individuals I've had the pleasure of knowing and calling a friend," he says. "He was a mentor of mine in the early days I was at the NAB, and he was smart enough to recognize the strength and power of this business at a time when some people were not doing well and had given up. When people didn't seem to know where the business was going, he put together this company called Clear Channel and he's never looked back since that day.

"Lowry always had — and still does have — a very large presence when he comes into a room," says Steve Hicks, former president and CEO of AMFM Broadcasting. "You could just feel his energy. Not only his size and stature, but also the respect he commands. He was a real presence from the first time I ever met him, and he's been that way all the way through his career. People will always credit him with great vision and stature in the industry."

"Lowry Mays is a true Texas gentleman," says former RAB President/CEO Gary Fries. "He also had vision and saw where consolidation was going. He had been very influential at the NAB and getting deregulation passed, and really saw what this could mean for radio and what kind of company could be built." Fries says that Lowry Mays understood the basic underpinnings of the radio industry, something that many people seemed to forget during the rapid-fire consolidation process. "He really grasped the connection between advertising on the radio and getting results for the client," he explains. "Lowry was talking about that before it became fashionable, and it was just symbolic of his great knowledge of how sales take place and the drivers behind selling radio advertising time."

Kraig Kitchin, former president of Premiere Radio Networks, describes Lowry as a natural leader of individuals. "From the time you meet him, you believe you are the favorite member of his team," he observes. "You believe he has specifically chosen you to run a very specific part of his business empire, and he has great confidence that you will do really well when the wind is at your back — and that you will work that much harder when the wind is blowing in your face. You believe him because you have seen him work through 25 years of real hardship to get to where he is. He is a risk-taker but he also has a very financially conservative way of keeping enough money in the bank for tomorrow, should there be a rainy day."

New Radio Group President and CEO Mary Quass says she first was introduced to Lowry Mays in 1999, when she was receiving *Radio Ink's*

Broadcaster of the Year award and he was being honored as the magazine's Radio Executive of the Year. "That was the first opportunity I'd had to speak with him, and the one thing that very much impressed me was that he truly had a profound love of the radio business. He's a man who hasn't had to worry about where his next meal is going to come from for a very long time, and he's in this business not because it's been financially beneficial, but because radio affords him the opportunity to have an idea and translate it into a real outcome." Quass says that, like it or not, Clear Channel "has done more to make radio higher profile in the last five to ten years than any other single entity since Marconi. They have brought a respectability from an investment standpoint, and they've added value to the business in terms of buying and selling in ways that couldn't have happened without them."

Perhaps no one has been better situated to view Lowry Mays' fiscal acuity than Clear Channel's Chief Accounting Officer Herb Hill. Noting that the company's critics continue to characterize Lowry as an MBA bean-counter, Hill maintains that Mays' insistence on tight corporate financial control has led to the company's longevity and success. "Lowry is a very shrewd investor," he explains. "He knows how to evaluate deals and opportunities, and he has a unique knack for business. He is comfortable taking risks, and uses that to enhance his deal-making."

Hill cites the company's expansion into the independent television business as an example of how Mays' focus on numbers and cash flow was able to drive future acquisitions. "When we began to do those Fox television deals, I began to realize that this was going to provide a lot of seed capital for further ventures," he recalls. "I saw that if we did this again and again this was going to multiply. The system for finding underperforming assets, going in and doing a better job marketing them and providing a lot better control environment was a recipe that worked very well. Of course, it also required some shrewd M&A deals and a good, strong capital structure, but with all those elements in place I saw early on that this was going to work."

MEET THE PARENTS

When people see Lowry Mays listed as one of the world's wealthiest businessmen, the immediate reaction is to imagine New York penthouses, Palm Beach mansions, and ocean-going yachts with helipads and jet skis. Nothing could be further from the truth. When Lowry is not at home or in the office he most often can be found with some, if not all, of his four children and 16 grandchildren at his ranch outside San Antonio, where his favorite mode of transportation while relaxing amidst the Texas sage is an aging 30-year-old Willys Jeep whose primary feature is rust.

While Lowry receives most of the credit for building and operating Clear Channel, Peggy deserves equal recognition for raising four accomplished and family-oriented children. "Peggy is just a great person," Lowry says. "Not only is she a leader in the community, but she is a great mother. She really was an anchor to the family because back when I was in the investment banking business I traveled a lot, and when I got into the radio business I traveled a lot. She was there all the time. She's a wonderful woman and we've had a wonderful marriage — it's lasted almost 50 years."

Through those 50 years, some of which were more prosperous than others, Lowry applied the same fiscal principles both in business and at home. This translated to somewhat of a Brady Bunch existence, with a modest home, a modest car, modest vacations, and plenty of household chores. "When I was twelve years old we finally moved into a new house, which was great because it meant that we didn't have to share rooms anymore," recalls Kathryn Mays Johnson, the eldest of the four Mays children. "It wasn't a huge house; in fact we still shared bathrooms until we moved out and went to college. But all of a sudden we had our own space, and I remember going to garage sales and picking out furniture for my room. I got to sand it down and paint it whatever color I wanted. To this day I can't believe my mother would let me do that. It was a very ugly room — pink, green, and orange — but at the time I thought it was just fabulous."

Kathryn says that while her father always worked long hours, first at his investment banking company and later at the radio company, her mother was always home, taking care of her four kids. "She's a perfectionist," Kathryn says. "She may not admit it, but she is — and so am I. It's definitely in my genes. She became the power behind the man, no question about it, because she had that stabilizing effect, and was always there for us kids."

"Even though Dad worked a lot when I was growing up, we always had dinner together as a family," observes Linda Mays McCaul, the second-oldest of the four Mays children and the only one never to work at Clear Channel. "My mom always was there just like all moms are, and family was real important to them. She used to make cakes for birthdays parties and she would bake them from scratch. One time she even made a cake in the shape of a baseball glove with a baseball in it." She says that, as close as the family was, all four children were taught at an early age to be independent — something Linda took more to heart than her sister and brothers. Instead of pursuing a career in finance, she obtained a degree in oceanography and traveled the world as a marine scientist, and later settled in at the Pentagon as an operative in naval intelligence. "We all flew the coop pretty early — our mother wanted to teach us independence; she wanted to make sure that her girls could take care of themselves," says Linda, who today lives in Austin with her husband, Republican Congressman Michael McCaul, and their five children.

Beginning with those early years and continuing up until today, life in the Mays household was all about family. Vacations were family affairs, often involving road trips that were not all that different from the Griswold's in *National Lampoon's Vacation*. "Whenever we traveled somewhere we drove in cars that always broke down," Kathryn says. "On our first trip out to Disneyland — sometime in the early-'70s — our station wagon gave out in the middle of the Arizona desert. It was summer and there was no air conditioning." In order to keep the kids occupied while Lowry tried to get the car repaired, Peggy bought five Tootsie Pops and gave one to each of her four children. "The objective was for each of us to take our time eating it, because whoever had theirs the longest would get the last one."

As with most families where a stay-at-home mom must juggle a large brood of children, Peggy Mays was the owner-operator of the family taxi business. "Mom was always there to chauffeur us around," Kathryn says. "All of us kids were involved in at least two activities, and she seemed to always be driving us around, dropping us off and picking us up. On top of that she cooked breakfast, lunch, and dinner, and we always ate together. To this day whenever we get together, if somebody's not there it doesn't work for her. She wants every single piece to the puzzle to be there, and if someone is missing, you can tell that picture is not complete." With four grown children and 16 grandchildren, bringing the entire family together in one place poses some logistical challenges, but it does happen — and almost always during the holidays.

Of course, as a young girl Kathryn had no idea that her father was going to end up creating the largest radio company in the world, but it didn't at all surprise her when it happened. She also was struck by his penchant for listening rather than talking, which she says was his way of letting people work through their own issues rather than trying to apply his own solution to a problem. "When I was young I naturally thought my father had a lot of vision," she says. "At that age children usually do. In my eyes he could do no wrong. But even when I was a young girl he had this great capacity for listening. He's not as much of a talker as he is a listener. When I was growing up I would ask him, 'What do you think I should do here?' And he would answer, 'Well, what are your options — lay it out for me.' He always wanted me to think things through. He'd just sit back in this green chair he had and listen to what I had to say. At work he was the same way. If he had a budget meeting he would always ask questions, and then he'd ask more questions. Sometimes you didn't know what was going on in his head, but I think it was during much of that listening that he generated a lot of his forward-thinking ideas."

As parents, Lowry and Peggy Mays worked hard to instill in their children a strong sense of values that is evident today, both in the closeness of the extended family and the way the business is operated. "We're really a very ethical family," Kathryn says. "I've never lied to my parents about anything, ever, and I never lied to my brothers. I would never have stolen money out of my dad's wallet. He would give it to me if I needed it, but it wouldn't even cross my mind to do something like that. It was driven into my core that you didn't tell the teacher that somebody chewed up your homework. We just never felt comfortable telling anything but the truth. Even now I never take pencils home from the office."

"Our dad is probably one of the most humble people I have known in my life," says Linda McCaul. "You'd never know from the old tattered shorts he always wears at the ranch that this is a guy who has a lot of means. One of the principles that he taught us growing up was that it's just as important to be nice to the janitor in the school as it is to be nice to the principal. That's a founding principle by which we all live, and I try to impress that upon my kids, as well."

Linda says that both her parents also tried to instill in their children the importance of community service and responsibility. "My mother works endlessly to give back to the community in every way she can," she says. "Whether they're cancer projects or art projects, she's always right there right in the middle of things. That's how she was raised. Those two principles really sum up who our parents are."

One might think that the chairman of a company that generates close to $7 billion of revenue a year might sit behind a massive desk in a high-rise office the size of an end zone. Wrong on both counts: Lowry Mays still uses the same oak desk he has sat behind since his early days in business, and his second-floor office has a view of a golf course that has been folded into the remnants of an old quarry carved out of Texas sandstone. His book-shelves are crammed with photographs of his family and friends, as well as an oversized collection of murder mysteries and thrillers. "Dad is very much not the corporate mogul," says Mark Mays. "Far from it. We've always lived a very moderate lifestyle. Someone once described him as having deep pockets and short arms. He's always been hard-driving, and he instilled that sense of spirit and work ethic in all of his kids, and that was always a big part of our growing up. We all had chores, we all con-tributed, and we all learned the value of the dollar. Dad had a great trait, which was that as soon as we were out of school every year we had to go to work. There were no allowances or anything. If we wanted any spend-ing money, we had to go earn it."

By the time Mark Mays reached high school his father still didn't give him an allowance, but he did provide him go-fer employment at the two Clear Channel stations in town. "In the late 1970s, when I was about fif-teen or sixteen, my summer job was as a schlepper," he recalls. "I was told to 'take this here, take that there.' I carted the music, I cleaned the machines, I put up the reel-to-reel tapes. One summer the company was moving the studios here in San Antonio and I ended up doing some con-struction work for one of the radio stations. If my dad was trying to teach me a life lesson, it worked, because I decided I sure didn't want to work construction the rest of my life."

While the corporate spotlight has been pointed at Lowry over the years, Peggy Mays always functioned just off stage, raising the kids and keeping the family running. "Mom deserves just as much of the credit, if not more, just from the perspective that she always was around," Mark insists. "Mom was always doing everything, and she was involved with all of the local charitable organizations. I think that's where we got our sense of compassion and community spirit, which is an integral part of what drives not only the company, but the family, as well."

Youngest son (and sibling) Randall Mays was seven years old when his father entered the radio business, and says he only had a vague aware-ness at the time of what his father did for a living. "I do remember that he had an office in a building next to the St. Anthony Hotel downtown, and there was a lunch club there called the St. Anthony Club," he recalls. "You had to be a member to go eat lunch there, and once a year he would invite me down to go to lunch at the St. Anthony Club with him. That was a big thing for me. But it probably wasn't until I was about thirteen that I really even started understanding that we were in the process of building the studios that we have now. Over that summer I did construction and helped build out those studios, and Dad paid me about half of minimum wage. I was too young to even know that there was a minimum wage, but I know I wasn't getting paid it. My mom dropped me off and picked me up at the end of the day, and that was kind of my first exposure to what he even did."

While the two Mays sons share their father's corporate vision and business sense, they are not carbon copies of either Lowry or each other. "Mark and Randall do things very differently," Kathryn explains. They make a perfect team because their assets blend beautifully. Of course, I've seen arguments where I literally have had to close my ears. They're very honest with each other, and they let you know if they don't agree, but the best idea always wins. They go over all the pros and cons, and each listens to the other. Instead of trying to convince the other that he is right, they will listen to the other's ideas — and sometimes they'll tear those ideas apart — but in the end they'll always make a decision that's best for the company."

If asked, most people who know Mark and Randall will say that Mark is more of a "people person" than his brother, while Randall is the king of the numbers. "Mark is a talker," says Kathryn, who confesses to having taught Mark how to dance when he was a child. "He lets things roll off his back very easily, and he doesn't hold a grudge. Yet he is very focused on the bottom line. Both he and Randall are goal-oriented, but that particularly describes Mark." So much so that at the end of the year he will take his own mental retreat where he can sit down and analyze what he accomplished — or did not accomplish — in the past twelve months and then write down all his goals for the next year. "Mark is always looking forward, and he encourages all the people who work for him and around him in his life to do the same thing."

Despite the type-A focus on all things business, however, Mark's family is very much his purpose. He arrives at the office early, but divides his day so that he can devote quality time to his wife and six children. "Mark will leave the office at 5:30 or 6:00 in the evening, go home, bathe and feed his children, and put them to bed," Kathryn says. "He knows that his wife has been with them all day, and she needs a break and he needs to be with his kids. He absolutely is the 'dad of the year' — he has coached every one of his sons in three different sports: soccer, basketball, baseball. And he's always the coach, not the assistant coach."

So what about Randall? "Well, he's definitely a genius," Kathryn says. "And while I say that very seriously, I also say that very jokingly. He is five steps ahead of you when he's thinking. He already has an answer to your third question, which you haven't even thought of yet. He really does think out of the box, which is what helps to stir things up. When Dad and Mark are being conservative, Randall would be thinking out of the box." As children, Kathryn and her sister Linda referred to him as "Infoman" because of his vast knowledge of things both important and not. "He knows things that nobody else even wants to know," Kathryn continues. "He is really good at dissecting things and figuring out what is at the root of a problem. Randall has a real gift for taking something that's complicated and explaining it in very simple terms. He can take a complex issue and compare it to riding a bike or raising kids. He puts it into a perspective that you can understand."

"Mark is one of the most amazing people that you'll ever meet," boasts his sister Linda. "For several years now he's run the company, but even as he's done that he has made time to coach the Little League teams, and then bring dinner home for his wife and bathe his kids. He is incredibly even-tempered, and when we were growing up he was always the clown of the family. Randall is more on the serious side, and in that role he does a wonderful job for the company."

Lowry understandably is proud of all his children, but when it comes to business he speaks particularly fondly of Mark and Randall. "They're very different individuals, so you can't lump them together," he says. "One thing they do have in common is they're very bright people. They're a helluva lot smarter than I am, and that is a tremendous advantage in our father-son relationship. When the kids are really bright and they're pulling their own weight, everybody recognizes that it's pretty easy to justify any position they might have within the company. That was the great benefit I had: I knew I was bringing in people whom other people would recognize were extremely beneficial to the company."

All assumptions to the contrary, Lowry insists it never was his plan to have either of his sons work for the company, aside from the odd summer jobs when they were young. But at one point in the late 1980s, when the radio industry was experiencing skyrocketing prices and Clear Channel was entering the television business, Lowry realized that he needed help. Not just any help, either, but help in the form of an individual he knew he could speak with honestly — and, more than anything, trust implicitly with the company.

At the time, Mark was working in New York at Capital Cities/ABC, handling affiliate relations for the radio network division. Several years earlier he had graduated from Vanderbilt University, where he was a double major in economics and mathematics. He subsequently moved to Dallas where he worked in investment banking for two years before moving to New York, where he earned advanced degrees in economics and finance from Columbia Business School. "Dad's feeling always was that you had to understand the language of business, which is the numbers," he says. "He believed that if you don't understand them someone else will, and they'll use it to their advantage. And I always had a mind for math." Indeed, corporate staff at the company's San Antonio headquarters is aware of his fondness for statistics and all things analytical. "I've always had a very quantitative mind," he admits.

In any event, Mark never saw it as his destiny to work for his father's company. "Dad never pressured us to work for Clear Channel," he says. "Sure, every once in awhile he'd remind Randall or me that he had this great company, but he always encouraged us to go do something else. He wanted us to follow our instincts, find our own interests, and get exposed to a lot of different things."

As the adage goes, life is what happens when you're busy making other plans. In Mark's case, while he may have been preparing for a life in investment banking or Wall Street analysis, market pressures in the broadcasting industry were beginning to heat up merger and acquisition activity in both the radio and television businesses. Lowry kept coming back to the fact that he needed the assistance of someone who would not just be a nameplate on a wall. "Mark had been to business school and he'd worked in the investment banking business — all those things that I did," he says. "And I really needed him because I was certain that we shared the same values. Plus, he was a known quantity."

Lowry didn't exactly make his son an offer he couldn't refuse, but he did make a very persuasive case for Mark to move back home to San Antonio. Enticing Randall to join them, however, was an entirely different matter. "I couldn't talk Randall into coming into the business," he says. "I wanted to bring him in as treasurer as Mark moved up to an operating role. By this time he was graduating from business school, and I tried to persuade him to join the company. And he asked, 'Well, what will you pay me?' And I said, 'Well, I think I could justify paying you about twice what you're worth, and that would be about $55,000.' And Randall said, "Well, Goldman Sachs has already offered me $100,000 and a signing bonus of

$20,000.' At that juncture I told him that if money was the most important thing, he'd better go there." Whether Lowry was calling his bluff or not, Randall did, indeed, accept the position at Goldman Sachs, where he worked for nearly two years.

While both sons as teenagers participated in hourly wage work, Randall actually had already performed some consulting work for his father while he was a freshman at Duke University. "He asked me to analyze radio markets for him, and specifically look for any markets we ought to think about getting into," Randall remembers. "It wasn't anything sophisticated — I just looked at population growth rates, per capita income, how many stations were in the market, what the revenue-per-station was. I went through the top hundred markets and came up with a list of the ten best markets that we ought to try to get into. This was before the days of Excel, so I developed it on graph paper, working it out with a calculator."

After his freshman year at Duke University, Randall transferred to the University of Texas, where he earned a degree in business administration. After graduating he moved to Dallas and worked for Trammell Crow, leasing and selling real estate before following in his father's footsteps and attending Harvard Business School. Goldman Sachs came next, and as Randall remembers it, one day in 1992 he was sitting in his office when the phone rang. "It was Mark, who told me that the FCC had just passed new ownership rules that were going to allow the company to grow. At that point Dad felt very strongly that radio properties were great cash flow machines, and he wanted to own as many of them as he could because he knew they were going to be pretty profitable."

Mark informed his younger brother that Clear Channel's chief financial officer was leaving, and the company was looking for someone to come into the company in that role and oversee the anticipated acquisitions. "He explained that he and my father wanted to bring me in, but if I wasn't interested that would be fine — they'd just hire someone else," Randall recalls. "When I got off the phone I sat back and thought about it and realized that I'd always known I'd come back and work for the company. But my father was really good about it: He never ever put pressure on us to work here. I considered the whole thing for all of about an hour, and decided that this clearly was what I wanted to do." In retrospect Randall says that the move back to San Antonio couldn't have been more fortuitous, in terms of the M&A activity that was about to erupt across the radio landscape. "The timing couldn't have been better in terms of access to the capital markets, which gave us the ability to buy stations, take out the costs, target specific audiences, and sell those audiences to advertisers," he says. "There was really a tremendous amount of cash flow generation that happened through that consolidation process."

"There's a real interesting dynamic with Lowry, Mark, and Randall," Clear Channel Radio CEO John Hogan says from his office, which is situated immediately next door to Randall's. "They trust each other completely. They've known each other forever, they communicate extraordinarily well, and they provide a wonderful sounding board. It allows them to explore different ideas, to get feedback in different ways. As dominant a personality as Lowry has, Mark and Randall are unique in their own way. Randall is very smart, simply amazing in the quantitative sense, and he is extremely well cast in his role as the president and chief financial officer. He spends a lot of his time focused on the investment community, and he has a great ability to communicate with them.

"By contrast — although not too much — Mark is an extremely bright guy," Hogan continues. "He has a great handle on numbers and analysis, he's very quantitatively oriented, and he exploits those strengths very well in his role. He and Randall have an amazing partnership. There is complete trust and ongoing, candid, open, and direct communication. They both are unbelievably adept at identifying and assuming their responsibilities, based on skill set or necessity. It's all very seamless." Hogan says that the first time he ever spent any "quality time" with Mark was on a golf course. "At the end of those four hours Mark knew a lot more about me than he had known when we started, and I knew virtually nothing more about him," he laughs. "Mark was very adept at drawing me out, and it was very pleasant. We had a great time, but I came home thinking that I didn't really get much insight into Mark. That's one of his characteristics: he keeps things very close to the vest."

While Mark and Randall are viewed as the two Mays offspring who were groomed — consciously or not — to come into the Clear Channel fold, Kathryn Mays Johnson actually was the first to work for the family business full-time. She began as a receptionist at WOAI-AM in San Antonio one summer in the late 1970s, and also served as traffic director for a while. "My job was to answer the phones and manually log every commercial that was scheduled to go on the air," she recalls. "Sometimes I helped write the ad copy, and I really began to enjoy all of the marketing and creative aspects of the business. Plus, it was fun."

The following year Kathryn moved to Dallas to attend Southern

Methodist University, where her father strongly suggested that she earn a degree in business. "When I was a freshman my dad said to me, 'Kathryn, you're a woman of the '80s, and that means you really should major in finance,'" she recalls. "I told him I didn't want to major in finance — I wasn't a numbers person — but he insisted that I needed to be a numbers person, so I should major in finance. But because I had worked at WOAI I really liked marketing. A lot of people still don't see the importance of how it can make or break a company, but I did — and that's what I liked." Reaching a compromise with her father, who was writing the tuition checks, Kathryn says she decided to pursue a major in both fields.

After graduation Kathryn worked in Dallas for about a year, then moved back to San Antonio with the expectation that she'd be able to work in some aspect of radio marketing — but not necessarily at Clear Channel. "I had heard that WOAI had an opening for a promotions director, so I went in and interviewed with John Barger," she recalls. "I told him I had a degree in marketing and I told him I was perfect for the job, but if he didn't hire me I'd walk around the corner and work for the competition." Barger was intrigued by her attitude and approach, and he gave her the job. "I went to work at barely minimum wage, doing all the promotions for the stations. I did everything from setting up booths, ordering phone lines, setting up tables and banners, putting together events for our clients."

At the time, Lowry Mays was somewhat reluctant to hire his children to work at the company, partially because he didn't want to create the impression that he was "gifting" them with jobs. "John Barger suggested to me that we hire Kathy for the WOAI promotion job," he says. "Neither of the boys worked for the company at that time, and I said, 'Well, as the promotion manager for one radio station, maybe that would be okay.' She became manager of promotions — the first one the company ever had — and she did a great job." Kathryn's position eventually evolved into Clear Channel's senior vice president of corporate relations and she is involved in corporate philanthropy as well as producing the managers' meetings and other company events.

Then there's Linda Mays McCaul, the daughter who moved away and spied on Russian submarines for a decade before moving to Austin. "When Linda got out of school she worked at the CIA and the Pentagon and ended up marrying a Texas boy who was a lawyer at the Justice Department," Lowry says, adding his personal perspective. "They make a great team and she's got five kids, including triplets."

"My father used to harass my husband Michael and me to no end, trying to get us to move back to Texas," Linda McCaul remembers. "Eventually Michael was offered a job by [Texas Republican Senator] John Cornyn, and I told him that if he ever thought he was going to take me back to Texas, this was it. So we moved to Austin, and my husband — who always wanted to go into politics — asked me if I would support him if he ran for Congress. I told him, 'Hey, as long as I get to live in Texas I'll be happy.'" Michael did win his election bid in 2004, and continues to represent Texas' 10th District in the U.S. House of Representatives.

"Lowry really is a self-made man and in my view exemplifies the American dream," says Congressman McCaul. "His father died when he was very young, and he went on to build one of the most successful businesses in the world. My father died about twenty years ago and Lowry has sort of become a second father to me. He and Peggy raised a wonderful family and they obviously instilled in the children a profound sense of values, and we're trying to pass those values on to our kids, as well."

"All in all, it's a neat family," Lowry says with a proud gleam in his eye. "We're very focused on our family and have been all our lives."

Some of that focus understandably was shaken on the morning of April 30, 2004, when Lowry Mays awoke to a strong sensation of numbness on his left side. As his son Mark revealed the following Tuesday at the start of the company's quarterly conference call, Lowry had been admitted to the hospital for testing. "The doctors found some swelling of his brain caused by localized bleeding and a small blood clot," Mark explained. "He underwent surgery Friday afternoon to relieve pressure caused by the swelling. The surgery was successful and he is in good spirits and is mentally alert. He even started grilling me about the business shortly after he came out of surgery. We and his team of doctors expect a complete recovery."

Mark says that the next few months were very difficult for the family, although not for the company's operations. "Whenever someone close to you encounters any type of illness — particularly as serious as my father encountered — you become very concerned," he says. "It all ended up well, but at the time there was a lot of anxiety and worry. When a guy you've spent your whole life with, particularly those 16 years working side by side, goes down, that's a tough day for you. For the first few months I'd wake up every morning at 5:00 and go to the hospital so I could get the doctor's reports and make sure we were doing everything we possibly could. It was a tough period."

"The natural reaction anytime something like that happens is to immediately take a look at how you prioritize what you're doing in your life," adds Randall Mays. "You begin to ask yourself whether you're spending your time on the things that truly make a difference. Whatever the exogenous event is — whether it's 9/11, having a good friend die, or having something happen to a family member — those things tend to have a very clarifying effect in terms of trying to focus on what really is important in your life. That was the biggest thing it did for me."

The sudden shift from seeing Lowry rushing around Clear Channel headquarters, directing the company's operations, to lying in a hospital bed was a shock not only to company employees, but also to the four Mays siblings. "When Dad went into the hospital we were given an opportunity to spend a lot of time with him," says Linda Mays McCaul. "His father died when he was very young, and I remember my dad telling me one day in the hospital that he wasn't given that kind of opportunity. He was just told one day that his dad was gone and his life was changed forever. We knew our father was going to recover, but that sort of incident really wakes you up and makes you think."

The road to recovery has been slow but steady. Eleven months after being stricken by what has been described as a subdural hemotoma, Lowry attended the National Association of Broadcasters' annual convention in Las Vegas to receive that organization's Distinguished Service Award. The honor, which in the past has been bestowed upon such industry luminaries as Oprah Winfrey, Dick Clark, Charles Kuralt, and Walter Cronkite, recognizes those broadcasters who "have made significant and lasting contributions to the broadcasting industry." As Eddie Fritts, the association's president/CEO at the time said, "Lowry Mays built from scratch a media and entertainment company that has changed the face of broadcasting and mass communications. His passion for excellence, his commitment to community, and his support for civic causes make Lowry the perfect choice for this year's DSA Award."

While most folks in the broadcasting industry were familiar with Lowry's well-publicized health issues, many found it unnerving that morning in April to see him wheeled out onto the stage to receive the award. The man who four years running had been hailed by Radio Ink magazine as the "most powerful person in radio" seemed significantly weakened by his ordeal, and many friends and colleagues voiced their concerns and offered their best wishes to him following the presentation ceremony. Despite his physical limitations he insisted that his health was improving every day, explaining that, "Mentally I was always completely recovered so I don't have to worry about any speech defects or mental problems at all."

Months of extensive physical therapy have greatly reduced any visible signs of the initial stroke. He comes in to the office five days a week, except when he's out at his ranch or traveling to an industry function. "When I had the stroke I couldn't even move my arm or leg, but I'm getting back to 100 percent with everything," he says. "Whether I'll ever totally get rid of the wheelchair is still to be seen, but if and when I can, I'm thinking about having a ceremony at a railroad track near my home."

"After Lowry had his health challenge, he was so fortunate to have Peggy beside him to help climb that road to recovery," says longtime friend and former Texas Congressman Tom Loeffler. "The way she immersed herself in that process with a full heart and total commitment was amazing."

Despite the fact that Mark and Randall have assumed much of the company's day-to-day financial operations, Lowry still is very much a presence in Clear Channel's San Antonio headquarters. "Dad loves what he does — that's the number one reason he's successful," Kathryn says. "He got to where he is the hard way. After his father died he had to sack groceries just so his mother could put food on the table. Building this company into what it is today is the American dream, and he got it — and deserves it — because he worked hard. I think I could take the 'big-company' criticism better if he was a flamboyant mogul, jet-setting his way around the world. But he isn't, and neither is Mom. She still washes Ziploc bags out. Most of the time they're both dressed in old blue jeans, spending time with their grandkids. When Mark, Randall, and Dad get together they trust each other implicitly."

"Lowry and Peggy are very close personal friends, and my wife Nancy and I have shared a lot of fun times with them," says Tom Loeffler, who now is a partner in Loeffler Tuggey Pauerstein Rosenthall in San Antonio. "We met through the course of my very early political career when I first ran for Congress, and they were two of my major supporters throughout my entire public career in elective office. As a husband and father, Lowry truly is an outstanding family man. He cares so much for his wife, kids, and grandchildren, and there isn't anything he enjoys more than spending time with all of them at the family ranch north of San Antonio. Peggy is one incredible individual who will roll up her sleeves and put herself to work in whatever capacity is necessary for any cause she chooses to be involved with. The two of them without question are one heck of a team."

"To say it's a pleasure to be involved with a family like the Mays family wouldn't be strong enough," observes Red McCombs. "It's more than that — it's a great privilege. They are a really active, energetic, fun family. They all have very strong work ethics, and they have very strong moral codes. It's a wonderful family to be around. Having said that, you like to be around them for the fun of being there." It's often said that the apple doesn't fall far from the tree, and most close associates of the Mays family will say that this homily is easily applied to Mark and Randall Mays. "I've watched them come out of school, grow in the company, and show great judgment in management, operations, everything about the business," McCombs says.

CHAPTER FOURTEEN

FORGING A NEW
INDUSTRY LEADERSHIP

BY 2005, THE RADIO INDUSTRY — WHICH STILL WAS PRIMARILY AN ANALOG broadcast business — increasingly was coming under attack from new, digital media. Radio stations "broadcasting" on the Internet under the brands of Yahoo!, AOL, and Microsoft, and devices like Apple's iPod, had given radio listeners and music lovers new options — and they were taking them. Industry executives were faced with the interesting responsibility of lifting the tide so all boats could rise, while remaining in competition with all those other vessels.

Clear Channel consistently had taken a leadership position within the radio industry, dating back to when Lowry Mays was active on the National Association of Broadcasters' board of directors. And now Mark and Randall Mays were emerging as leaders who also could balance their corporate quest for cash flow with altruism for the industry, says Drew Marcus, vice chairman of the Media & Telecom Group at Deutsche Bank in New York and a longtime radio analyst.

"Mark has always come across as someone who's very detail-oriented, very hard-working, and very intense," Marcus says. "Also, he was trained in the under-promise, over-deliver mode. Likewise, Randall has this image of someone who had a great strategic vision. He has a great understanding of complex situations, and together they have established a very decentralized management structure, which allowed them to have more profit centers than most other companies were comfortable with."

Whatever skills they bring to acquisitions and operations, much of it was learned at the knee of their father. Most long-term radio broadcasters will agree that Clear Channel has always taken a leadership position within the radio industry, dating back to when Lowry Mays was active on the National Association of Broadcasters' board of directors.

Radio & Records Publisher/CEO Erica Farber agrees, noting, however, that Clear Channel often finds itself in a damned-if-you-do, damned-if-you-don't situation. "This industry needs some visionaries who are compassionate, who get it, and who also have fun with it. There have been several cases where Clear Channel has taken a distinct leadership role, but often the response from the industry has not been to necessarily embrace that leadership. The industry sits there and says, in a somewhat derisive tone, 'Look at what Clear Channel is doing.' Well, the fact is, they're doing a lot more than a lot of other companies. There are a lot of other companies that haven't made anywhere near the efforts that Clear Channel has made."

Because of its sheer size and influence, the company is expected to be a guiding force as the industry struggles with revenue growth and new media competition. But Clear Channel executives reject the notion that they, as a single company, can carry the industry. While Clear Channel does have the clout to affect the way business is done, Clear Channel Radio CEO John Hogan maintains that it is up to every broadcaster to have the discipline to go out and "sell the benefits and value" of radio.

"If our industry and company revenues are going to grow, it is going to be because of our focus on the things that we can control," he explains. "It is incumbent upon us as individuals, then as a company, and then as an industry to recognize that our success will be determined by our efforts. We have a great medium, but we can't expect people to gravitate to it just because we think it's great. It's a very competitive environment out there; there are many more choices today than there were just five years ago. One of the great things about our industry is that we can create opportunity. We are limited only by our own desire and our willingness to work at selling it."

"The biggest challenge we have today is that the radio industry really needs to look to itself — and that's certainly what we're doing at Clear Channel," Hogan continues. "Our industry absolutely has to do a better job of letting advertisers, agencies, investors, regulators, and legislators know what our radio stations can do. We have to let them know about the successes we produce every single day." Additionally, he says, as other new media become fixtures in the consumer experience, radio broadcasters must work with manufacturers of new digital audio equipment to ensure that the industry doesn't get left out of an increasingly complex picture.

Indeed, in a world where the next new thing quickly displaces the last new thing, young media buyers increasingly have been urging their advertiser clients to direct more marketing dollars into new media platforms that they believe could target consumers most efficiently. "Accountability" and "return on investment" steadily emerged as buzzwords that demand mandatory inclusion in any effective media plan, and digital technologies also spawned new measurement systems that allowed for instant online tracking that can document "click-through" traffic and purchase activity.

Starting in 2004, Clear Channel began taking broad steps to correct what it saw were industry ills.

LESS IS MORE

Radio's post-consolidation tendency to increase commercial spot loads — a pattern that began in earnest when venture capitalists opened the dot-com floodgates in the late '90s and continued as long as ad dollars would support it — raised some red flags among advertisers who saw signs of fatigue among radio listeners. Consequently, audience research began to suggest that listeners were associating radio with "too many commercials" and "too much clutter," a relationship that the industry could ill afford as revenue was showing signs of stagnation.

"The radio industry in general — and Clear Channel in particular — really violated the relationship we have with our listeners," John Hogan admits. "We clearly had oversaturated the airwaves with commercials, and this is something that everyone in radio is going to have to deal with."

In July 2004, John Hogan announced a plan to trim the number of commercials and promotions that were playing on each of its stations nationwide. Specific commercial ceilings would apply to every Clear Channel Radio station and would vary by format and daypart. The plan, dubbed Less Is More, also advocated the use of thirty-second (and shorter) spots in addition to the radio commercial standard of sixty seconds.

Radio spots in the rest of the world had already migrated to 30-second spots, and television had used the 30-second commercial as its staple spot length for years. So the fact that U.S. radio would be the last to accommodate the shorter attention spans of younger media consumers was not lost on the company.

A statement released at the time reported that "Clear Channel Radio is placing a new and significantly lower ceiling on the amount of commercial minutes that are played per hour across its radio group, as well as limits on the length of commercials in a spot break. In addition to reducing commercial capacity, Clear Channel Radio will also reduce and limit the amount of promotional interruption on all of its radio stations."

"Clutter is a major issue in our industry and our decision to limit the amount of commercial time and length of breaks, while reducing promotional interruptions, will benefit listeners, advertisers and the industry as a whole," John Hogan observed at the time. "Despite radio's great underlying listener trends, and the fragmentation in other media, radio is still discounted relative to other media. We're taking this step to close that gap and make radio more competitive, compelling, effective, and valuable. And we actively encourage the rest of the industry to do the same."

This new policy was expected to improve the listening product for consumers while providing advertisers more effective opportunities and value for their advertising dollar. And over time, all of that did happen.

But as they say on Broadway, the initial reviews were mixed. The LIM initiative, as it came to be known, alternately was met with praise and ridicule. Some radio broadcasters lauded the company's move, while others said that commercial clutter was an issue for only those few companies that overloaded on spots to begin with. While some group heads publicly observed that any move to reduce radio spot loads should be commended, behind closed doors a few condemned the plan as just another way for Clear Channel to exert pricing pressure on advertisers and agencies. And the response from major advertising and media-buying groups who felt jolted by such a major change was less than positive.

The move also was controversial inside the company. Compensation for sales professionals was changed to create incentives to sell the shorter-length spots. And a new metric, "yield per minute," was created to measure success. For sales professionals used to selling only 60-second ads, and measured on gross dollars, the changes were significant.

JOHN HOGAN INSISTED AT THE TIME THAT, "GIVING LISTENERS A BETTER experience, and giving a better environment, inarguably is a benefit — and a step forward. Part of radio's challenge is not just on the sales and marketing side; it's on the audience and consumer side. People have more choices today and they have different lifestyles today, so as they are evolving, radio has to evolve. That's what LIM is all about."

Today, Hogan characterizes Less Is More as the foundation for making radio more attractive to listeners and, in turn, to advertisers. "LIM is an umbrella term for the evolution of our radio stations," he explains. "The evolution is to make them more meaningful, more valuable, more connected to our audiences. If we do that and then offer advertisers a better environment and more choices in spot length, spot price, and spot position, that's a huge win."

Ultimately, Less Is More changed the way that radio advertising was bought and sold. But Madison Avenue did not instantly jump onto the Clear Channel bandwagon, and many agency directors and media buyers raised some very real concerns about how a shift from 60-second commercials to those that were 30 and 15 seconds in length might affect consumer awareness. The concerns were so real that Clear Channel funded studies and developed a Creative Services Group to help advertisers and agencies create spots that drove listener retention.

Still, many were intrigued by what shortened commercial pods would mean, since it was long believed that a spot break that contained seven or eight commercials in a row was detrimental to those advertisers that were not the first or second to be heard in that cluster. Additionally, Less Is More forced many creative directors to rethink how they were writing and producing radio commercials, since they now had to convey a sales message in half as much time as they previously worked with. While television for years had sold 30-second commercials, some people had settled into the thinking that, since radio only has an audio element to work with, the message had to be twice as long.

The noise that resulted from the announcement and implementation of LIM stems from the very nature of change, John Hogan says. "It was different," he explains. "It was unfamiliar. It represented a major challenge for people, and it was difficult for them to get their arms around it. But it's like arguing whether a diet is a good thing for an overweight person. There is no argument: If you are overweight, if you are bloated, if you are not taking care of the body, the machine, or the structure, you are going to have problems. So you can argue about whether it should be the Atkins Diet or the South Beach diet, but there is no argument that by dieting you are improving things."

Broadcasters who fiercely criticized LIM are examples of the lag-behind mentality that still seems to pervade the radio industry, Hogan says. "The very same people — both inside the broadcast industry who acknowledge that clutter was an issue and who acknowledge the need for change and leadership — have really done nothing. This is one of the things that historically has limited our ability as an industry to collaborate on common challenges. We're always going to be competitive, but people are delusional if they think that running 15 commercial minutes an hour, or spot breaks that run 8 or 9 units deep, aren't very real obstacles to our future."

"The original responses to Less Is More were pretty choppy," recalls Gary Fries, who was president of the Radio Advertising Bureau when LIM was launched. "Initially there was a lack of understanding of what it all meant, which led to a lot of misinterpretation."

There is universal agreement that the initiative directed a bright spotlight on the radio business within the advertising industry, pointing out the "commercial creep" that had occurred over the past ten decades. Some broadcasters resented Clear Channel for conceding to Madison Avenue that they had been inserting more and more advertisements in order to achieve double-digit revenue growth, and more than a few maintained that not they, but other groups, were guilty of this practice.

Meanwhile, the LIM initiative was introduced at a time when the radio industry was experiencing almost flat revenue growth, causing a further financial displacement that lasted well over a year. The plan reduced the amount of commercial time on Clear Channel radio stations alone by an average of 19 percent — handing almost one-fifth of its revenue-producing time over to the DJs and program directors.

"Less Is More caused some real difficulties in a very tough advertising environment," Fries says. "If this had taken place five years earlier in the heat of the Internet era, when radio just couldn't get out of the way of the business, it just would have gone right through without comment. But unfortunately we happened to hit a financial downturn, and that may have led to a lot of negativity and fear within the industry."

"Clear Channel took a lot of heat for Less Is More, but history will show that they were absolutely correct," says Entercom CEO David Field. "Part of LIM was the company's willingness to exorcize the excess inventory, and part of it was their recognition that radio needed to evolve to a medium with shorter spot lengths. In a world where the 60-second commercial is grossly superfluous in most advertising applications, by creating 30- and 15-second commercials we end up providing a more effective way for our advertisers to reach listeners and provide a much more listenable product. It's a win-win for everybody, but it required some short-term pain for long-term gain. And as the industry leader they stepped up and did that. Clear Channel was the only company, other than CBS Radio, that had the wherewithal to truly drive the marketplace toward that desirable outcome."

Any time there is change, people have varying reactions to it — and many are highly resistant, Hogan concludes today. "We saw that on a number of fronts, but our job was to stay the course and make sure that we did this as intelligently and thoughtfully as we could, and work hard to get the right results. I had as much riding on this as anyone. I certainly have had a big target on my back. But I also have the great fortune to work for people who are visionaries: Mark, Randall, and Lowry Mays. It would have been very easy for them to take the short-term view and get unsettled by the financial challenges we had at the start of LIM. But they are absolutely looking at radio for the long-term. They understand and support the ideas that make up this initiative, and while they are eager to increase our revenues and our profitability, they have been extraordinarily supportive."

"Without question it was the right decision," says Mark Mays. "The consumer research clearly showed that people didn't like the clutter on radio stations, and that was leading to a huge consumer backlash to traditional radio. We had to fix that if we were going to improve our long-term prospects."

And they did.

Arbitron ratings released after the first full year of LIM bear out the belief that listeners notice commercial clutter — and will tune in when that clutter is reduced. And after four gloomy quarters of negative radio revenue in 2005, Clear Channel in May 2006 announced that its first-quarter radio revenues were up 5 percent, to $808.9 million. During the company's quarterly conference call, Mark Mays said that both national and local ad revenue increased during the quarter, and indicated that there was growing popularity for 30- and 15-second commercials, as well as increases in revenue per minute and average unit rates. The rest of the industry was down low- to mid-single digits for the same quarter.

After a year of uncertainty and debate, most advertisers and agencies have come to recognize it as a positive for all concerned. "After some initial belief that Clear Channel was simply trying to raise rates, they've come to understand the importance of creating a better advertising environment," says Stu Olds, chief executive officer of Clear Channel-owned rep firm Katz Media Group. "They believe in the increased value of shorter pods, and now that we're seeing increased audience numbers, the rest of the industry is beginning to reduce inventory, as well. The advertising community clearly believes that radio is doing things differently and that Clear Channel is leading that charge."

Clear Channel easily could have ignored the problem of slow but steady audience erosion in the face of commercial clutter. But rather than try to maintain modest revenue and cash flow growth while collectively wringing their hands about the shift of audience to new technologies, Hogan — and the rest of the company's leadership — looked beyond the quarterly perspective of Wall Street in favor of a longer-term outlook.

"It would have been very easy for us to outperform our peers had we not instituted LIM," Hogan says. "But had we not done this, I guarantee that the radio business today would not be talking about the industry's long-term viability. We would have been stuck in the same rut."

LET'S GET DIGITAL

In the late 1980s and early '90s, as digital audio technology evolved from a drawing-board fantasy to a reality, engineers in the U.S. and overseas began to envision a revolution unlike anything the media had ever seen. Ever since Thomas Edison invented and developed the phonograph, all audio had been recorded and stored in "analog" mode. As advancements in computer coding and solid state electronics began to make digital audio not only possible, but a reality, the traditional "needle-in-grooves" technology that was developed in Edison's Menlo Park, New Jersey, laboratory shifted to a new technology known as the compact disc. Recognizing that digital audio provided a more satisfying sound for most music lovers (except those who professed to enjoy the pops found on old vinyl records), the recording industry made a hasty evolution to compact discs. This decision was fueled by the recognition that many audiophiles would seek to convert their music libraries from LPs to CDs, igniting sales of catalog product and driving significant profit to the record labels' bottom lines. Reacting to consumer demand, electronic equipment manufacturers developed generations of new CD players that could play these innovative new discs. The first models, which cost well in excess of $1,000 and had few features, soon were replaced by multi-disk units that were capable of sophisticated functions and whose price points dropped considerably as more and more units were sold.

Meanwhile, the radio industry climbed on the digital bandwagon, with many stations proclaiming that they were "all-digital, all-the-time." Studio turntables were tossed into the dumpster and replaced by systems that either played directly from compact disc or transferred the digital audio directly to tape cartridges. The audience soon caught on to this new digital listening experience, scooping up Sony's new portable Discman (and competing systems) almost as fast as they could be produced.

There was one problem: As digital as a radio station's studios and control room may have been, the digital signal ended at the transmitter. No matter how pure and sweet a digital signal might be to the human ear, by the time it was broadcast over the AM and FM band it had reverted to its analog sound, with all the accompanying hiss, fade, "picket-fencing," and tunnel effects. The radio broadcast that came out of the dashboard of a listener's car virtually was no different from what it had been ten or twenty years before, and to consumers who now were listening to digital everywhere else, the difference was obvious.

That difference was particularly obvious to audio engineers, who realized that the only solution to this analog discrepancy was to convert radio signals to digital. It might sound simple, but the challenge lay in the fact that the audio spectrum is sliced into a wide variety of uses, only one sliver of which is reserved for transmitting radio signals. FM stations transmit within 88 and 108 megahertz, while AM stations broadcast within 535 and 1700 kilohertz. Other common uses of radio frequencies outside the FM and AM band include shortwave radio, television stations, garage door openers, cell phones, air traffic control radar, and global positioning systems.

The engineering challenge was to find a way to broadcast a digital signal either on a sliver of available but unused spectrum, or to "piggy-back" that signal on top of a broadcaster's existing radio frequency. In 1990, a European-sponsored consortium of government and broadcast industry scientists successfully demonstrated a digital audio broadcast in Canada, using what in engineering circles is referred to as the L-Band. Unlike standard AM and FM signals, broadcasts on the L-band are virtually immune to interference, which means there are no "multi-path" echoes caused by signals bouncing off buildings or natural topographical features.

The National Association of Broadcasters initially supported this system of digital audio broadcasting for adoption in the U.S., but two problems with the L-Band quickly emerged: First, the U.S. military uses that particular slice of spectrum for telemetry purposes; second, American broadcasters preferred a system that would have kept the digital broadcasts "closer to home." In other words, they wanted to find a solution that allowed the new signal to be broadcast "in-band and on-channel" (IBOC) within the same frequency that they currently used to transmit their AM or FM programming.

Development of this IBOC digital radio technology in the U.S. began in 1991, when CBS and Gannett established USA Digital Radio Partners; Westinghouse Corp. joined the partnership shortly thereafter. In 1998 USA Digital Radio Partners changed its name to USA Digital Radio, and a group of major U.S. radio companies invested $20 million to incorporate the new company. In 2000 the firm merged with Lucent to become iBiquity Corp., and over the next year the company developed and tested its IBOC system.

In 2002 the FCC approved the technology, and iBiquity branded the system publicly as High Definition Radio (HD Radio). The following year a number of broadcast companies announced that they would begin converting their stations to HD, despite the fact that electronics manufacturers had yet to commit themselves to building HD-capable receivers.

Meanwhile, some savvy radio engineers discovered that if the new HD digital signal were to be split, a radio station effectively could broadcast its FM programming on one HD channel and have enough frequency left over to broadcast an entirely different digital signal — and perhaps two or three. At the same time, consumers were growing comfortable with the digital sound emanating from their iPods and satellite radio receivers, it became obvious to a few radio industry leaders that it would be fatal to just "hurry up and wait."

Thus, in December 2005 the radio industry experienced a first: The CEOs of eight rival broadcasting companies came together to announce a joint initiative — the HD Digital Radio Alliance. This *ad hoc* group's sole mission would be to invigorate the roll-out of HD radio — accelerating the production of receivers, retail availability, in-vehicle installations, and consumer interest — and to make sure that the industry didn't miss what was perceived as a very small window of opportunity to make the switch to digital broadcasting.

If it weren't for some carefully applied pressure and arduous negotiations, the HD Digital Radio Alliance might never have seen the light of day. As Randall Mays says, "Neither Mark, Lowry, nor I ever try to pat ourselves on the back or take credit, but make no mistake, there would not be an HD Digital Radio Alliance if it weren't for Clear Channel. iBiquity was floundering and they were not going to be able to get additional capital. Plus, the auto manufacturers and the receiver manufacturers had basically given up. So I sat down personally with [iBiquity Chairman] Bob Struble, and said, 'What does it take to get this going?' And he said, 'Well, we've got to raise this much money, and we've got to get the auto manufacturers and the receiver manufacturers back on board.' So I asked him, 'Well, what do you need to do that?' And he answered, 'I need a commitment from the industry to roll this out, and for you guys to convert to HD.'"

One of the stumbling blocks to conversion was the fact that, as a for-profit corporation that owned the proprietary system through which the digital signal could be broadcast, iBiquity was charging license fees to each radio company in order for them to use the digital algorithm. Usage was licensed on a sliding scale dependent on revenue, although iBiquity had offered a low "early adopter" start-up fee in order to get broadcasters to invest in the technology. Still, some broadcasters — Clear Channel included — were not pleased with how these rates very likely could escalate in the future, and they wanted assurances that if they committed to HD conversion they would not be gouged at a later date.

"I said to Bob, 'Okay — what are you going to give me?'" Randall Mays recalls. "And he said, effectively, 'Well, I'm not going to give you anything.' At which point I said, 'Well, that doesn't fly. We will not as an industry be held hostage to an outside service provider. We've already got that with Arbitron right now, and let me assure you, it doesn't work.'"

Mays says that he and Struble had a bit of a stare-down but, at the end of the day, they had a deal. "We got long-term imbedded pricing that's tied to a formula where the better we do, the better they do," he notes. "And they got a commitment from us and a lot of other broadcasters to roll out HD Radio as quickly as possible."

Now the task fell on Clear Channel to get other broadcasters to agree. Randall Mays credits Entercom CEO David Field with getting much of the HD Alliance deal done, noting that he truly was a catalyst in terms of helping bring people on board. "David made it happen," he says. "But if there hadn't been Clear Channel, I guarantee it wouldn't have happened." Mays concedes that some entities in the radio industry might be either intimidated or afraid of Clear Channel, and he says that's probably for good reason. "I'm not sure they shouldn't be a little wary of us, but I think they're finally understanding that if we weren't here, they would be a lot worse off than having us here."

"Several of us spent a lot of time talking about HD Radio, and in conversations with Mark, we both agreed that an alliance was by far the most effective means of ensuring that HD Radio would be successful in the marketplace," Field says. "Mark and Randall have done a great job shepherding that effort, and as an industry we're doing a great job accelerating the deployment of that technology."

"We needed bold leadership on this issue," observes Peter Smyth, president and CEO of Greater Media and a member of the Alliance management committee. "People at the major companies who would stand up, take risks, and defy the standard operating mentality. Mark and Randall did that, effectively saying, 'This is a new day, this is the value of our medium, and we need to start to believe in it for what it's worth.'"

CHAPTER FIFTEEN

BACK TO
THE FUTURE

MORE THAN 85 YEARS AFTER THE FIRST COMMERCIAL RADIO PROGRAM WAS transmitted over the air in Pittsburgh, extreme change has come to the broadcasting landscape. Near-logarithmic evolution in digital technology and broadband communications has introduced a vast array of new devices that allow consumers to obtain news and entertainment in ways that even Gene Roddenberry and George Lucas could only dream of. The last few years have introduced serious technological transformation into the consumer marketplace, and as iPods, cell phones, PDAs, and other as-yet unimagined appliances are set to capture more and more out-of-home time spent listening (and viewing), traditional mass media are being forced to reconsider their business models and compete in a new media world order. The "new media" genie is out of the bottle and there's no getting him back in.

No media company is more pressured by this technological shift — and possibly better-positioned to deal with it — than Clear Channel. How the firm adapts to and grows with these changes will determine its health and longevity.

"We're really in the business of delivering information and entertainment," says John Hogan. "With the proliferation of news, information, and entertainment outlets today, it would be crazy to think of ourselves simply as radio operators. We have a team of people who evaluate technological advances and opportunities so we can stay at the forefront. Radio is vastly different today from when we were growing up, which was very different from when our parents were growing up. We need to remember that so much can change so quickly, and make sure that we remain flexible and — most important — are willing to change along with it."

The first glimpse of change came during the late 1990s, when early adopters began to see the opportunities — and challenges — presented by the Internet. At that time a few radio stations began to experiment with the booming medium by offering online "streams" of their programming, including Clear Channel's. But as high-speed connections continued to be scarce except at the most cutting-edge companies, web-based listening was slow to catch on.

That didn't keep other entrepreneurs from creating online radio stations that offered niche programming that was perceived to be glaringly absent from over-the-air broadcasting, and a number of these survived the implosion that came when the bottom fell out of the dot-com fantasy world. Still, the web was not yet ready for drive time, and many radio broadcasters heaved a collective sigh of relief that they had dodged a competitive threat. They had been here before — the situation was similar to the development of television in the early '50s and the introduction of in-dash 8-track tape players in the '70s. Indeed, a common sentiment heard at radio conventions was "radio survived those technologies, and we will survive these new competitive threats, as well."

Except that, aside from Clear Channel, most radio broadcasters were not moving in anticipation of the high number of new audio and video devices that were about to appear in rapid succession. Shortly, radio was ceding the out-of-home field to consumers, who now enjoyed enormous choice over where and how they could obtain their music, news, and information. Apple's iPod allowed users to rip and store thousands of their favorite songs in a device about the size of a fat credit card, ostensibly obviating the need for a program director to develop a station playlist. Cell phones quickly followed suit, evolving into tiny appliances that not only allowed people to communicate with one another, but also to take photographs of their friends, send text messages, and play music, videos, and games in a way that radio was not equipped to handle. The introduction of WiFi and its Herculean cousin, WiMax, promises to provide even greater conductivity and consumer choice.

"What we're seeing is convergence and divergence at the same time," says Clear Channel's Jeff Littlejohn. "We need to come up with divergent ways of distributing audio. Broadcast free over the air analog radio is going to be the major listening device for some time to come; there are a lot of other things coming down the pike. XM and Sirius are part of this, and so are podcasting, cellular phones, the Internet, and HD Radio. There are just a lot of different ways that people can receive media now." Littlejohn stresses that it's critical not to worry about how audio content is being delivered, but instead to produce the best content available and distribute it in as many ways as possible. "Younger consumers are looking to get what they want when they want it, and we need to be able to give it to them," he points out.

To the radio industry this shift in focus may appear to be both monumental and staggering, but it is typical of any industry in which a new product or service is introduced to the marketplace. Any time in the 20th century that a distribution system in an industry has faced a new technological threat or point of competition, the incumbent industry as a rule reacts with responses designed to reduce the damage or threat. This is true when airlines posed a threat to trans-Atlantic liners or the railroads, when electronic media went up against newspapers, and even when the U.S. Postal System was confronted with such overnight services as Federal Express or DHL. Established industries almost always respond in the same way, with the incumbent industry burying its head in the sand. When that fails to work, the incumbent industry tries to cut costs in order to preserve its historical margins. The next thing that happens is that the older industry invests in the new technology or in a competitor of that new technology. It could be said that the radio industry today is somewhere between steps two and three.

In order to extract itself from this traditional recovery process — one that is not all that dissimilar to the five stages of grief — radio needs to pursue aggressively alternative methods of distribution and revenue. "For radio companies to do well in the future, they need to protect their brands and deliver a critical mass audience," says Deutsche Bank's Drew Marcus. "They need to have a strategy to maximize the Internet, which could be a $50 billion advertising pot over the next ten years. It's equally important to have a mobile strategy, given the increased functionality of mobile devices. Then it's critical to think about how certain products fit within a bundle, which could provide a triple or quadruple play. Finally, radio needs to see how its content can be made more valuable so its revenue can be maximized."

So where does this leave radio, and the companies that have invested millions of dollars in studios, transmitters, and towers? Some, like Clear Channel, see it as an opening.

"I see nothing but huge opportunity for radio to build a complementary experience in the online and mobile space," says Evan Harrison, whom Clear Channel hired away from AOL in 2004 to lead the company into the on-demand world. "My task is to take the strength of our brands — we have 1,005 of them that speak to an audience in a passionate way on a local level — and build out a complementary relationship using a new medium."

In an on-demand world, the online environment presents numerous opportunities to pick off some low-hanging fruit, and Harrison's first task was to identify opportunities that could be generated from Clear Channel's existing properties. "I saw that we could use our KISS FM brand in L.A. not only to keep our listeners connected with the on-air broadcast, but, if they were using the computer in their bedroom instant messaging their friends while doing another twenty things, they not only could listen to the radio but watch videos that we could deliver on demand," he says. "All of a sudden this allowed us to be in the business of visual programming, both on the programming side and the advertising side."

In other words, it's all about brand extension. Broadcasters who understand that each of their radio stations represents individual brands within the minds of listeners are those who will be able to bridge the gap successfully between traditional and new media.

"The opportunity lies in taking the strengths of the Clear Channel brands and reinventing what those brands mean," Harrison says. "We reach 110 million people a week, and we reach them in a way that creates an excitement level that a passive medium can't. Being able to offer an experience that is complementary to radio is a one-two punch that few other broadcasters or media companies rarely have an opportunity to do." Harrison notes that, while many broadcast executives lose sleep at night worrying about what everybody else is doing, he loses sleep because he's thinking there may be an opportunity lurking out there that he is not taking advantage of.

So it's ironic that radio was one of the first industries that descended on the Internet, almost *en masse,* during the dot-com boom of the late 1990s — yet since then, many radio websites outside the Clear Channel network have yet to evolve past the embryonic stage. This has happened for a number of reasons, not the least of which was the prohibitive rights fees imposed on entities that use the web to stream music. But the fact remains that many are used primarily as online billboards, highlighting the station's on-air staff and upcoming events, a purpose that serves the station well but might not have sticking power with the user. That was true of Clear Channel's sites at one time, and Harrison says that one of his first responsibilities when he came on board was to clean them up and make them clutter-free, just as was happening at the company's radio stations. The next step was to increase greatly the number of stations that were streaming their on-air content online — but with a twist. "It's the same programming that is being broadcast over the air, but it's not necessarily the same advertisements," Harrison says. "We don't simply pass an advertiser through online; those commercial messages have a value all their own. Some Clear Channel advertisers buy online but they don't buy on-air, some buy both, and some only buy on-air."

Harrison says that one of the biggest misconceptions within the radio industry is that the Internet is limited to streaming a station's existing program content. While that does allow for significant brand extension, a little out-of-the-box thinking — and the resources to implement it — can extend the station's brand to additional levels. "All of our stations have websites, and many of those websites go way beyond streaming," he explains. "For example, we have a proprietary show called Stripped that's our own production. We've done several dozen of them, including shows with Kanye West, Big & Rich, Gretchen Wilson, Rob Thomas, Melissa Etheridge, Sugarland, and James Blunt. This allows us to offer on-demand programming on our websites, and we've been able to expand our playlists by using our websites to talk about new artists and extend the number of artists we promote. People can watch an entire performance, listen to it in audio, and access the archives to view previous Stripped performances of other artists. Some websites also feature full-length streams of albums on demand; for instance, Jamie Foxx, Rod Stewart, and Paul McCartney all have debuted their CDs on our websites. Sometimes the only place you could hear the entire body of work for four days was on our station's websites." Additionally, some Clear Channel stations offer podcasts of various programming elements, allowing users to download directly to their iPods anything from segments of popular morning shows to comedy bits to short vignettes. "So far we've already moved tens of millions of pieces of content through podcasting," Harrison says. "It's simply another way to get people to come to our sites to get content on demand."

The online platform also allows stations to expand beyond the tight structure of their format. For instance, a news/talk station that traditionally programs a lineup of political talking heads need not restrict itself to the same sort of content on its website. Recognizing that many news/talk stations attract a predominantly male audience, that station can offer additional content that appeals to its core listener. "You'll find a talk station promoting the fact that the only place to hear the new Bon Jovi record is on their website," Harrison says. "People who listen to talk shows also are into music."

Critics who alleged — inaccurately, as it turns out — that Clear Channel diminished the number of formats and the opportunities for up-and-coming artists to get national exposure will be intrigued by an artist development program the company has introduced. Known as "New," the program makes available songs from emerging and unsigned artists. Also, the company has built an online vault of some 4,000 record company-created music videos. "All of this stuff is available at any given time on our websites, and that's giving people a reason to come back," Harrison says. "We've already sold visual ads to our advertisers, something that has never before existed in radio. All of a sudden big name companies like Corona, along with the neighborhood hair salons and restaurants, are buying fifteen-second visual ads on radio station websites. Not only are our listeners coming to our websites, but since we've only just begun to really let our audiences on air know what's available, we expect that growth curve to continue to expand rapidly. We've already seen NBC, Orbitz, and major automotive companies buying our streaming as a network. We're seeing exponential growth that's already into meaningful numbers, and it's going to continue to be more so as online grows about 30 percent a year."

The changes bore fruit immediately and in October of 2007, Clear Channel's Online Music & Radio unit took the number-one position among all online music and radio players in the crucial workday time period* — the time period during which the majority of online radio listening occurs. In doing so, the company passed Yahoo!, AOL, and others who had effectively popularized the medium.

Human resistance has never been able to stop technological change, and the same will be true of all the emerging technologies that threaten to slice and dice the public's time spent with any medium — new or traditional. While many "old-line" broadcasters remain in denial about the changing media landscape, it's useless to try to contain the radio industry within a decades-old business model. As Harrison notes, "It's going to become very clear that consumers are going to have a range of choices for getting infor-

*According to audience statistics tracked by ComScore/MediaMetrix.

mation and entertainment on a variety of devices." To that end, he says that Clear Channel's major focus is to "continue to create great programming and continue to package that programming in new ways. But we also have to create new programming that no radio company would ever be creating. Satellite radio clearly has tipped their hat to the fact that programming is king, although the way they're paying for programming and trying to keep an ad-free environment can't sustain their business model."

Along with Tom Owens, Harrison co-heads Clear Channel's content research and development division, which he maintains is a clear indication that the company already recognizes that radio is a constantly evolving medium. "Our strength is our local connection and relationship with the listener," he says. "But the lines have really blurred as to how we package and deliver the content. Radio used to be a live broadcast, and it really was a one-way medium. Now we're in the on-demand world, delivering content in ways that radio never has done before. People can listen to us on air, or they can go to our websites and receive packaged content that's appropriate for that delivery mechanism." Harrison says that the most exciting aspect of the multi-platform world is radio's ability to create full user interaction. "When this system is fully integrated, our websites will be the destination for an infinite variety of possibilities," he explains. "Things like ring-tone ticketing and digital commerce opportunities will come to life on our sites, and as a result, we'll have deeper partnerships with our listeners and our advertisers.

"The greatest threat would be to put our heads down and deny the value of new media," Harrison continues. "The greatest upside clearly is to take chances and embrace new technology and new opportunities in order to extend our reach and our relevance, and to find more meaningful ways for radio to reach its audience. Radio has always been a medium that can generate excitement due to that local relationship and the ability a jock has to really bring something to life. To now complement that with all of the new devices and distribution platforms is only an opportunity for our listeners to have a deeper relationship with the station — and for advertisers to find new ways to reach our listeners. As this change continues we will see a constant evolution of devices and an expanding number of choices for consumers to get their information, their news, their sports, and their entertainment. And we are going to be there, regardless of the device."

"Many younger listeners are early adopters of new technology," says Tom Poleman, Clear Channel's New York senior vice president programming and marketing. "They've never known a world without the Internet. They're part of a push-button, instant-gratification generation. We're living in an attention-deficit society, where every moment counts." As a result, listeners demand more from their media choices, and Poleman insists that radio needs to continue to find ways to integrate new technology with programming, giving listeners more choices, more interactivity, more customization, and more exclusive and specialized content. "Our products need to be more compelling than ever," he observes. "We have to grab their attention and keep them." To that end, in the fall of 2007, WHTZ-FM in New York launched "Z100 Mobile," an interactive service through which listeners are able to listen to the station live via cell phone. They also can download podcasts and wallpapers, rate photos of other listeners, access traffic reports on demand, and receive a text message alert when their song request is about to air.

Randall Mays says that Prophet Systems, a music scheduling system created in 1989 and now owned by Clear Channel will play a critical role as the company moves into the distribution of personalized media. Prophet essentially is an automation system that schedules a station's programming and commercial elements, eliminating the need for a board operator to physically play CDs or insert audio tape cartridges into playback machines. In addition to streamlining a station's on-air operations, the Prophet system also allows for stations to stream their programs on the Internet, after stripping out specific components.

"When we first started to stream programming on the web there were restrictions on some of the commercials and music," Mays recalls. "We started to strip out the commercials, which gave us two separate streams. Then I began to wonder whether, if we could create two streams, it would be possible to create a third stream." The answer turned out to be "yes"; in fact, Prophet allows the creation of an infinite number of programming streams — which, across a platform of 1,005 radio stations, presents some interesting opportunities.

As Joel Denver, president of All Access Music Group, observes, "One of the smartest things John Hogan has said is 'we're no longer in the big stick business. No longer just tall towers in big fields. We're in the branding business.' That's incredibly brilliant and observant — and that's what radio needs to begin to believe. Radio has many listeners to win back and maintain their listenership for longer periods. We have this infrastructure that's called the Internet, and as long as we have access to it and can market our brand, people will find a way to listen to it."

"The line between audio content and the radio business is closing in every day," says Jimmy Risk, president of LoyalEars and a major proponent of radio's use of podcasting. "Anyone who thinks this is just a passing thing hasn't thought enough about the future. The barriers to entry for podcasting are so low that the numbers are just going to be overwhelming." Risk says that radio's current greatest hope — HD radio — is still a good five years away from achieving critical mass, and notes that a lot can happen to consumer media within that time frame. "My suggestion to radio is to start podcasting right now and use it as a training ground for HD, or for whatever new technology might outstrip everything else five or seven years from now. In that regard, Clear Channel is probably the most aggressive, terrestrial radio company, especially with Evan Harrison running that show."

"The launch of HD Radio gives us the opportunity to show that radio is still a very vibrant medium," says Randall Mays. "The impact of digital audio will be significant, and the people who believe satellite radio is going to put terrestrial radio out of business will be proven wrong."
Indeed, Bridge Ratings in March 2006 predicted that HD Radio would experience "hockey stick" growth, with 1 million HD receivers in use by the end of 2006 and 9 million by the end of 2010. While XM and Sirius were expected to hit 8.5 million and 6 million subscribers, respectively, by the end of 2006, HD Radio's late surge very well could offset the gains made by the two satellite players. While some radio companies don't see a need for converting to HD and, therefore, "might not make the bend in the road," Randall Mays says that Clear Channel is poised to take advantage of all things digital. "What will become very clear over the course of the next two to three years is that the satellite companies are in a digital oasis," he says. "Satellite has a huge formatic advantage over us today because of the spectrum that they were allocated, and they get to pump 120 stations in every market while we get eight."

Despite satellite radio's ability to broadcast scores of channels to paying customers while terrestrial radio is hamstrung by technological and ownership limits, the deployment of HD Radio will allow radio companies — particularly Clear Channel — to narrow dramatically that discrepancy. "Not surprisingly, 85 percent of satellite listening is to 20 percent of the channels — and the majority of all their listening is to rebroadcasts of commercial radio," Randall says. "Everybody thinks that people buy satellite radio for the commercial-free music, but if you study what people really listen to, you find that they're actually tuning to commercial programs. As we further diversify formats via HD radio, people are going to start saying, 'Why am I paying $15 a month for this?' If they can get what they really want on their iPods, and if they don't mind listening to commercials, they can get it for free on terrestrial radio."

Mays believes that in the media landscape of the future, where listeners will look for customized listening experiences, "a fixed pipe from the sky isn't going to get it done." But terrestrial broadcasters, in order to compete, are going to have to provide a more customized experience that satellite will be unable to fulfill. "Ultimately, the satellite companies will not be able to provide what consumers want and need, and they're going to have a very difficult time migrating off the satellite platform, because they have no competitive advantage to do so. How can paying Howard Stern $100 million a year be a competitive advantage?" While XM at one time boasted that it would hit 10 million subscribers some time in 2007 — a number that in late 2006 clearly seemed out of reach — Clear Channel currently has 110 million listeners per week, Randall points out. "*That,* to me, is a competitive advantage," he says. "One of the reasons you see XM and Sirius working at Herculean rates to get subscribers is that they know they have very limited time to get to where they need to be."

Mays points out that, as XM and Sirius have failed to hit their respective subscriber quotas, their stock prices have experienced a significant reality check. "At some point these companies are going to come crashing back to earth," he observes. "At the same time, radio needs to grow in order for the industry to experience an expansion in its cash flow multiples. But when radio does start growing — and it will — the media landscape will come back to being level." Mays concedes that a number of analysts and money managers believe that radio's consolidation game — and thus the industry's real growth potential — has already been played out, and any reversal of this outlook will take hard work and some risks. He also says that broadcasters who wring their hands and say "woe is me" while doing nothing to change their approach to the radio business are playing radio roulette. "We can't all just sit around and say 'radio is great!'" he says. "We have to do a lot better job of self-examination. It's like a person who's been coughing and coughing but refuses to go to the doctor because he thinks he's going to be fine. Well, at some point you have to go get a check-up and find out what's wrong with you. That's what we did with Less Is More: We looked at the research, which said that listeners thought radio was good, but we were running too many commercials and interruptions. So we decided we were going to make a drastic change, and we wanted to make sure we did it in a dramatic fashion rather than doing it a little bit at a time over five years. We wanted to do it now so we could correct it for the future."

Satellite radio, MP3 players, and cell phones aren't going to replace radio, but they will present very real competition, Mays continues. "These new technologies aren't going to put us out of business, but we need to have a better environment for both our advertisers and our listeners," he says. "People have a lot more things to do in the car, whether that's talking on the cell phone or listening to an iPod or tuning in to a satellite radio. Within this environment we have to make radio a compelling place for people to want to be."

To do that in an increasingly competitive marketplace, radio also will have to return to one of its basic core assets: the on-air personality. As Sean Compton, Clear Channel vice president of programming, observes, "When television came to life, radio stations playing the hits became the big guys while stations with orchestras and sound effects became archaic. Over time new music formats evolved and AM music stations moved to FM. AM stations rebounded by launching news, talk, and later, sports programming. Now we are faced with portable technologies, such as satellite radio, WIFI radio, and iPods moving into our cars, homes and workplaces. In order to compete with these technologies, radio will have to rely on more personalities in the coming years."

Compton notes that radio cannot compete with emerging technologies simply by increasing the number of songs played in a row. "Successful radio hosts are doing more and more podcasting, have significant web presence, and some of them even have TV shows," he says. "It's the cross-promotion that reinforces their brand on radio. It comes down to entertaining and informative local programming and nationally successful personalities. This does not mean that music radio will disappear, but music will eventually become secondary to the personality."

Not surprisingly, countering the negative spin from competing industries is a priority.

"If you listen to all these press pundits, everything else out there is sexier and hipper and better than radio," says Mark Mays. "After awhile that starts to weigh on the consumer's mind. We need to do a better job of marketing radio, providing consumers with messages about why radio is great. At the same time we need to provide great radio."

Of course, much of radio's success in the new media world will be in bringing advertisers along with it. Recent history has shown that consumers are less than enthusiastic about having to pay for music content either online or for their personal listening devices, which means that an advertiser-based model of some kind must be extended to future media endeavors.

Katz Media's Stu Olds categorizes the advertising environment by breaking it into three distinct segments: new media, traditional media, and static media. "New media is that which is online, video games, cell phones, iPods — all of which are very targeted," he explains. "On the other side of the equation is the static stuff like magazines, cinema, direct mail, and event marketing. Between those two you have traditional media, which is radio, the TV networks, broadcast syndication, cable networks, newspapers, yellow pages. In the last couple of years all the growth has really come on the new media and the static media side." The reason for this, Olds says, is that advertisers and agencies are geared more and more toward measured impressions and measured responses. "We're all trying to scramble to get ourselves into that 'return on investment' world," he explains. "We can do this through new distribution channels, improving the ad environment by reducing inventory, introducing a creative flexibility that didn't exist a couple of years ago, and applying a lot of research that shows the advantages of using radio. All these elements will give radio a new buzz, some new excitement and enthusiasm, and some increased accountability. That's what the ad world is looking for these days, and it's absolutely critical that we give it to them."

"With all its influence, Clear Channel has the ability to shape the future of the radio industry," says Gary Fries. "The leadership at Clear Channel has started investing in that future, realizing that they have a tremendous obligation to research where things are going to go and what this industry is going to look like five or ten years from now. They also know that neither they — nor the industry — can run it the way it's been done before. We're playing a whole new ballgame today."

Although radio stands to be affected directly by this new media convergence, virtually all traditional media are experiencing similar growing pains. Digital transformation is causing intense fragmentation across all media, and radio will be no stranger to this shift. "The towers in big fields will always be there, but no one really knows where the digital world is going to be ten years from now," says Greater Media's Peter Smyth. "If they say they do, run away from them as fast as you can because they're wrong." That said, Smyth believes that radio will continue to be a dominant part of American culture, noting that, "As long as everyone in this industry begins to recognize that they're in the audio entertainment business and not the radio business, we're going to be fine. If everyone thinks we're in the radio business and not the audio entertainment business, we're in trouble. It's the same analogy with the railroads: If they had thought they were in the transportation business, they'd still be successful."

"There's no question that media companies have to evolve," says Deutsche Bank's Drew Marcus. "The disruptive forces of the digital age are severe, and they will continue to be so. Still, if you looked at radio in 2006 — at a time where the effect of satellite radio and Internet radio probably have been the greatest ever — the decline in radio listenership had actually decelerated. It seems as if the positive effects of running fewer commercials has more than compensated for the negative effects of a fragmented audience, which means that if radio continues to deliver a good product, it should always be able to maintain its critical mass. Ninety-three percent of all Americans listen to the radio each week, and I believe it will always maintain that critical mass. The business is not going away."

While the radio industry is faced with myriad ongoing challenges, outdoor advertising's short- and long-term prospects are somewhat clearer. "We are cautiously, unbelievably excited about the digital conversion in outdoor," adds Randall Mays. "If you consider that any advertising medium is only as good as it is in helping an advertiser sell its product, any changes that fundamentally improve the ability of the advertiser to do that are truly groundbreaking. Digital unquestionably allows advertisers to better utilize the medium to target consumers, because you no longer have to have an advertiser who has the maximum marginal utility for a board, 24 hours a day, 7 days a week, on an individual sign." In fact, digital technology allows advertisers to rotate through available inventory in certain time slots, and on certain days of the week. "This allows us to move copy much quicker in a seamless, real-time manner," he says. "That's a tremendous change from when it would take 30 days to create a vinyl and get it posted on the display, and it truly speaks to the value of the medium to an advertiser."

CHAPTER SIXTEEN

A CLEAR AND CLOSELY HELD VISION

TWENTY-THREE YEARS AFTER LOWRY MAYS TOOK CLEAR CHANNEL INTO THE public market, he and his sons engineered a strategy — with the help of a partnership composed of two private equity firms — to re-enter the private sector. While the public market offers advantages such as access to significant sums of capital, the persistent scrutiny of short-term-focused financial analysts, shareholders, and others can serve to diminish some of the financial glow. Additionally, for companies in a regulated industry such as Clear Channel, government regulators and other oversight bodies pile on pressures that can make it difficult to operate in any sense of an entrepreneurial fashion. For Clear Channel, the ability to make quick, sound decisions in a rapidly changing business environment was always the top priority.

"The attraction of being a public company always has been the access to capital, but now we have access to capital in a much different way," says Mark Mays. "Today, it's possible to get the benefits of being a public company when you're privately held. And being a private company has a lot of its own advantages: the chance to have a deeper focus on the business; being able to move quickly; the alignment of interests among everyone involved — all those things make this a very solid arrangement for us. Eliminating the distractions of the public market at this point in our company's development is very appetizing and exciting, and it allows us to focus on growing the business."

Moving forward, Mays sees little difference in the company's focus: Leadership in its business and creative and opportunistic day-to-day operations. "The one thing that will remain consistent in our business is change," he says. "Over the last five or six years, this company has driven enormous change in the industries in which we operate and we've changed dramatically to succeed. To think that it won't continue to do so would be naïve. We will continue to perform and do our best every day. The operating environment in which we do business will continue to change dramatically, and we're going to continue to change dramatically so that we remain the leader in our respective businesses."

That leadership, Mays continues, will also require the company to be as forward-leaning as it has always been.

An area of continued intense focus: the creation and distribution of content. "Digital technology and online platforms have been, by far, our fastest-growing revenue segment, and we believe that will continue into the foreseeable future," Mays says. "We fully committed this company to digital several years ago, and we're doing some pretty creative things in both our Radio and our Outdoor divisions.

"Clearly, we've done more to bring outstanding and modern audio, and even original video, content into our stables than any other company over the last five years," he maintains. "We're committed to continuing to develop content that isn't necessarily thought about in the conventional radio business. We very much see our properties as audio brands, extending from the AM/FM dials through to iPods and cell phones and the Internet. We see no boundaries."

Indeed, in late 2007, Clear Channel revealed its collaboration with Apple Computer and iBiquity Digital Corporation in creating so-called iTunes "tagging." Here's how it works: New HD digital radio receivers from Polk Audio and others are equipped "with iPod docks and special 'tag' buttons." When pushed, the button "tags" a song using a special inaudible digital code embedded within the radio broadcast. Once the iPod is re-synced with iTunes, the song is recalled and either downloaded, played back or purchased via the music service.

An equal focus: the content that moves over those media. "We've always had a passionate connection with our listeners," he observes. "We have to make sure we don't take that for granted, especially with our younger audiences."

In early 2007, the Radio division began a beta rollout of extensive social networking facilities bringing local listeners even closer to on-air personalities and each other. More than 100,000 listeners signed up in the first five pilot markets in the initial 90 days.

For Outdoor, the future is equally ambitious. "Our vision for our Outdoor division is to connect with viewers of our billboards and other outdoor signage in very creative ways. Ideally, in ways that inspire them to become customers of our advertisers."

It's that passion to innovate, combined with a deep sense of purpose for all of the company's customer segments, Mays concludes, that will continue to drive the company's success.

SEGUE

THROUGHOUT CLEAR CHANNEL'S METEORIC HISTORY MUCH HAS BEEN WRITTEN or said about this media entity. Many of these words have originated with individuals and organizations who have attempted to characterize the company according to their own personal motivations or political agendas, often without regard to the truth. Further, as people tend to believe what they read or hear, the rumors and innuendoes take on lives of their own and spread like viral infections. In a world increasingly divided by negativity, it seems more and more important for certain people and groups to criticize those people and groups with whom they have differing opinions or moral differences.

As stated throughout this book, Clear Channel admittedly made its share of mistakes as it was going through a tumultuous period of consolidation and growth. Most of those errors were unintended and minuscule, and similarly, were the product of inexperience, not the malevolent actions of a company with a runaway management team or overriding political agenda. Still, because of Clear Channel's sheer size and the way it changed the radio and outdoor advertising businesses virtually overnight, it makes a good target for those factions that prefer to take aim at an easy target rather than take the time to research and validate the underpinnings of their accusations.

When I began writing this book I didn't know what I was going to learn about Clear Channel, so I approached the task with a keen sense of ambivalence. As a career journalist covering the radio industry, I had written about the company and its "hockey-stick" growth pattern for several decades. During this time I was afforded the opportunity to meet Lowry Mays and many of the rest of the Clear Channel cast and crew, and always had been struck by their profound sense of professionalism and their business acumen. Still, as the editor-in-chief of several broadcast industry trade publications in the late 1990s and the early 2000s, I'd heard the stories of Clear Channel's reputed transgressions, and found myself beginning to question the veracity and intentions of this company that appeared hell-bent on a modern-day course of slash and burn. During this post-deregulation period, I had been the unwitting "anonymous source" of more than one general press article that promised to expose the company to the public, and on more than one occasion I was just as shocked to see how my own words — "deep background" as they were — had been shaped to fit a story, as I was to see how those stories had darkened Clear Channel's intentions with a cloak of evil malfeasance.

Writing this book was an opportunity to set the record straight, both in my own mind and throughout the broadcasting industry. Certainly, I had heard the stories about how Clear Channel approached each new station or company it acquired with a "my-way-or-the-highway" style. I had heard the misrepresentations about the incident in Minot and the alleged zeal with which Clear Channel's entertainment division was laying waste to the concert industry. I had heard about Randy Michaels' brash management style, how the company allegedly was eliminating on-air jocks in favor of voicetracking, and supposedly was cozying up with independent record promoters. But writing a book presents an author with a unique, front-row seat, and throughout an extensive process of interviewing, researching, and digging, I began to form a perception of a company that was far different from what I anticipated. That is the perception that you find in this book.

Of course, had I approached this project with an agenda of my own — essentially, to regurgitate the same tired rumor and accusations that have very little basis in fact — this would have been an entirely different volume altogether. And I suspect that someday, someone will be motivated to write such a book, simply because Clear Channel provided such an easy target. But I also suspect that whoever writes that book will not have the privilege of getting to know the principal players in the story, at least not in the same way that I have. And for that reason, they will miss the heart of the story, because — as mentioned in the introduction of this book — it is all about the people. Of course, it could be said that engaging in this project has shifted my personal balance of subjectivity and objectivity, and in a sense I would tend to agree. But it would be impossible to enter into a mission such as this and not come away with a profound appreciation for the men and women who are a part of this company, and have made it what it is.

It is my sincerest hope that, by reading this book, you will have done the same.

REED BUNZEL
March 2008

ACKNOWLEDGMENTS

RESEARCHING AND WRITING ANY BOOK CANNOT BE ACCOMPLISHED IN A VACUUM or within the confines of a lonely writer's garret. It is a combined effort of many individuals who have been gracious and courteous enough to contribute their time, their opinions, their hard work, and their patience to a journalist whose persistence and perseverance has to border on annoying and, at times, exasperating. While I might not have always shown it at the time, I am tremendously grateful for every ounce of assistance that comes my way — and that's what this section is all about.

I must begin this recognition process by saying that I could not have written this book without the support, trust, encouragement, and total confidence of Clear Channel's Chief Communications Officer, Lisa Dollinger. Having worked in the radio industry for my entire career, I have come to identify and appreciate those individuals who possess an extreme level of commitment and dedication to their work, but Lisa's incredible professionalism has led me to create a new category all unto itself. There is no finer colleague with whom I would have wished to work on this project than you, Lisa. Thank you.

Obviously, this book would not have been possible without the full cooperation of the principle players at Clear Channel. Thanks, first, to my colleague and friend Lowry Mays, who endured my endless, probing questions and shared his life's story over a number of months and long conversations. Many thanks also to his sons, Mark Mays and Randall Mays, two of the finest gentlemen I have ever come to know in the radio business. All three of you are true leaders within this industry, and for you to place your trust and faith in me as I examined all of Clear Channel's many facets is an opportunity I will long remember. Kathryn Mays Johnson: You are an amazing woman, and your candor, sincerity, and continued assistance are most appreciated. Additionally, I want to extend my gratitude to Linda Mays McCaul: Thank you for permitting me to invade your privacy and share your thoughts and views without reservation or hesitation.

Then there's Red McCombs: Red, you are a true Texas gentleman, an entrepreneur, salesman, and inspiration. As I mention in the course of the book, you are the sort of person other people want to hang around just in the hope that some of your business acumen wears off on them. Thank you so much for opening your life to me and making sure that this story was told straight from the heart.

Of course, many other men and women inside Clear Channel took that giant leap of faith by allowing me to invade their offices and set my tape recorders on their desks, hit the record buttons, and ask those prying questions that journalists love to ask. To that end, and in no specific order, I want to thank John Hogan, Andrew Levin, Sean Compton, Bob Cohen, Paul Meyer, Michael Forte, Evan Harrison, Kraig Kitchin, Glenn Beck, Herb Hill, Rick Stensby, Tom Owens, Gabe Hobbs, Tom Poleman, Stu Olds, Don Perry, Jeff Littlejohn, and Dick Lewis. Additionally, for their help in verifying quantitative and qualitative data, I'd like to extend my gratitude to Randy Palmer and Rich Meyer.

Numerous other individuals shared their stories, memories, and viewpoints during the research and writing of this book. Again, in no specific order, I thank you all: Steve Hicks, Donald Trump, Stan Webb, Eddie Fritts, Gary Fries, Bill Stakelin, Peter Smyth, Lew Dickey, Larry Patrick, David Field, Mary Quass, Dan Mason, Ken Beck, Baron Hardelin-Doherty, Drew Marcus, John Barger, Casey Kasem, Marion Oettinger, Erica Farber, Thom Mocarsky, Pierre Bouvard, J. Steven McCusker, Steve Meyer, Jimmy Risk, Joel Denver, Gary Krantz, Howard Nolan, and Robert Struble.

I also would like to thank Monica King for her tireless effort in pulling together volumes of information and research material, setting up appointments and interviews, and making sure that the thousands of little details that accompany a project this large were dealt with smoothly and efficiently. Many thanks also to Alexander Guerri, who spent hundreds of hours transcribing scores of interviews just so I didn't have to. I also extend my sincerest appreciation to Sandra Harrod, who made sure that Lowry Mays was available to chat whenever it seemed I wanted to; Zen Gomez, for making the same arrangements with Mark, Randall, and John; Cindy Talbot, for handling numerous requests for corporate data and hundreds of photographs; and to Kippy Schaefer, Sharon McGuire, Susan Madden, and Katie Forte. Also many thanks to Michele Clarke at Brainerd Communicators and to Amir Forester at Premiere Radio Networks for all their continued assistance.

Additionally, many thanks to my publisher, Ruina Judd at Bright Sky Press; Dave Kaplan and Dixie Nixon, my editors on this project; and Julie Savasky who put it all together. Heartfelt thanks also go to Dennis Wharton, Steven Mitchel, Kris Jones, and Kathryn Roberts at the National Association of Broadcasters, and to Suzy Thomas at McCombs Enterprises. I also extend my sincerest gratitude and appreciation to my good friend and colleague Joyce Tudryn, for her intuitive counsel, her balanced business sense, and her photographic eye.

From a personal perspective, I would not have been able to start this book, much less complete it, had it not been for a few fine individuals who helped to shape my career over this long and winding road. With that in mind, I want to thank the late "Radio" Wayne Cornils, who gave me my "big break" at the National Association of Broadcasters many years ago; Dwight Case, who hired and mentored me during my years at *Radio & Records;* and Eric Rhoads, who granted me broad editorial latitude during my tenure at *Radio Ink.*

Of course, I must save the most important recognition for last, and in that regard I have to thank my wife Diana and my daughter Jennifer for their love, their never-ending support, and their belief in me — and what I do for a living.

REED BUNZEL
March 2008